STEFAN PAPASTEFANOU

Patentability and Morality

Studien zum vergleichenden Privatrecht

Studies in Comparative Private Law

Band / Volume 22

Patentability and Morality

A Comparative Perspective on How Legal Culture
Shapes Morality within Patent Law

By

Stefan Papastefanou

Duncker & Humblot · Berlin

The Bucerius Law School Hamburg
accepted this work as thesis in the year 2022.

Bibliographic information of the German national library

The German national library registers this publication in
the German national bibliography; specified bibliographic data
are retrievable on the Internet about http://dnb.d-nb.de.

All rights reserved. No part of this book may be reproduced, translated,
or utilized in any form or by any means, electronic or mechanical,
without the expressed written consent of the publisher.
© 2024 Duncker & Humblot GmbH, Berlin
Typesetting: 3w+p GmbH, Rimpar
Printing: CPI books GmbH, Leck
Printed in Germany

ISSN 2364-8155
ISBN 978-3-428-18859-8 (Print)
ISBN 978-3-428-58859-6 (E-Book)

Printed on non-aging resistant (non-acid) paper
according to ISO 9706 ∞

Internet: http://www.duncker-humblot.de

To Jake & Amir

Acknowledgements

First, I wish to show my appreciation to my supervisor Prof. Dr. Dana Beldiman of the *Bucerius Law School*. Her guidance, support, and encouragement have been invaluable throughout this project. I am deeply grateful for her assistance at every stage of the research project. In particular, aspects of the U.S. legal system were much more approachable with the unrelenting patience and support of Prof. Beldiman. Her encouragement made it possible for me to realize my first international academic research projects.

Additionally, the assistance provided by Prof. Dr. Kung-Chung Liu of the *Singapore Management University* was greatly appreciated. His help and insights regarding Chinese patent law, in particular, were of utmost significance. Without his understanding and wisdom, it would not have been possible to identify and analyze original Chinese sources to the same extent. Furthermore, Prof. Liu provided me with significant networking opportunities throughout China and Southeast Asia. I owe the direction of my academic career, in large part, to the efforts of Prof. Liu.

My gratitude extends to the *Friedrich-Naumann-Stiftung für die Freiheit* for the generous scholarship to undertake the research project and to allow me to take part in several international research conferences. These conferences offered substantial insights in academic thinking and provided important networking opportunities. In particular, the networking events and academic conferences were hugely important in helping me to achieve independent publications on a national level.

Furthermore, I would like to thank the *Applied Research Centre for Intellectual Assets and the Law in Asia* of the Singapore Management University. Their generous scholarship opportunity enabled the research required for the inclusion of the part of this thesis on Chinese law. The PhD program provided by the research center was of immense academic and personal value.

Finally, I wish to express my gratitude to *Schmidt, von der Osten & Huber*, law firm in Essen, Germany. They provided a significant scholarship for this project and offered academic as well as personal support through their scholarship program and networking opportunities.

Hamburg, August 2023 *Stefan Papastefanou*

Contents

Preamble 15

A. Introductory Remarks 17
    I. Research Questions and Scientific Interest 20
    II. Methodology and Content 21
        1. Methodological Approach 21
            a) Methodological Structure 23
            b) Concept of Ethics within the Thesis 26
        2. Scope 27
            a) National Security and Patent Secrecy 27
            b) European Unitary Patent 27
            c) EU "Biotech Directive" 27
            d) Theories of Law 28
            e) Philosophical Approaches to Morality 28
            f) Patentability Assessments of Specific Technologies 29
    III. Overview of Sources 29

B. The Interplay of Technology and Morality 32
    I. Examples of Recent Technological Development with Moral Considerations ... 32
        1. Biotechnology as a Trailblazer of Patent Morality 33
            a) Basics of CRISPR Gene-Editing 34
            b) Moral Debate Regarding CRISPR Gene-Editing 35
            c) Similarities between CRISPR Gene-Editing and Stem-Cell Research ... 38
            d) Summary 40
        2. Weapon Technology and Moral Concerns 40
            a) Global Relevance of Modern Weapon Technology 41
            b) Fundamental Differences to Conventional Weapon Technology 43
                aa) Railgun Basics 43
                bb) Laser Weapon System Basics 44
                cc) Advantages of the Emerging Weapon Systems 44
            c) Areas of Moral Concern 45
    II. Potential Moral Considerations with Regard to Modern Weapon Technology ... 45
        1. Moral Concerns of the Heat Ray 46
        2. UN Convention CCW 46

Contents

      3. Significance of International Treaties 47
      4. Potential Violations of National Law 48
          a) Potential Violation of Sect. 311, 309 StGB 49
          b) Applicability 49
          c) Ionizing Radiation 50
          d) Potential to Violate Regulations on Ionizing Radiation 51
      5. Relationship of Legal Violations and Patentability 51
          a) International Treaties and Patentability 51
          b) National Law and Patentability 52
  III. Conclusion 53

C. Moral Considerations in Patentability in European and German Patent Law ... 55
  I. Art. 27 (2) TRIPS and Respective Regulations 55
      1. Relevance of Art. 27 (2) TRIPS for the Interpretation of Subsequent Regulation 56
      2. Regulatory Approaches in the EU and Germany 58
      3. Art. 53 (a) European Patent Convention 58
      4. Sect. 2 (1) PatG in German Law 60
  II. Ordre Public and Morality on a European Level 62
      1. Determining the Meaning of Ordre Public and Morality 62
      2. Relevant Contracting States 64
          a) Differences in the Understanding of Ordre Public within the EPC Contracting States 66
              aa) Lowest Standard – Validity of the Patent in One Contracting State .. 66
                  (1) Comparison of Art. 53 EPC and Art. 139 EPC 70
                  (2) Relationship of EPO and National Interpretation 70
                  (3) Relevance of the Report by the EU Commission 71
              bb) Medium Standard – Validity in the Designated State of the Application 73
              cc) Strictest Standard – Validity in All Contracting States 74
          b) Discussion of the Legal Arguments 76
          c) Conclusion 78
      3. Jurisprudence 78
          a) *Brüstle* Case 79
              aa) Factual and Legal Background 80
              bb) Legal Procedure 81
                  (1) Role of the European Court of Justice 82
                  (2) Referring the Case back to the German Federal Court of Justice 83
          b) Analysis of the Reasoning 84
              aa) Dogmatic Criticism of the Decision 84
              bb) General Criticism of the EU Biotech Directive 86

Contents

- 4. Conclusive Summary and Relevance 87
  - a) Fundamental Principles of Ordre Public or Morality 88
  - b) Characteristics of Human Dignity in Biotechnological Inventions 88
  - c) Specific Arguments Concerning Ethics in Biotechnological Inventions .. 93
  - d) Identifying Abstract Characteristics 95
- III. Fundamental Considerations of Morality in German Legal Literature 96
  - 1. Factual and Legal Background of the German Provision 96
  - 2. General Considerations Regarding the Morality Provision 97
    - a) Fundamental Objections to the Provision 97
    - b) Arguing in favor of the Morality Provision 100
  - 3. Subject of the Examination Process 101
    - a) Relevant Moment and Geographic Scope 102
    - b) European Union vs European Unity 104
  - 4. Understanding Ordre Public in Morality in German Legal Culture 105
    - a) Ordre Public and Morality as Ethical Considerations 107
    - b) Ordre Public and Morality across the German Legal System 111
    - c) Morality as a Social Concept Instead of a Legal Concept 113
    - d) The Unique Relationship of Immorality and Illegality in Patent Law 115
    - e) Interim Result 116
    - f) Identifying Elements of Morality and Ordre Public in Patent Law 117
      - aa) Essential Constitutional Principles as a Significant Element? 118
      - bb) Approaches to Define Ordre Public in German Legal Literature 120
  - 5. Meaningful Distinction of Morality and Ordre Public? 121
    - a) Attempts to Distinguish between the two Terms 121
    - b) Concepts of Proportionality in Ordre Public and Morality 124
    - c) Technicality of Patents in Relation to Morality as an Independent Approach 126
    - d) Limitations of the Proposed Differences between Morality and Public Order 126
    - e) Conclusion 129
- IV. Commercial Exploitation as a Requirement of Moral Violations 130
  - 1. TRIPS Considerations and the Term itself 130
  - 2. Standard for Commercial Use 132
    - a) German Jurisprudence Regarding Commercial Use 133
    - b) Legal Discussion of Commercial Use 135
    - c) *Romandini's* Case Group Solution 137
  - 3. Relevant Moment of Commercial Exploitations 140
    - a) Black Letter Analysis of Art. 53 EPC and Art. 27 (2) TRIPS 140
    - b) Black Letter Analysis of the German Patent Act 143
    - c) Interim Result 145

V. Conclusion 145

D. Patentability and Moral Concerns in U.S. Patent Law 147
    I. Historic Development 147
        1. Genesis of the Moral Utility Doctrine 148
        2. Specific Decisions Regarding the Moral Utility Doctrine 149
            a) Gambling Devices 149
                aa) Legal Analysis of the Reasoning 150
                bb) Historic Development of Morality with regard to Gambling Devices 151
            b) Deceptive Devices or Devices with Mischievous Tendencies 152
                aa) Legal Analysis of the Reasoning 153
                bb) Decline of the Moral Utility Doctrine 154
        3. Recent Development and Status Quo 155
    II. Rise of Biotechnology and Genetic Engineering 157
        1. Jeremy Rifkin as the "Most Hated Man in Science" 159
        2. Re-Introducing Morality Concerns into U.S. Patent Law 160
        3. Myriad Breast Cancer Genes Patent Case 162
        4. Ultimate Place of Morality within the Patent Subject Matter Doctrine? ... 166
        5. Influence on Canadian Jurisprudence 167
    III. The Role of Human Dignity in the U.S. Patent System 170
        1. Historical Development within the U.S. Legal System 170
            a) Historical Background of the Introduction of Human Dignity 171
            b) Legal Assessment of Human Dignity within the U.S. 172
            c) Comparing U.S., German and European Approaches to Human Dignity   174
        2. Relevance of Human Dignity for the Patent Law System 175
            a) Discussing the Legal Reasoning 176
            b) Human Dignity in the Context of Biotechnology as a Precedent 177
        3. Summary 178
    IV. Differences in Judicial Arguments 179
    V. Morality and Patentability in Relation to State Powers 180
    VI. Conclusion and Recommendations 182

E. Morality and Patentability in Chinese Patent Law 184
    I. Chinese Legal Culture and Patent Law 184
    II. Development of Patentability Concerns in China 185
    III. Morality and Chinese Legal Culture 187
        1. Governmental Influence on the Legal Culture in China 188
        2. Moral Considerations in Chinese Culture 189
        3. Morality in the Context of Legal Culture 191
    IV. Conclusion 197

F. Summary and Comprehensive Assessment 199

Bibliography 204

Index 228

Preamble

The main impetus for undertaking a study of this research topic was the fact that it is, inherently, both complex and simple. Patent law regulation and patentability requirements are complex legal ideas. They raise difficult legal questions that have global relevance because intellectual property is not restricted by physical borders or even physical objects. Yet, being untethered from physicality, these complex constructs also lend themselves to easy and logical answers within their own legal systems. Simultaneously, moral questions are much simpler to ask. Framing a question about the morality of human enhancement or weapon technology is relatively easy and does not require a legal education. However, the answers to these questions can be extremely complex. Moral considerations originate from philosophical, religious and metaphysical viewpoints. As such, the topic of patent law and morality illustrates how different cultures take account of moral considerations in their own understanding of patent law. The beauty of this topic is that it combines difficult questions with arguably simple answers and simple questions with impossibly complex answers.

Once the research concept had been developed further, it became clear that there was virtually no limit to the extent of the different theoretical approaches. In addition, the implications of this for technological advancement and practical significance became apparent. As such, a decision was made to restrict the thesis to a specific theoretical approach. That approach was the cultural aspects of patent law systems and more specifically, the legal culture and its substantial influence on patent law. Therefore, the analysis was focused on the different national and supranational approaches towards morality in patent law. Selecting practically relevant but also culturally different legal regimes in a comparative analysis was chosen as the most promising approach.

The development of the academic discussion was not without challenges and dead ends. Organizing and structuring an analysis on various different cultural, legal and moral aspects of several national patent systems was much more difficult than anticipated. Language and translation issues represented another difficulty, especially in the context of Chinese patent law. Even attempts to identify consistent terms that adequately expressed each national understanding of "morality" or "ordre public" turned out to be futile. Parts of the thesis required countless rewrites to include shifts in academic perspective. Additionally, the fundamental approach of the thesis turned out to be academically underdeveloped in the existing legal literature and jurisprudence.

While these difficulties and challenges existed, it was possible to overcome them or to regard them as opportunities as the thesis developed. In the end, the project provided a result that had diverged significantly from the initial ideas. However, ultimately, the dynamic development of the thesis also substantially contributed to the fun and excitement of the entire endeavor.

A. Introductory Remarks

In many of the world's significant patent systems, the implementation of aspects of public policy relating to morality within the patenting procedures has been subject to substantial legal discussion and controversial development. Conventionally, the concept of an "invention" in patent law was defined according to the creation and alteration of inanimate matter.[1] However, morality concerns in patent law have been dealt with in many varying ways in past centuries. With the emergence of advanced biotechnology and controversies surrounding it, all major patent law jurisdictions have had to address the issue either by legislation or through case law. The recent development of CRISPR gene-editing remains one of the most controversial areas of research. Therefore, biotechnology has become the center point of legal discussion about morality in patent law. However, other areas of technology also raise moral concerns which have not been subject to a broader legal review or a discussion of the implications for patent law at all. Following on from the controversies around biotechnology, patentability requirements based on moral concerns have become more important. National and supranational patent patentability approaches differ significantly. Addressing the differences in the patent law regimes requires an overview of the different and, in particular, less well-established cases of moral ambiguity in technology. A review of recent controversies and developments would contribute to this as well.

In all the relevant patent law jurisdictions around the world, essential elements of patentability are much more similar than the essentials in other areas of law and even intellectual property law. Those elements of patent law usually include a decision on what kinds of inventions are patentable in general. Therefore, a comparative analysis of the aforementioned moral concerns is very pragmatic and could provide useful insights into patent law and fundamental principles in general. Once such elements are identified, the emphasis of each element in each national patent law will be analyzed.

The aim of this project is to showcase how legal culture influences morality within patent law regimes. It also provides insights into the challenges arising in the area of patent law and morality. Ultimately, the thesis suggests approaches to better understand the concept of morality in patent law and how to address moral issues in a more consistent manner.

---

[1] *Mills*, Biotechnological Inventions: Moral Restraints and Patent Law 7; *Peng*, Patenting Stem Cell Inventions in China, 21.

Since patent law is generally similar across the most significant law regimes, it is an ideal research subject for elucidating the influence of legal culture. The reason for this is two-fold. First, the concept of a patent is based on an international treaty; therefore, it has a common background in the relevant jurisdictions. Secondly, the concept of morality is extremely different in different national legal cultures but simultaneously influences patent law to a certain extent. Therefore, the subject combines aspects of universal legal concepts and cultural peculiarities on a national level.

One of the fundamental issues addressed in this analysis concerns the incentivizing function of patent law. It is generally accepted that a patent functions as an incentive to promote inventions and research. Beyond that, the ultimate goal of incentivizing research is subject to debate. One opinion argues that an invention is an end in itself and no higher societal benefit is needed. Another approach suggests that the fundamental function of any patent legislation is the advancement or fruition of the well-being of society.[2] Usually, the differences in both views are practically irrelevant to the activities of any national or supranational patent offices. Patents with moral concern are rare. Yet, with the emergence of the new biotechnologies, the question arises again, offering the perfect opportunity to assess the concept in general and in greater detail.

The underlying concerns around potentially morally ambiguous inventions are identical on a global level. Hence, it is possible to describe the general moral controversies of certain technologies in a single introduction. It is, however, impossible to assess the technological specifications of a particular piece of technology, because most of the inventions are currently under development or subject to strict secrecy. For the general purposes of this thesis, however, it is also unnecessary.

Technological advancements and technologies prompt the analysis, but the subject goes beyond a specific technology and focuses on the inner workings of patent law and its fundamental functions.

In a very broad overview, this thesis will first present an introduction to the current patent regulation within Germany and the European Union and its challenges, followed by a summary of the development of morality within the U.S. patent system. Afterwards, the thesis will illustrate how the same issues are addressed in the Chinese patent law system which has a vastly different legal and cultural background.

Even though the patent system in the U.S. has a longer history than the modern patent approaches of continental Europe, this order seems reasonable. The explicit abandonment of morality concerns in U.S. patent law is directly opposed to the European approach of incorporating aspects of morality directly into patent litigation. Additionally, European and German patent law provisions allow for a classic black letter approach, while the situation in the U.S. requires a more in-depth review which includes the historic development.

---

[2] For a balanced protection: *Nägele/Jacobs*, Mitt. 2014, 353; *Straus*, GRUR 1992, 253.

Furthermore, controversies in Europe and Germany regarding morality in patent law usually revolve around human dignity. The significance of human dignity is due to the value hierarchy apparent in most European countries following World War II. To identify the role of human dignity in patent law, this thesis will subsequently review the significance of human dignity in each legal system and its relevance in patent law. Human dignity as a significant value additionally supports the order of the analysis. Addressing the U.S. legal system in a subsequent step makes the most sense, given the very different use of the concept of human dignity in the U.S. context. This comparative review also serves as an ideal way to observe value construction and value conceptualization in the U.S. and the U.S. constitution.

Following this discussion of the concept of values and legal culture, in the third section, the analysis will move towards the Chinese patent system. First, the concept of human dignity plays a very different role in Chinese legal culture, given its roots in mostly Western conflicts and cultural history. Additionally, the concept and significance of intellectual property in Chinese patent law have been subject to very recent development compared to the U.S. and European patent law jurisdictions. Apart from these recent developments, China's legal culture is also very different from a Western perspective, especially since the concept of IP law is foreign to the Chinese legal system. With regard to the value-based analysis, Chinese legal culture offers more insights, because it might seem that only a few moral restrictions apply in Chinese patent law. Yet, carefully analyzing the fundamental cultural principles that shaped the Chinese legal system, it can be observed that more complex connections exist between aspects of patent law and Chinese legal culture.

Ultimately, the observations about the role of values and the concept of legal culture in patent law and morality will be the basis for the rest of the research project. This allows for a more micro-functional comparative analysis and allows conclusions to be drawn about the overall topic. The results indicate that patent systems are not as different as they first appear but adhere to a broadly common concept and have followed a largely similar developmental trajectory that is shaped by fundamental legal culture. For example, some of the differences observed are actually rooted in different concepts and understandings of the separation of state powers and responsibility. The hope is that this summary will help to shed light on the underlying foundation of modern controversies and debates regarding morality concerns in patent law.

With these research interests in place and the illustration of the suitability of the research subject above, it is possible to formulate the research questions for this thesis more precisely. These research questions offer a structural outline to support the aim of the thesis (I.).

Following the research questions, this chapter also provides an outline of the Methodology and Content (II.) and gives an overview of the sources (III.).

I. Research Questions and Scientific Interest

The overall research question addresses the functionality and purpose of patent law and its interplay with legal culture. Why do nations grant patents for inventions and in which cases is patentability excluded? Since the exclusions are numerous and thus cannot all be covered by this analysis, the focus of this thesis will not be limited to any specific technology.

Furthermore, the most relevant exclusion within the analyzed national patent regimes stem from general clauses of exclusion from patentability. Those exclusions usually include terms such as "morality", "public order", "legal order", "ordre public", etc. While those terms have been subject to lengthy and detailed discussion in the context of biotechnological inventions, other fields of technology have not been subject to recent advancements which have prompted such scrutiny. In particular, military weapon technology seems to be addressed in part by those general provisions. Yet, the general scope and standard of those vague terms remains shrouded, for the most part, in intangible definitions. With this in mind, it is useful to identify an overarching question that will build the basis for the analysis:

How does legal culture affect the perception of morality in patent law regimes and can a better understanding improve the imprecise relationship between the two?

To articulate a meaningful answer to the overarching question, it is helpful to formulate specific sub-questions. The individual questions will allow issues to be addressed in a more detailed way. Combining the answers will then allow the overarching question to be answered:

First it is necessary to understand how morality affects patent law. This question focuses more on practical examples of technology than on theoretical or purely legal considerations (Chapter I.).

1. *How is morality shaped in the context of patent law?*

The next step addresses the fundamental functions of patent law and how its functions vary according to legal culture:

2. *What role does legal culture play in the foundation of patentability?*

Comparing very different patent law regimes offers an opportunity to address aspects of historic development. This raises the question of whether a patent law systems simply develop a certain understanding of morality over time.

3. *Is there a specific timeframe necessary to develop a morality doctrine within a patent system?*

Addressing morality within patent law requires a regulatory decision, or, at the least an assignment of regulatory power for the scope of patentability is necessary. In a modern state, such a decision can be made by the legislative, administrative or judicial branch of government. It would thus be interesting to analyze the effect of the concept of separation of powers on patentability decisions:

4. *How can basic ideas of separation of powers influence the understanding of patentability?*

The relationship between legality and morality has been the subject of research for a considerable time. Several other areas of law, including intellectual property law, take account of legal considerations relating to morality to some extent. However, patent law has a unique understanding of morality. What those differences are and how they affect the question of patentability are relevant considerations within the scope of this thesis:

5. *What makes the application of morality in patent law more difficult than in other areas of law? What is the relationship between immorality and illegality in this specific context?*

In a final step, the results of the previous questions offer a list of issues that characterize the relationship between morality and patent law and inform the following question:

6. *How can the current situation of applying morality in patent law be improved?*

How the overarching question and the respective sub-questions are addressed is outlined in the following chapter on methodology and content.

II. Methodology and Content

To thoroughly analyze the fundamental considerations of each patent law regime, it is necessary to address the various challenges and answer the research questions for each separate national regulatory framework. The main methodology in this thesis encompasses black letter analysis and micro-functional comparative discussion. The most significant reason for choosing comparative analysis is that the three patent law jurisdictions of Europe, the U.S. and China are similar enough to allow the different effects of legal culture to become apparent.

1. Methodological Approach

It is often observed that patent systems "share common principles".[3] The Chinese patent system, however, is, in essence, an exotic intellectual property system. China only recently incorporated patents into its legal system.[4] Therefore, it is only in the

---

[3] *Drahos*, 21 European Intellectual Property Review 441, 442 (1999); *Paradise*, Patents on Human Genes: an Analysis of Scope and Claims, 307 Science 1566, 1588 (2005).

[4] *Yu*, Building the Ladder: Three Decades of Development of Chinese Patent System, Drake University Law School Research Paper (2012); *Peng*, Patenting Human Stem Cell Related Inventions in China, 14; *Liu*, 12 The Journal of World Intellectual Property 122, 127 (2009); *Pan*, In Vitro Neuronal Differentiation of Cultured Human Embryonic Germ Cells, 327 Biochemical and Biophysical Research Communications 548, 561 (2005).

last few decades that China has begun to adopt lessons from other patent regimes in industrial nations on how to utilize patents to incentivize innovation. Patents function fundamentally as innovation starters within all relevant jurisdictions.[5] Simultaneously they raise social and public concerns regarding morally ambiguous technologies, especially biotechnological inventions.

Additionally, China has very recently adopted some form of CRISPR research in the context of human germline editing which is highly controversial within the scientific community.[6] So, not only is Chinese patent law legally interesting, but the Chinese scientific research community has been subject to international criticism for allowing the use of morally questionable biotechnology.

The European (and specifically Germany) and U.S. patent systems were chosen since their principles, in terms of morality and patentability, have been established for a much longer time and are sometimes therefore considered to be more advanced.[7] The U.S. is interesting in itself since the patent jurisdiction does not include a moral requirement in its codification even though it has a long-standing history of addressing moral concerns in patent jurisprudence. The difference in legal culture makes the comparison to the mostly civil law regimes of Europe and German patent law more interesting because those jurisdictions include morality requirements within their patent law. Additionally, in the European context, moral issues about

---

[5] The relationship of patent law and innovation has been subject to great debate: *Galasso/Schankerman*, Patents and Cumulative Innovation: Casual Evidence from the Courts, 130 The Quarterly Journal of Economics 317 (2015), 320 et seq.; *Grundmann*, The Economic Arguments for Patents and Their Validity for Developing Countries, 19 Indian Economic Journal 193 (1970); *Heller*, The Tragedy of the Anticommons: Property in the Transition from Marx to Markets, 111 Harvard Law Review 621 (1998); *Heller/Eisenberg*, Can Patents Deter Innovation? The Anticommons in Biomedical Research, 280 Science 698 (1998); *Huang/Murray*, Does Patent Strategy Shape the Long-run Supply of Public Knowledge? Evidence From Human Genetics, 52 Academy of Management Journal 1193 (2009); *Kitch*, The Nature and Function of the Patent System, 20 Journal of Law and Economics 265 (1977); *Ko*, An Economic Analysis of Biotechnology Patent Protection, 102 Yale Law Journal 777 (1992); *Köllner/Weber*, Mitt. 2014. 106; *Kunczik*, GRUR 2003, 845 et seq.; *Locke*, Second Treatise of Government (CB Macpherson ed., Hackett Publishing Company 1980); *Marx*, Theses on Feuerbach (Vol. 5) (Karl Marx & Frederick Engels ed., Lawrence & Wishart 2010); *Maskus*, The Role of Intellectual Property Rights in Encouraging Foreign Direct Investment and Technology Transfer, 9 Duke Journal of Comparative & International Law 109 (1998); *Merges*, Contracting into Liability Rules: Intellectual Property Rights and Collective Rights European Patent Organizations, 84 California Law Review 1293, 1300 (1996); *Rai*, Fostering Cumulative Innovation in the Biopharmaceutical Industry: The Role of Patents and Antitrust, 16 Berkeley Technology Law Journal 813, 823 (2001); The Information Revolution Reaches Pharmaceuticals: Balancing Innovation Incentives, Cost, and Access in the Post-Genomics Era, 2001 University of Illinois Law Review 43, 50 (1998); *Tur-Sinai*, Cumulative Innovation in Patent Law: Making Sense of Incentives, 50 Idea 723, 727 (2009).

[6] *Lander* et al., Nature 567 (2019), 165.

[7] *Peng*, Patentability of Stem Cells in China, 14; *Merges*, Intellectual Property in Higher Life Forms: The Patent System and Controversial Technologies, 47 Maryland Law Review 1051 (1987); *v. Renesse/Tanner*, Mitt. 2001, 5.

patentability have been highly debated for a long time regarding human embryonic stem cell research.

Given all these different approaches and cultural backgrounds, the initial research will focus on black letter analysis of case law and statutes and continue with an in-depth comparative analysis including academic commentary and consideration of the existing literature on legal culture and the interplay of values and law.

The second research step identifies the fundamental intentions of legislative power and judiciary shaping the regulatory framework. Those fundamentals are based on the aforementioned analysis of each national law and separate application thereof. Patent law generally serves to incentivize technological advancement by providing an exclusionary right on the one hand, but also requiring publication of the invention in the form of the patent specifications. Since the patent regimes examined usually include similar requirements, it is possible to use previously identified patent fundamentals within the ongoing analysis. Cross-referencing specific regulatory differences with fundamental differences in the patent regimes of Europe and Germany, the U.S. and China allows for a more natural flow of the argument.

a) Methodological Structure

Besides these introductory remarks, the thesis consists of six chapters. The thesis will begin with an overview of the interplay of morality and technology (Chapter B.). This relationship will be exemplified by two areas of technology and respective patentability concerns based on morality. The first example is biotechnology and the related and very intense legal and moral discussions. The second example is concerned with weapon technology. Moral concerns surrounding weapon technology are far less commonly subject to open controversy. Therefore, analyzing both of these areas of technology provides a good basis for how legal concerns about general patentability are rooted in morality and legal culture. This analysis provides insights which help to answer Research question 1.

The second part (Chapter C.) of the thesis builds on these first observations. Its goal is the establishment of a fundamental analysis of case law and the legislature in specific patent law systems. This analysis begins with a hierarchical approach from international treaties (TRIPS) to supranational, European patent law. Moving from European patent law, the focus then switches to German patent law. In addition, the relationship between German and European patent law and its respective challenges are addressed. Given the similarity of both jurisdictions, most of the issues which arise are comparable. The analysis focuses strongly on the *Brüstle* decision.[8] The *Brüstle* decision reveals the fundamental understanding and shortcomings of the European and German approach to morality with regard to patentability. Fur-

---

[8] With a similar analysis: *Overwalle/Berthels*, Patents & Venus: About Oocytes and Human Embryonic Stem Cells, in: Stem Cells and Women's Health – Cellules souches et santé des femmes – Stamcellen en vrounwengezondheid (Anthemis-Intersentia 2007).

thermore, this chapter ultimately establishes the connection of the said approach and fundamental considerations to the legal culture of the German and European patent systems. It indicates that the understanding of morality is tethered to the concept of values, especially human dignity, arguably the highest value. The results are relevant for answering Research Questions 2 and 3.

In Chapter D., the analysis uses the results of the value-oriented morality approach described in Chapter C. in the context of the U.S. patent system. This analysis expands the foundation to address Research Questions 2 and 3. The legal history of morality in the U.S. is much older than the current approach in Europe and Germany. Therefore, the analysis focuses on the development and legacy of the U.S. "moral utility doctrine". Furthermore, this section observes that the legal culture in the U.S. and its respective approach to human dignity have a direct effect on the fundamental understanding of patent law. The impact then extends to the principles of morality within U.S. patent law requirements. This chapter concludes that the U.S. patent system is much less impacted by the value of human dignity than the European patent system. The significantly lower level impact of the concept of human dignity in the U.S. patent system gives insights into the influence of legal culture and morality regarding patentability. The micro-functional analysis with the results of Chapter C. reveal insights about the role of separation of power within the legal system. Applying the results to the role of patent law specifically allows Research Question 4 to be answered.

Following these results, in Chapter E. the analysis focuses on the historic introduction of the patent system to China. Based on general observations made during the preceding chapters, this chapter elaborates on the public perception of patents in Chinese society. This perception significantly influences the question of whether to affirm patentability to all subject matter or to make exceptions based on moral concerns. The conclusion lays the groundwork for answering Research Questions 3 and 4. The Chinese public does not have any strong moral concerns about patentability especially in the connection with human dignity. However, some moral concerns are expressed within the concept of Chinese legal and moral culture. The analysis concludes that historic development and legal culture heavily influence the concept of morality within a patent system. In particular, this is the case since patent law is a comparatively new subject in Chinese legal culture. Although the analysis in this chapter focuses mainly on Chinese patent law, in some cases other jurisdictions, such as Singapore, Taiwan and India, will be included. The reason for this is twofold. Not only do these jurisdictions share similar historic developments of patent law but they are also culturally different from Western patent law jurisdictions. Therefore, they provide more insight into the effects of different legal cultures on patent law. This chapter provides additional insights for Research Questions 4 and 5. The goal is to assess how patentability requirements or a lack thereof have been applied or construed by either the administrative agencies (the European Patent Organization (EPO), the German Patent and Trademark Office (GPTO), the United States Patent and Trademark Office (USPTO) and the China National Intellectual Property Ad-

II. Methodology and Content

ministration (CNIPA)) or the courts (such as the Court of Justice of the European Union (CJEU) or the Appeal courts in the U.S.). It is observed that the U.S. seemingly focuses on scientific and economic issues, but in Europe and China moral issues are more directly addressed.

Subsequently, the chapter discusses whether such an (prima facie) abandonment of moral assessment in patent law is necessary or ideal. However, the focus of the entire analysis is not on an assessment of morality in patent law as a whole, it provides more of an overview of the current situation and how it should be developed. In conclusion, a complete abandonment of moral considerations within patent law does not seem ideal and is not practiced by any of the previously mentioned jurisdictions, even if they officially declare otherwise. China has a different degree of administrative regulation and domestic development of research and industry than the EU. Yet, it is not suitable for Chinese patent law or any jurisdiction to either completely exclude certain inventions or accept any invention unconditionally despite possible moral concerns. The analysis of Chinese patent law indicates that jurisdictions will develop their own standards based on legal culture. Combining several results from previous questions offers a foundation for addressing Research Question 6.

After the comparative analysis, the final chapter, Chapter F., presents the main findings of the thesis by providing a conclusive answer for each research question. The results demonstrate how difficult the implementation of moral restrictions in patent law are in their application. Since all jurisdictions are subject to the TRIPS agreement which includes the possibility of moral considerations within patent law, the concept of morality in national patent law is entirely different from other areas of law of each jurisdiction that are not based on an international treaty. Consequently, morality in patent law can be considered a "legal artifact" or even a paradox. Its nature as an "artifact" makes its practical application difficult. Therefore, the concept of morality in patent law is developed and shaped by principles of legal culture. Ultimately, the results of the micro- and macro-level analysis in each national patent law chapter are more deeply evaluated in this section. The conclusion to Research Question 6 is based on the identified solutions. The thesis provides conclusions and summarizes the recommendations from the separate jurisdictions. Ultimately, incorporating the recommendations of Research Question 6 makes it possible to assess the overarching goal of the thesis.

The overview of each national patent law system is semi-separate, while the comparison and summary offer a framework for the entire analysis. Application and comparison of each patent law regime are not strictly separated, since it is more practical and efficient to engage in a micro-functional comparative analysis. This method of analysis is first used during the application of the U.S. legal system in Chapter C. and will address significant differences and their consequences directly. Such a procedure allows for a more direct comparison. The significance of each difference and how they relate to the function of patent law are also addressed. Immediate responses to the comparisons makes it easier to identify relevant differences in the regulatory approaches and legal backgrounds. Findings and the most significant differences or similarities are then be summarized in the final sub-chapter. Those results are also subject to a short assessment.

b) Concept of Ethics within the Thesis

The basic idea of moral philosophy is the concept of right and wrong conduct.[9] This definition is virtually infinitely broad and hardly suitable for direct transfer into a legal system. Law itself is an attempt to answer the question about right and wrong while also framing the answer within a binding system.

Contemporary definitions identify three major areas within general ethics. While meta-ethics[10] are a very interesting topic for theoretical transfer in legal systems, both applied ethics and normative ethics are more relevant in this case.

Normative ethics describe the study of ethical action based on an attempt to construct an overarching moral principle that might be applicable to resolve any moral decision.[11] Applied ethics, ultimately, describes the philosophical examination of a particular issue which is a matter of moral judgement.[12]

Normative ethics appear to be the most relevant sub-area for the research questions, since they focus on developing an overarching or fundamental standard. The legal question centers on finding a similarly overarching standard for patent law when it comes to patent protection.

However, the issue of patent protection is very specific and any possible overarching standard is only relevant to general patentability provisions. Therefore, it is actually more appropriate to address the issues relating to legal culture in combination with applied ethics. The use of applied ethics is supported by the fact that public order and principles of morality are subject to public scrutiny within a society.[13] Fundamentally, such an approach is called descriptive ethics. Descriptive ethics are based on an empirical investigation that evaluates the moral beliefs of a certain demographic. Such an empirical investigation might be of use for the evaluation of a specific invention. However, the standard for morality assessment has to be distinguishable from the dynamic nature of momentary opinion within a population.

Hence, the following analysis is based on the modern approach of applied ethics, which is relatively focused on the issue at hand but also relies on an overarching principle. A normative approach is not included for the reasons above, i. e. it is too far removed from the general concept of legal culture.

---

[9] *Baier*, Values and Morals, 231; *Murray*, Social Science & Medicine, 1987, 637 et seq.
[10] *Baier*, Values and Morals, 240 et seq.
[11] *Diamond*, Human Lives, 26 et seq.; *Murray*, Social Science & Medicine, 1987, 638.
[12] *Murray*, Social Science & Medicine, 1987, 641.
[13] *Diamond*, Human Lives, 17; *Baier*, Values and Morals, 244.

2. Scope

The research subject examined in this thesis includes broad legal and philosophical terms. To prevent the thesis from meandering, it is necessary to restrict its scope to ensure that the content of the research project is focused in a meaningful and concise manner.

a) National Security and Patent Secrecy

Technology that raises moral concerns might simultaneously raise issues of national security as well. Most prominently, weapon technology does both to a significant degree. The relationship between national security and patent law is commonly known as patent secrecy. The law of patent secrecy tries to balance the interests of national security with the economic interests of the inventor. National understandings of this balance differ substantially. The differences within those approaches are influenced by the focus and relevance of national security. It is certainly an interesting topic that relates to the theory of patent law and its application; however, it is much more a political than a legal issue. In addition, it does not relate to morality directly or address issues of legal culture. Furthermore, concerns of national security usually arise only in relation to weapon technology. Since this thesis is not limited to a specific type of technology, there is insufficient overlap between the research subject and the legal issue of patent secrecy. Therefore, issues relating to patent secrecy and national security are beyond the scope of this thesis.

b) European Unitary Patent

The European Patent with unitary effect ("Unitary Patent") poses a variety of challenges. The Unitary Patent builds on the European Patent Convention. Therefore, the pre-grant phase is exactly the same as for European Patents. Accordingly, the patentability requirements are identical. In addition, since the Unitary Patent has only very recently been implemented, no independent jurisprudence or administrative guidelines exist. As such, analyzing the Unitary Patent system within this thesis would not add any additional insights.

c) EU "Biotech Directive"

In 1998, the EU harmonized patent law relating to biotechnological inventions. Directive 98/44/EC on the legal protection of biotechnological inventions, commonly known as the "Biotech Directive", was implemented by all Member States by 2000. Its intention was to clarify which biotechnological inventions are patentable on ethical grounds. However, it is generally accepted that its actual goal was to harmonize patentability throughout the EU as certain Member States had already initiated their own patentability provisions for biotechnology. The directive focuses on a specific field of technology, whereas this thesis explicitly takes a much more general approach. Therefore, the insights about morality and patent law in general within the Directive are mostly limited to specific biotechnology. In addition, given that the directive was adopted in 1998, numerous in-depth analyses of the legal and political issues have already been undertaken. Hence, this thesis does not provide a detailed analysis of the Biotech Directive. Its contents are the subject of certain chapters, however, where it provides insights about EU jurisprudence and general legal concepts of morality.

d) Theories of Law

At the center of the thesis is the theory of law as a social contract. Therefore, the intention of patent law and other legislative approaches are addressed primarily from this viewpoint. Other law theories, such as law as a tool of power or control are also relevant in certain chapters that involve government control, most notably the sections on U.S. and Chinese patent law. The analysis is conducted with an awareness that provisions regarding morality and public order have been subject to government abuse. However, patent law is usually considered to be removed from direct government control. Patents also offer very little in terms of influencing a broad group within a society or addressing a minority specifically. Accordingly, different theoretical approaches to law are not substantially relevant to the research questions. Hence, the political and philosophical challenges of law as a social contract are not fundamentally addressed within this thesis.

e) Philosophical Approaches to Morality

Morals are usually defined as "values that we attribute to a system of beliefs that help the individual define right versus wrong, good versus bad. These typically get their authority from something outside the individual – a higher being or higher authority (e.g. government, society). Moral concepts, judgments and practices may vary from one society to another."[14]

Ethics, on the other hand, are described as more of a concept, also known as moral philosophy. As a philosophical discipline, they are also concerned with good and bad or right and wrong.[15] Within the legal profession, the term "legal ethics" has been established to refer to "principles of conduct that members of the profession are expected to observe in the practice of law".[16] Clearly, such a definition exclusively addresses individuals who are under pressure or facing a moral dilemma. Therefore,

---

[14] *Navran*, What Is the Difference Between Ethics, Morals and Values? Ethics Research Center, 2017, 149.

[15] *Lerman*, Ethical Problems in the Practice of Law, 4.

[16] At Id.

such ethics codes or guidelines for ethical behavior in the legal profession are only relevant on an individual scale in relation to specific moral challenges.

The research question, however, concerns general considerations that shape the understanding of morality and ethics within a given society. A specific analysis of a state's ethics code can therefore only be viable as far as it allows for conclusions regarding the overall standards of ethics. Unfortunately, most guidelines or ethics codes are not centered on a set of fundamental considerations. Instead, they follow a more topic-related system, which usually includes "conflicts of interest", "truthfulness", "lawyer's duties and interests", etc.[17] While it might be argued that these specific cases within the guidelines or ethics codes include similar considerations, the guidelines generally do not go into great detail as to what those considerations are. Ultimately, the benefit of such an analysis for this thesis is mostly insignificant. In addition, ethics codes are intended to govern the conduct of lawyers in specific situations and are therefore concerned with a complex sanctioning system. The functionality of an ethics code is consequently identical to that of a criminal code, which also offers only limited insight into the general standard of morality within a society.

Ultimately, morality as a general term is so broad that it can be approached from a myriad of different viewpoints. It is not the intention of this thesis to offer any finite definition – inside or outside the context of patent law. The analysis only addresses the functionality and role of morality in terms of its relationship to legal culture. Anything that goes beyond this theoretical approach is not covered by this thesis.

f) Patentability Assessments of Specific Technologies

Several emerging technologies are addressed in this thesis. Some of those specific technologies have not been subject to broad legal discussions or patentability disputes. Therefore, it might be of practical interest to assess the patentability of these new technologies. However, this thesis does not focus on any specific technology, nor does it provide an assessment of the patentability of said technologies. Furthermore, the thesis does not specifically cover dual-use technology, such as rocket technology. Dual-use technology describes the problem of having multiple potential uses for a certain type of technology. The issue of potential uses is addressed in this thesis without specifically analyzing dual-use technology.

III. Overview of Sources

Chapter Bibliography provides a bibliography with a detailed list of all the materials that have been used within this research project. This section gives a general overview of what the most significant sources are and how they are relevant for the

---

[17] *Lerman*, Ethical Problems in the Practice of Law, 14.

thesis. The selection and availability of sources provide insights into the legal culture surrounding the issues of patentability and morality.

Sources on patent law and morality regarding European law focus mainly on legal discussion and the ECJ case of *Brüstle*, as well as some minor administrative decisions. *Brüstle* is the case that is closest to the issue of patentability and morality. Sources such as *Bastia*,[18] *Staunton*,[19] *Plomer*,[20] *Taupitz*[21] and *Trips-Hebert/Grund*[22] argue based on the facts of the *Brüstle* case. Most notable in the area of EU and German patent law is the very detailed analysis of *Romandini*.[23] He assesses the patentability of embryonic stem cells in a comparative approach. His thesis covers the German, EU and Italian patent law approaches. This multi-national and supra-national approach provides an excellent and unique jumping-off point for part of this analysis. Therefore, Chapter C. focuses in part on his findings regarding specific stem cell technology across several patent jurisdictions. Analyzing the considerations relating to specific technology allows for a better understanding of the general concepts of morality and patentability. Beyond these concepts, focusing on and advancing *Romandini*'s research also allows for insights into the relationship between national and supra-national regulatory approaches. This unique combination of topics and the quality of *Romandini*'s research contribute fundamentally to the section of this thesis analyzing European and German law.

U.S. law sources focus mostly on jurisprudence and the historic development of the moral utility doctrine. This indicates the case law legal system of the U.S. as well as the age of its patent law regime, being the oldest among the three analyzed legal systems. The legal discussion surrounding the issues of morality and U.S. patent law specifically address the *Rifkin* patent case from 1997. *Rifkin* intentionally addresses moral issues in patent law in a general sense. Given this general disruption of the patent landscape in the U.S. legal system, the analysis is fundamental for Chapter D. Other significant research projects on morality are from *Keay*[24] as well as *Beyleveld*[25] and *Pelligrino*.[26] The latter examines the role of human dignity within the U.S. legal

---

[18] *Batista*, GRUR Int. 2013, 514.

[19] *Staunton*, Brüstle v Greenpeace, Embryonic Stem Cell Research and the European Court of Justice's New Found Morality, 21 Medical Law Review 310 (2013).

[20] *Plomer*, After Brüstle: EU Accession to the ECHR and the Future of European Patent Law, 2 Queen Mary Journal of Intellectual Property 110 (2012).

[21] *Taupitz*, GRUR 2012, 1.

[22] *Trips-Hebert/Grund*, PharmR 2007, 397.

[23] *Romandini*, Die Patentierbarkeit von menschlichen Stammzellen – Eine vergleichende Betrachtung des europäischen, deutschen und italienischen Patentrechts [The patentability of human stem cells – A comparative analysis of European, German and German patent law], 2012.

[24] *Keay*, Morality's Move within U.S. Patent Law: From Moral Utility to Subject Matter, AIPLA Quarterly Journal 2012, 409–439.

[25] *Beyleveld*, Human Dignity in Bioethics and Biolaw, Oxford University Press 2001.

[26] *Pelligrino* et al., Human Dignity and Bioethics, University of Notre Dame Press 2009.

III. Overview of Sources

system. Human dignity plays a substantial role in European and German morality issues. Research on the topic in the U.S. context gives further insights into the legal culture that shapes the concept of morality in patent law.

Sources in Chapter E. covering Chinese patent law are significantly different from the other chapters. Patent law is a new concept within the Chinese legal landscape and therefore very little jurisprudence or legal discussion exist. However, several sociological studies on the legal understanding of patent law within the population have been carried out by *Wang*,[27] *Weng/Weng*,[28] and *Liu*.[29] These studies, as well as the fundamental analysis of stem cell patents in China by *Peng*,[30] provide an ideal background for this thesis. In particular, the original Chinese sources offer essential insights into the legal culture of China.

---

[27] *Wang*, Woguo Zhuanxingqi Gonggong Zhengce Guochengzhong de Gongmin Canyu Yanjiu – Yizhong Liyi Fenxi de Shijiao [Study on the Participation of Citizens in Public Policy Making During China's Transition: From the Interest Analysis Perspective], 8 Zhongguo Xingzheng Guanli [Chinese Public Administration] 86 (2005).

[28] *Weng/Weng*, Zhishi Jingji Shidai de Daxuesheng Zhishichanquan Yishi he Renzhi Zhuangkuang Yanjiu [A study on University Students' Awareness and Cognition of Intellectual Property in an Era of Knowledge-based Economy], 24 Journal of Nanjing University of Science and Technology 96 (2011).

[29] *Liu*, Shengwu Jishu de Falü Wenti Yanjiu [Studies on Legal Issues for Biotechnology] (Kexue Chubanshe [Science Publishing House] 2007).

[30] *Peng*, Patenting Human Embryonic Stem Cell Related Inventions in China, Singapore, 2018.

B. The Interplay of Technology and Morality

To get a better idea of the different areas of technology that are subject to moral considerations, the following part of the thesis presents several examples. The examples primarily illustrate the interplay of technology and controversy in patent law.

This chapter begins with an introduction of various controversial technologies and explains the different kind of moral concerns (I.). It is observed and analyzed how some technologies establish open and intense controversies while others raise moral issues in a more subtle way.

To better understand the latter, the analysis then focuses on moral considerations in modern weapon technology (II.). This analysis addresses potential moral concerns which are expressed in legal regulation – international and national. Examples of legislation are the core element of this research chapter. The link between morality and the legal system is much stronger in weapon technology than within the biotechnology controversies. Therefore, this section introduces and explores the role of legal culture in greater depth.

The results of this chapter (III.) provide the basis for the legal considerations discussed in the subsequent chapters.

I. Examples of Recent Technological Development with Moral Considerations

While numerous areas of technology have sparked public debates, the examples given here cover the most discussed and debated technologies as well as devices that are not central to the public debate. However, the latter potentially provide more insight into the complex relationship between patentability and morality. Also, this section outlines the potential of modern technologies to be subject to debate. Both biotechnology and weapon technology reveal underlying societal and legal opinions about the functionality of patent law and the role of morality within it.

Controversies within the patentability debate are fueled in part by different understandings or misunderstandings of patent law. Technically, patent law simply provides an exclusionary right and not a positive right of use. However, the general public usually fails to make this distinction and therefore vacillates, in terms of intensity, over possible morality violations. Even within the legal literature, the perceived intensity of a possible moral violation ranges from indirect and tangential to direct and obvious.[1]

On the far end of the spectrum, those who argue for the indirect nature of the possible violation oppose moral considerations in patent law all together. They assert that no moral considerations should be included in the process of determining patent eligibility. This legal opinion can be found in all patent law regimes covered in this thesis. In the U.S. legal system, this line of reasoning has even been a main contributor to the shift in the patentability paradigm – from a strict morality to doctrine to the (allegedly) complete abandonment of moral considerations.

Unsurprisingly, the argument on the nature of patentability surfaces during the discussion on advanced biotechnology – the *Brüstle* case in the EU or the *Rifkin* case in the U.S. Biotechnology is still the primary subject of most controversies with regard to morality and patentability. Therefore, the following chapter starts with an overview of recent biotechnological advancements that have been the subject of heated debate. Following on from the review of biotechnological technology, the more subtle moral issues of modern weapon technology are considered.

1. Biotechnology as a Trailblazer of Patent Morality

Biotechnology generally refers to a wide range of research and development in which biological material is altered by means of biological methods.[2] Controversies have usually arisen in the field of advanced biotechnology where the subject of the alteration was a complex living being. In the case of human individuals or the human genome as research subjects, the debate has been especially intense.[3] The controversy

---

[1] Misunderstandings of this key principle of patent law make the societal debate much more difficult and "heated". The confusion usually stems from the idea that patent law allows a certain use when it actually does not.

[2] *Peng*, Patentability in Stem Cell Research, 37; Convention on Biological Diversity (Rio de Janeiro, June 5th, 1992); *Brevini/Gandolfi*, Parthenotes as a Source of Embryonic Stem Cells, 41 Cell Proliferation 20 (2008), 23; *Holden*, A Seismic Shift for Stem Cell Research, 319 Science 560 (2008); *Hoppe*, Pharma Recht 1997, 392; *Hübel*, Limits of Patentability: Plant Sciences, Stem Cells and Nucleic Acids (Springer Science & Business Media 2012); for the European Uniform Patent Approach: *Pehlivan*, The Creation of a Single European Patent System: From Dream to (Almost) Reality, 34 European Intellectual Property Review 453, 469 (2012); *Sander*, The Gatekeepers of hES Cell Products, 23 Nature Biotechnology 817, 828 (2005).

[3] *Bagley*, A Global Controversy: The Role of Morality in Biotechnology Patent Law, in: Intellectual Property and Information Wealth: Issues and Practices in the Digital Age (Vol. 2) (Peter K. Yu ed., Praeger 2006); *Busche*, Mitt. 2001, 4 et seq.; *Bagley*, Patent First, Ask Questions Later: Morality and Biotechnology in Patent Law, 45 William and Mary Law Review 469 (2003); *Bregman-Eschet*, The Ripple Effect of Intellectual Property Policy: Empirical Evidence from Stem Cell Research and Development, 19 Journal of Technology Law & Policy 227 (2014), 230; *Erramouspe*, Staking Patent Claims on the Human Blueprint: Rewards and Rent-Dissipating Races, 43 UCLA Law Review 961 (1995), 963; *Feuerlein*, GRUR 2001, 561, 562; *Goebel*, Mitt. 1995, 153; *Haedicke*, Jus 2002, 113; *Hurlbut*, Ethics and Em-

has moved from direct human stem cell research in the 1990s and 2000s to a more dynamic use of germline editing in the form of human enhancement.[4] Such methods for altering biological matter at the cellular and molecular levels based on human genetic transfer have only been developed in recent decades. The research has been advancing rapidly with the law and societal morality struggling to keep up.[5]

With the emergence of CRISPR gene-editing, biotechnology has very recently come into focus as morally questionable research and technology. The scientific advancement has even been combined with other modern technologies.[6]

a) Basics of CRISPR Gene-Editing

CRISPR gene-editing is a genetic engineering technique in molecular biology which allows the genomes of living organisms to be modified.[7] Genome editing has been possible since the 1980s, though the methods employed had proved to be inefficient and impractical to implement on a large scale. The ease with which researchers can use CRISPR gene-editing in order to silence or cause point mutations at specific locations has proved invaluable for the quick and efficient mapping of genomic models.[8] It is also relevant to other biological processes associated with various genes in a variety of cells.[9]

---

bryonic Stem Cell Research: Altered Nuclear Transfer as a Way Forward, 21 Biodrugs 79 (2007); *Ilic*, Derivation of Human Embryonic Stem Cell Lines from Biospied Blastomeres on Human Feeders with Minimal Exposure to Xenomaterials, 18 Stem Cells and Development 1343 (2009); *Isasi/Knoppers*, Towards Commonality? Policy Approaches to Human Embryonic Stem Cell Research in Europe, in: Embryonic Stem Cell Patents: European Law and Ethics (Aurora Plomer & Paul Torremans eds, Oxford University Press 2009); *Kollmann*, Taking the Moral High Road: Why Embryonic Stem Cell Research Should be Strictly Regulated, 2 Faulkner Law Review 145, 150, 152 (2010); *Peng*, The Patentability of Human Embryonic Stem Cell Technology in China, 34 Nature Biotechnology 37, 45 (2016); *Ruse/Pynes*, The Stem Cell Controversy: Debating the Issues (Prometheus Book 2006).

[4] *Lander* et al., Nature 567, (2019), 165; *Cyranoski*, Nature, 548 (2018), 272.

[5] *Brownsword*, Human Genetics and the Law: Regulation a Revolution, 61 The Modern Law Review 593 (1998), 601; *Busche*, GRUR Int. 1999, 299; *Dederer*, GRUR 2013, 353; *Demaine/Fellmeth*, Reinventing the Double Helix: A Novel and Nonobvious Reconceptualization of the Biotechnology Patent, 55 Stanford Law Review 303 (2002), 306; *Ferrer*, The Scientific Muscle of Brazil's Health Biotechnology, 22 Nature Biotechnology DC8 (2004); *Isasi/Knoppers*, Mind the Gap: Policy Approaches to Embryonic Stem Cell and Cloning Research in 50 Countries, 13 European Journal of Health Law 9 (2006); *Kleine/Klingelhöfer*, GRUR 2003, 1; *Kretschmer*, GRUR 1992, 155.

[6] *Pontin*, The Genetics (and Ethics) of Making Humans Fit for Mars, Wired (8 July 2018); *Regalado*, The DIY designer baby project funded with Bitcoin, MIT Technol. Rev. (1 February 2019).

[7] *Cohen*, J. (October 7th, 2020), CRISPR, the revolutionary genetic "scissors," honored by Chemistry Nobel, Science; *Heidenreich*, M./*Zhang*, F. (January 2016), Applications of CRISPR-Cas systems in neuroscience, Nature Reviews, Neuroscience, 17 (1): 36–44.

[8] *Young*, S. (11th February, 2014), CRISPR and Other Genome Editing Tools Boost Medical Research and Gene Therapy's Reach, MIT Technology Review.

I. Examples of Recent Technological Development with Moral Considerations

The technique is considered highly significant in biotechnology and medicine as it allows genomes to be edited *in vivo* very precisely. In comparison to conventional stem cell research, CRISPR gene-editing requires less effort and is more cost-effective. The areas in which it can be applied are diverse, ranging from the creation of new medicines and genetically modified organisms to controlling pathogens and pests.[10]

In terms of basic functionality, the technique uses what resemble genetic scissors. A Cas9 nuclease opens both strands of a targeted DNA sequence to introduce a genetic modification. Knock-in mutations, facilitated via homology directed repair (HDR), represent the traditional pathway for targeted genomic editing approaches.[11] This allows for the introduction of targeted DNA damage and repair. HDR employs the use of similar DNA sequences to drive the repair of the break via the incorporation of exogenous DNA to function as the repair template.[12] Knock-out mutations caused by CRISPR-Cas9 result in the repair of the double-stranded break by means of non-homologous end joining (NHEJ). NHEJ can often result in random deletions or insertions at the repair site, which may disrupt or alter gene functionality. Therefore, genomic engineering using CRISPR-Cas9 gives researchers the ability to generate targeted random gene disruption. Consequently, genome editing is of great concern. Genomic editing leads to irreversible changes to the genome.

Similarly to stem cell research, the use of CRISPR gene-editing in human germline genetic modification is highly controversial. Many bioethical concerns have been raised about the prospect of using CRISPR for germline editing, especially in human embryos.

b) Moral Debate Regarding CRISPR Gene-Editing

In March 2015, multiple groups had announced ongoing research, laying the foundations for applying CRISPR to human embryos for human germline engineering. Labs intending to offer this technology were located in the U.S., China, and the U.K.[13] In April 2015, Chinese scientists reported on the results of an attempt to alter the DNA of non-viable human embryos using CRISPR to correct a mutation

---

[9] *Barrangou*, R./*Doudna*, J. A. (September 2016), Applications of CRISPR technologies in research and beyond, Nature Biotechnology, 34 (9): 933–941.

[10] *Zhang*, J. H./*Pandey*, M./*Kahler*, J. F./*Loshakov*, A./*Harris*, B./*Dagur*, P. K. et al. (November 2014), Improving the specificity and efficacy of CRISPR/CAS9 and gRNA through target specific DNA reporter, Journal of Biotechnology, 189: 1–8.

[11] *Bak* et al., Trends in Genetics, 2018, 34 (8), 605; *Vakulskas*, C. A./*Dever*, D. P./*Rettig*, G. R./*Turk*, R./*Jacobi*, A. M./*Collingwood*, M. A. et al. (August 2018), A high-fidelity Cas9 mutant delivered as a ribonucleoprotein complex enables efficient gene editing in human hematopoietic stem and progenitor cells, Nature Medicine, 24 (8): 1216–1224; *Ledford*, H. (June 2015), CRISPR, the disruptor, Nature, 522 (7554): 20–4.

[12] *Bak* et al., Trends in Genetics, 2018, 34 (8): 607; *Ledford*, Nature, 531 (2016), 156.

[13] *Regalado*, MIT Technology Review 2015, 124.

that causes beta thalassemia, a lethal heritable disorder.[14] The study had previously been rejected by both *Nature* and *Science* – both highly prestigious scientific journals – in part because of ethical concerns.[15] The experiments resulted in successful changes to only some of the intended genes, and there were off-target effects on other genes. The researchers stated that CRISPR is not ready for clinical application in reproductive medicine.[16]

In 2015, Experts from seven nations called for a CRISPR moratorium in order to establish an international governance framework for the technology.[17] The proposed moratorium has a focus on human germline editing which would enable the creation of genetically modified children.[18] There have already been attempts in China to apply this technology.[19] While a multitude of considerations come to mind, the most relevant for this thesis is the concept of moral considerations.[20] These moral con-

---

[14] *Liang* et al. (May 2015), CRISPR/Cas9-mediated gene editing in human tripronuclear zygotes, Protein & Cell, 6 (5): 363; *Kolata* (23 April 2015), Chinese Scientists Edit Genes of Human Embryos, Raising Concerns, The New York Times retrieved April 24th, 2015.

[15] *Cyranoski*, Nature, 548 (2018), 272.

[16] *Cyranoski*, Nature, 548 (2018), 272.

[17] *Lander*, Nature 2019, 165 et seq.; *Barad*, Human Embryonic Stem Cells vs Human Induced Pluripotent Stem Cells for Cardiac Repair, 30 Canadian Journal of Cardiology 1279 (2014), 1282; *Barfield/Calfee*, Biotechnology and the Patent System: Balancing Innovation and Property Rights (The AEI Press 2007); *Blackburn*, The Oxford Dictionary of Philosophy (2nd edition), Oxford University Press 2005; *Cohen*, Construction of Biologically Functional Bacterial Plasmids In Vitro, 70 Proceedings of the National Academy of Sciences 3240 (1973), 3244; *Fiechter*, Preface, in: History of Modern Biotechnology II (Armin Fiechter ed., Springer 2000); *Grund*, Mitt. 2000, 328.

[18] *Bergman/Graff*, The Global Stem Cell Patent Landscape: Implications of Efficient Technology Transfer and Commercial Development, 25 Nature Biotechnology 419 (2007), 420 et seq.; *Halliday*, A Comparative Approach to the Regulation of Human Embryonic Stem Cell Research in Europe, 12 Medical Law Review 40 (2004); *Krauß/Engelhardt*, GRUR 2003, 985; *Krefft*, Patente auf human-genomische Erfindungen, Schriftenreihe zum gewerblichen Rechtsschutz Band 122 (2003); *Rimmer*, Intellectual Property and Biotechnology: Biological Inventions (Edward Elgar 2008).

[19] *Peng*, The Morality and Ethics Governing CRISPR-Cas9 Patents in China, 34 Nature Biotechnology 616, 622 (2016); *Liang*, CRIPR/Cas9-mediated Gene Editing in Human Tripronuclear Zygotes, 6 Protein & Cell 363 (2015); *Li*, Chunliang, Efficient Derivation of Chinese Human Embryonic Stem Cell Lines from Frozen Embryos, 46 In Vitro Cellular & Developmental Biology-Animal 186, 188 (2010); a recent research project with significant Chinese support: *Chung*, Human Embryonic Stem Cell Lines Generated Without Embryo Destruction, 2 Cell Stem Cell 113 (2008).

[20] Other considerations are of scientific, technological and medical nature: *Heins*, Derivation, Characterization, and Differentiation of Human Embryonic Stem Cells, 22 Stem Cells 367 (2004); *Heller*, The Boundaries of Private Property, 108 Yale Law Journal 1163 (1999), 1170; *Kitch*, The Patent Policy of Developing Countries, 13 Pacific Basin Law Journal 166, 169 (1994); *Klar/Kunze/Zahradnik*, Journal für Reproduktionsmedizin und Endokrinologie 2007, 21, 22; *Liddell*, Immorality and Patents: The Exclusion of Inventions Contrary to Ordre Public and Morality, in: New Frontiers in the Philosophy of Intellectual Property (Annabelle Lever ed., Cambridge University Press 2012); *Lovell-Badge*, The Regulation of Human Embryo and Stem-cell Research in the United Kingdom, 9 Nature Reviews Molecular Cell

siderations are linked to the possibility of using CRISPR or other similar methods to alter a fundamental aspect of humanity for a particular purpose.[21] It is argued that such an alteration needs "broad societal consensus" and the engagement of "a wide range of voices". Such a sentiment hints at the concept of morality that was the foundation of the proposed moratorium. It highlights the concerns and caution reflected in the formulation of the moratorium. Societal impacts such as the potential stigmatization and discrimination of people with genetic differences or peer pressure for parents to enhance children are much more prominent than inherently ethical considerations – such as the concept of altering fundamental human biology. Additionally, other ethical considerations in the proposal are more medical in nature. The concern that "the introduction of genetic modifications into future generations could have permanent and possibly harmful effects on the species"[22] is one such example.

In February 2017, the United States National Academies of Sciences, Engineering, and Medicine (NASEM) Committee on Human Gene Editing published a report reviewing ethical, legal, and scientific concerns relating to genomic engineering technology. They concluded that heritable genome editing is impermissible now but could be justified for certain medical conditions. However, the usage of CRISPR for human enhancement was not considered to be justified.[23]

Consequently, different policy regulations for CRISPR-gene editing have been implemented. In February 2016, the UK gave permission for the genetic modification of human embryos using CRISPR gene-editing and related techniques. However, the permission does not allow embryos to be implanted and there is a requirement for such embryos to be destroyed after seven days.[24] In the U.S., the first organism that was genetically modified by CRISPR gene-editing passed U.S. regulation in 2016.[25] In the same year, the USDA sponsored a committee to consider future regulatory policy for upcoming genetic modification techniques.[26] In 2017, the Food and Drug Administration proposed a rule that would classify genetic engineering modifications to animals as "animal drugs". The classification subjects them to strict regulation if offered for sale and restricts the capacity for individuals and small businesses to make them profitable.[27]

Biology 998, 1001 (2008); *Rimmer*, The Attack of the Clones: Patent Law and Stem Cell Research, 10 Journal of Law and Medicine 488, 503 (2003).

[21] *Callaway*, Nature, 530 (2017), 16.

[22] *Lander* et al., Nature, 567 (2019), 165.

[23] *Brokowski*, The CRISPR Journal, 2018, 120.

[24] *Callaway*, Nature, 530 (2017), 18.

[25] *Waltz*, Nature, 532 (2017), 293.

[26] *Ledford*, Nature, 532 (2017), 158.

[27] The FDA Is Cracking Down On Rogue Genetic Engineers, Kristen V. Brown, Gizmodo, February 1, 2017; Guidance for Industry #187 / Regulation of Intentionally Altered Genomic DNA in Animals (PDF), February 11th, 2020.

In China, where social conditions arguably contrast with those in Western societies, genetic diseases carry a substantial social stigma.[28] Perhaps as a result of this, China has implemented significantly fewer policy barriers to the use of this technology. In November 2018, the Chinese gene biophysicist *Jiankui He* announced that he had edited two human embryos to attempt to disable the gene for CCR5. CCR5 codes for a receptor that HIV uses to enter cells. Yet, *He* said that the twin girls in whom the modification had been made still carried functional copies of CCR5 along with disabled CCR5 (mosaicism) and were still vulnerable to HIV. The work was widely condemned as unethical, dangerous, and premature.[29] In 2019, the People's Court of Nashan District of Shenzhen, China sentenced the biophysicist to three years in jail for "illegal medical practice".[30] He also received a considerable fine of 3 million yuan.[31]

In conclusion, both conventional stem cell research and CRISPR gene-editing raise moral concerns. Additionally, the concerns overlap substantially. By analyzing the similarities, it is possible to identify the underlying moral principles that influence the controversies. These principles are ultimately relevant for the question of patentability as well.

c) Similarities between CRISPR Gene-Editing and Stem-Cell Research

Human stem cell engineering raises similar moral issues to CRISPR gene-editing though not necessarily in terms of the biotechnology. Part of the controversy of stem cell research is related to the destruction of human embryos and its relevance for human life. CRISPR gene-editing does not necessarily require such destruction. However, the moral concerns are still similar since the research subject in each case is human. In addition, both methods have an effect on a human being and human attributes.

In both cases the controversy stems from the question of whether it is ethically permissible to change something inherently human in a fundamental way. Human embryonic stem cells are considered to be a fundamental unit of life. A certain type of stem cell, the so-called toti-potent stem cell is able to develop into a complete human being.[32] The general controversy is based on this potential, since most research on and

---

[28] *Cyranoski*, Nature, 548 (2018), 272.

[29] *Begley* (28 November 2018) Amid uproar, Chinese scientist defends creating gene-edited babies, STAT.

[30] *Cyranoski*, Nature, 577 (2020) 155.

[31] Approximately 400,000.00 EUR.

[32] *Peng*, Patentability of Stem Cells, 94; *Graeme*, Patenting Stem Cells of Human Origin, 26 European Intellectual Property Review 59, 60 (2004); *Bagley*, Stem Cells, Cloning and Patents: What's Morality Got to Do with it? 39 New England Law Review 501 (2004), 505; Bahadur/Morrison, Patenting Human Pluripotent Cells: Balancing Commercial, Academic and Ethical Interests, 25 Human Reproduction 14 (2010), 15; *Dederer*, GRUR 2007, 1055.

I. Examples of Recent Technological Development with Moral Considerations   39

with such cells requires them to be either altered or destroyed.[33] Destruction of stem cells leads to the objection that it indirectly alters or destroys human life itself, which is considered a highly ethically charged subject.[34] These debates have been ongoing for a very long time and most of the biotechnological details are generally well-known so it is not necessary to repeat them here.[35]

Using CRISPR for human enhancement and utilizing the self-renewal capacity of human embryonic stem cells have huge medical and commercial potential.[36] With such a huge potential comes the need to regulate in this area using patent law. Not only does it seem reasonable to incentivize[37] medical research to cure illnesses that have previously been considered to be incurable, but advanced biotechnology also generally requires a significant amount of initial investment. To make those investments worthwhile it is necessary to secure a phase of profitable commercial exploitation. Allowing for such a phase is one of the specific principle concepts of patent law – the use of the patent as an exclusionary right.[38]

Apart from significant skepticism that advanced biotechnology has been subject to, it has also had to deal with a large amount of controversy and numerous legal battles to attain the desired protection.[39] In particular, the controversies make it apparent that the question of morality in patent law addresses the very fundamental understanding of patent law. It touches upon areas of moral standards, values in a legal culture and the concept of state powers.

---

[33] *Keith*, The Developing Human: Clinically Oriented Embryology 38 (9th edition, Elsevier Saunders 2013); *Baharyand*, Generation of New Human Embryonic Stem Cell Lines with Diploid and Triploid Karyotypes, 48 Development, Growth & Differentiation 117 (2006), 120; *Mai*, Derivation of Human Embryonic Stem Cell Lines from Parthenogenetics Blastocysts, 17 Cell Research 1008, 1014 (2007); *Sander*, The Human Use of Humanoid Beings: Chimeras and Patent Law, 24 Nature Biotechnology 517, 524 (2006); *Resnik*, Embryonic Stem Cell Lines From Human Blastocysts: Somatic Differentiation In Vitro, 18 Nature Biotechnology 399, 404 (2000).

[34] *Peng*, Patentability of Stem Cells, 24; *Papastefanou*, GRUR Junge Wissenschaft 2018, 119 et seq.

[35] Further details are beyond the scope of the present writing, but can be found in the following literature: *Peng* 35 et seq. with a beginner-friendly introduction to the biotechnology of human stem cell research; *Bouvet*, Patentability of Inventions Involving Human Stem Cells in Europe, 9 Journal of commercial biotechnology 40 (2002), 42; *Resnik*, Owning the Genome: A Moral Analysis of DNA Patenting (State University of New York Press 2004).

[36] *Peng*, Patentability of Stem Cells, 43.

[37] *Falvey*, Intellectual Property Rights and Economic Growth, 10 Review of Development Economics 700 (2006) 702; *Fitt*, New Guidance on the Patentability of Embryonic Stem Cell Patents in Europe, 27 Nature Biotechnology 338 (2009); *Revazova*, Patient-specific Stem Cell Lines Derived from Human Parthenogenetic Blastocysts, 9 Cloning and Stem Cell 432, 451 (2007); *Winter*, DVBl 1986, 589.

[38] *Muscati*, "Some More Human Than Others": Assessing the Scope of Patentability Related to Human Embryonic Stem Cell Research, Jurimetrics 201, 202, 205 et seq. (2004); including global political issues: *Dolder*, Mitt. 2003, 350 et seq.

[39] *Peng*, Patentability of Stem Cells, 49.

d) Summary

In conclusion, biotechnology has changed over the years, yet, the core controversy remains the same: it centers on the principle of human life and altering human attributes in the form of human enhancement. Additionally, biotechnological advancements usually require significant investments. Therefore, patents are considered an appropriate means to ensure profitable exploitation. Ultimately, a patent application is very likely the first legal hurdle to take and ignites any moral debate. The societal and legal debates are subsequently very open and intense.

In comparison, it is interesting to see how other technologies approach ethical issues. To exemplify, weapon technology is usually developed in the "shadows". Controversies are much more subtle and sometimes even invisible. This is in the context of the fact that weapon technology is usually subject to state secrecy. Therefore, it might not even become the subject of a patent application process. Without a patent application, controversies surrounding weapon technology might arise outside of patent law or not at all. Nonetheless, the general principles of morality in patent law are legally applicable to any invention. The following chapter will analyze how moral principles in patent law can be addressed when issues of morality are less obvious and the debate is less heated. Analyzing both ends of the debate spectrum offers a good general idea of the concept of patentability and morality. In addition, the role of legal culture will be introduced into the discussion.

2. Weapon Technology and Moral Concerns

There are two main reasons why technologies other than biotech are not central in morality debates. First, issues of morality are often not as obvious as in advanced biotechnology inventions where of the terms "human nature", "human species" and "human dignity" are common. The question of patentability is then usually rephrased into a question of life and death or the position of power over life and death. Naturally, framing the issue from such a perspective and portraying it with such gravitas is much more likely to draw in the general public and special interest groups.

The second reason comes about due to the concept of patentability which allows even illegal inventions to obtain patent protection. Accordingly, generally dangerous inventions, which are intended for use in a defensive or offensive manner against human beings, are still patentable.[40] By expressing this idea as a general principle of patentability, one might be quick to draw the conclusion that patent law is fundamentally technology-neutral. Yet, this part of the thesis will address some modern and recent developments in weapon technology which certainly have the potential to

---

[40] *Straus*, GRUR 1998, 318; with more analysis on therapeutic methods: *Rigby*, Revocation of European Patent for Neural Progenitors Highlights Patent Challenges for Inventions Relating to Human Embryonic Stem Cells, 23 Expert Opinion on Therapeutic Patents 1397, 1402 (2013).

I. Examples of Recent Technological Development with Moral Considerations 41

raise moral concerns. In addition, the societal view of weapon technology and government funding has changed in some industrial countries. Most recently, the concept of autonomy in weapon technology has raised ethical issues. European countries in particular have expressed ethical concerns about autonomous weapon technology.[41] The United Nations Convention on Certain Conventional Weapons (CCCW) has also put lethal autonomous weapon systems on their agenda.[42] Other terms for autonomous weapon technology include "Lethal Autonomous Robots" and "killer robots".[43] Such terms indicate that the specific debate around lethal autonomous weapon systems is already emotionally charged to some degree. Therefore, for the purposes of this thesis, to identify a more general conception of the role of morality in patent law, the focus of this chapter is on weapon systems which are less commonly debated.

Introducing new weapon systems (aside from lethal autonomous weapon systems) with the potential to revolutionize modern warfare provides a variety of legal and ethical challenges. Patent protection is still of considerable interest for private investors, even if government-funded research may be subject to secrecy.

There are very few but prominent examples of weapon technology being considered morally questionable. Interestingly enough, the most well-known example, in the context of patent law, is anti-personnel mines. Such mines are specifically mentioned in the EPO guidelines regarding inventions which violate morality in patent law.[44]

To exemplify the impact of such technologies on armed conflict and thereby directly or indirectly on human life, this chapter discusses two recent developments: railgun weapons and laser weapon systems. First, this section provides a brief overview of the relevance of the global weapons market. This overview is then followed by the technical basics and finally the moral concerns which arise as a result of possible legal violations.

a) Global Relevance of Modern Weapon Technology

The two aforementioned technologies have been around for several decades – albeit mostly theoretically. However, in the past five to ten years they have been subject to more substantial and practical development.[45]

---

[41] PAX, Crunch Time, European positions on lethal autonomous weapon systems, 2018.
[42] Final Document of the Firth Review Conference, CCW, December 23rd, 2016.
[43] PAX, Crunch Time, European positions on lethal autonomous weapon systems, 2018, 30 et seq.
[44] EPO Guidelines for Examination – Part G patentability 4.1 "Matter contrary to 'ordre public' or morality".
[45] *Straus*, GRUR 1990, 915.

In the past decade, development and research regarding railguns have increased rapidly in Germany.[46] In 2015, the Federal Government in Germany admitted to having invested an amount exceeding 80 million Euro in the development of laser-based weapon systems. Before 2015, involvement in any such development had been denied.

Even though this is already a considerable investment, it pales in comparison to the U.S. investments. Prototypes of both systems were presented at the Naval Future Force: Science & Technology Expo in 2015.[47] The U.S. military intends a practical application of laser weapon systems[48] and has specified plans for industrial construction.[49] Another development in the U.S. is the LaWS (Laser Weapon System) which was prototyped in 2014 and is intended for practical application.[50]

Even China has been rumored to be engaging in the development of railguns.[51] However, since almost no official statements exist, reports have been based on satellite pictures.

---

[46] German defense supplier and arms manufacturer Rheinmetall Defence has been developing prototypes of directed-energy weapons since 2010 and managed to successfully test ground vehicle-borne high-precision laser systems in 2015. Another German arms manufacturer – MBDA Germany – also developed and field-tested several laser-based weapon systems in the recent 2010s http://www.flugrevue.de/flugzeugbau/mbda-deutschland-testet-hochenergie-laserwaffensystem/489136. The electromagnetic weapon version commonly known as a "railgun" has been the subject of research by Rheinmetall Defence since the 1990s and a prototype was installed in Germany in 1994: https://web.archive.org/web/20101220103203/http://rheinmetall-defence.com/product.php?fid=3844&lang=2.

[47] http://carzz.co/link/11600/the-navy-s-gigantic-railgun-is-almost-ready-for-prime-time/. Those plans were later changed to use a different warship, the USS Ponce but the concept was unchanged.

[48] The 2019 Navy fiscal budget proposal explicitly sets aside 45.8 million US Dollars to "applied research addressing the unique technical challenges inherent in the construction, assembly and operation" of the railgun prototypes currently tested by engineers at the Office of Naval Research and Naval Sea Systems Command: http://nationalinterest.org/blog/the-buzz/the-navys-electromagnetic-railgun-both-alive-dead-24616; https://www.military.com/defensetech/2018/03/09/navy-fully-invested-futuristic-railgun-top-officer-says.html

[49] https://news.usni.org/2015/01/05/navy-wants-rail-guns-fight-ballistic-supersonic-missiles-says-rfi; not surprisingly, no recent patents regarding these developed technologies can be found in the USPTO register or any patent register.

[50] US Navy developing laser weapons for ground vehicles, Gizmag, June 14th, 2014; http://edition.cnn.com/2014/12/11/tech/innovation/navy-laser-weapon; http://www.defenseindustrydaily.com/a-laser-phalanx-03783/. The U.S. Navy works in a joint program with the U.S. Air Force to build a high-powered radio frequency weapon for aircraft called High-Power Joint Electromagnetic Non-Kinetic Strike (HIJENKS): http://www.thedrive.com/the-war-zone/18489/despite-what-youve-heard-the-navy-isnt-ditching-its-railgun-and-budget-docs-prove-it.

[51] Early in 2018, rumors appeared that the Chinese military had taken steps to establish a first experimental deployment of a new "supergun" aboard a warship. Images began circulating in February 2018, which showed a Chinese amphibious assault ship – usually used to deploy troops and other material on a beach – with an enormous cannon on its bows http://www.news.com.au/technology/innovation/china-in-worldfirst-deployment-of-experimental-electromagnetic-rail-supergun-aboard-a-warship/news-story/6aab73b4402e064d41e7b1af463

I. Examples of Recent Technological Development with Moral Considerations   43

It seems as if all the significant military powers are engaging in a new arms race. Such competition and secrecy raise the question as to why such technologies are so desired. In addition, the new elements within those systems raise moral concerns as well. One of the main benefits of technological advancement is the economic cost-effectiveness of these weapon systems. Railguns and laser-weapons provide faster, lighter and cheaper projectiles than traditional defense systems and therefore, have the potential to replace the current traditional defense approach.[52] However, simple cost-effectiveness is not usually a cause for ethical concerns. Therefore, it is helpful to take a closer look at these emerging technologies and how they differ from conventional weapon systems.

b) Fundamental Differences to Conventional Weapon Technology

This presentation of the technology is intended as a scientific and technological overview and includes an introduction to the fundamental concepts. Subsequently, the potential conflict with standards of morality in patent law is addressed.[53] The descriptions are as short as possible while still giving a sufficient overview of the topic. Additionally, they are not meant to focus on any recent technology specifically.

aa) Railgun Basics

The construction of a railgun consists of two metal rails within a magnetic field with a power source supplying a current along each rail. A projectile is then inserted between the rails and completes the circuit between both rails. The connection creates an electric current which enables the contraption to behave like an electromagnet. The magnetic field created by the completion of the electromagnet circulates around each conductor. A simple straight line describes the flow of current in the direction of the magnetic field and resulting Lorentz force.[54] The Lorentz force then propels the projectile away from the power source along the rails. This kind of ac-

---

9c5ed. In an interview with the Science and Technology Daily component of the People's Daily, Chen Shuoren, a military commentator even addressed the competition with the U.S.: "Though the U.S. has been openly developing electromagnetic guns for years, it doesn't mean that China is far behind in this field, as the latter usually keeps quiet about its progress due to secrecy concerns. (…) If [the rumors] are confirmed to be true, this would be a milestone for China's electromagnetic weapons research program, with epoch-making significance." It is assumed that the Type 072 II landing ship named Haiyangshan has been fitted with a rail gun, stating the China Aerospace Science & Industry Corporation had announced a major breakthrough in electromagnetic research in 2015.

[52] *Keller*, The Navy's Much-Hyped Electromagnetic Railgun May End Up Dead In The Water, December 4th, 2017.

[53] It does not cover other patentability requirements such as novelty and technical feasibility.

[54] *Hawke/Scudder*, Physics and Technology, Magnetic Propulsion Railguns: Their Design and Capabilities, 1980, 148.

celeration and projectile system is highly similar to the barrel of a traditional gun. The inherent calculation of force and arch are identical.[55] The Lorentz force accelerates the mobile projectile along the rails which are mounted in a fixed place and are therefore not affected in a lateral direction by the Lorentz force which is produced. The amount of acceleration produced is affected by the length of the rails and the electric current.

In terms of weapon efficiency, such a projectile can easily reach extremely high velocities, nearly two magnitudes higher than traditional projectiles. Therefore, these projectiles carry an immense amount of kinetic energy that can penetrate any kind of available material protection such as a tank or bunker armor.

bb) Laser Weapon System Basics

A directed-energy system does not function in a fundamentally different way from a hand-held and commercially available laser pointer.[56] The magnitude of available power is simply increased significantly. The increase in amplitude and frequency of the electromagnetic radiation allows energy to be transported over long distances and used for a variety of different purposes. Since the range of potential applications is vast, it is not necessary or reasonable to include a more in-depth analysis. The main take-away is that the laser transforms electrical energy into electro-magnetic energy in the form of rays. Simple transformation of energy makes the equipment of warships or other military vehicles easier than with other weapon systems since it does not require any ammunition at all, just a powerful generator. The applications of such devices range from crowd-control measures to anti-missile systems or extreme precision strikes.

cc) Advantages of the Emerging Weapon Systems

The advantages of these weapon systems to conventional weapons relate to the fact that they do not require a traditional propellant or an explosive projectile. It makes them easier and safer to store and handle than regular ammunition. Furthermore, a requirement for gunpowder or any other propellant adds additional weight, increases volatility and limits velocity since the projectile cannot be accelerated to a greater speed than the gas expansion. Since military projectiles require energy to randomize a target area, explosives are commonly used. However, a railgun projectile can have very high kinetic energy which is comparable to commonly used explosive projectiles, rendering the inclusion of explosives obsolete. Railgun ammunition, in the form of small tungsten missiles, is relatively light, easy and safe to transport, handle and store. The potentially high velocities and range makes railgun missiles far less susceptible to wind shift observed in conventional artillery shells.

---

[55] Id at 150.
[56] *Kaushal*, Applications of Lasers for Tactical Military Operations, IEEE Access, 20739.

Finally, chemical propellant requires air to function by initiating the reaction of gas expansion and therefore does not work in outer space or on objects without an atmosphere. A railgun, however, requires no air or atmosphere of any kind.

The major research obstacle which had to be overcome in the development of such weapons was the amount of required energy. Recent technological advancements in electric motors have increased mobility, capacity and energy efficiency. Hence, the practical operation of both weapon technologies became much more feasible.

Apart from the kinetic and economic advantages, laser weapon systems are much more versatile in their application than conventional weapon technology. In particular, their potential uses as non-lethal crowd-control devices are relevant. Most prominently, the use of laser weapon technology leaves no trace behind, potentially not even on the target. Railgun systems also leave very few traces behind, mostly because no explosives are used and the projectile disintegrates on impact.

c) Areas of Moral Concern

The differences between the new weapon technology systems and conventional weapons are not limited to pure economic cost-effectiveness. Specifically, the increase in destructive power, the versatility of application, the potentially traceless deployment and the use of radiation are elements that might be morally concerning. In the following section, those elements are analyzed in comparison to conventional morality concerns for weapon technology. This will allow a general understanding of morality in the context of patent law – or lack thereof – to be identified.

II. Potential Moral Considerations with Regard to Modern Weapon Technology

While it is difficult to pinpoint potential morality concerns without looking at a specific piece of technology, the following provides some examples of morally ambiguous applications. As a starting point, it is helpful to address moral concerns that are expressed within legislation and international treaties. Some concerns were due to potential public and international condemnation. Other moral concerns are formulated according to international standards on warfare such as the Geneva Convention or The Convention on the Prohibition of the Use, Stockpiling, Production and Transfer of Anti-Personnel Mines and on their Destruction. Subsequently, it is necessary to relate a potential violation of an international treaty or national to patentability, given the illustrated nature of patents as exclusionary rights as opposed to rights of use. In a next step, the chapter addresses possible violations of national laws as a basis for morality concerns. Since the analysis of national laws is non-exhaustive and illustrative in purpose, German criminal and administrative laws are used.

1. Moral Concerns of the Heat Ray

A better-known example of public concern is the Heat Ray. It is basically a directed-energy weapon with a less intense and less focused ray of electromagnetic energy. Its operative principle is that of inflicting pain on a person without damaging the skin. The technology developed by the CIA was deployed during the Afghanistan War as a crowd control measure.[57] It works by heating deep body tissue. When used on a person, they experience a heating sensation which quickly turns painful and thereby forces them to leave a certain area. The ray is powerful enough to penetrate multiple layers of clothing but does not have enough energy to incinerate clothes or burn skin. During its deployment in the Afghanistan War, the weapon was never used in active combat because of moral concerns.[58] Since its application does not leave any evidence, it raised concerns and rumors that it might be used as a modern torture device. In addition, it has the capacity to inflict immense amounts of pain on restrained subjects. Therefore, its use was considered to be potentially too damaging to the United States Armed Forces or the CIA. The deployment therefore bore the risk of further decreasing support for the war among the American population.[59] As a result, the combat-ready weapons had no confirmed field execution. It is speculated that the use was intentionally avoided to fend off possible accusations of using torture devices in an already not widely supported war. These concerns and speculations were further increased because the weapon might be potentially harmful to the nervous system of the target.

Such an effect would make the 1980 Convention on Certain Conventional Weapons ("*1980 CCCW*") applicable. The device would be classified as a weapon that targets the central nervous system and cause neurophysiological disorders.

2. UN Convention CCW

The 1980 CCCW serves as a perfect example of international armed conflict regulations. It includes prohibitions or restrictions on the use of certain conventional weapons which may be deemed to be excessively injurious or to have indiscriminate effects. The Convention does not include a general morality clause but Protocol V, for example, restricts laser weapons that have the intent to blind human targets. However, laser weapon systems where blinding is an incidental or collateral effect, are not covered. Technically all the aforementioned directed-energy weapon systems are capable of blinding human targets. Yet, since the formulation of Protocol V of the Convention relates to intent and not capability, the regulation can be easily cir-

---

[57] *Shachtman*, January 25th, 2007, U.S. Testing Pain Ray in Afghanistan (Updated Again), wired.com, June 19th, 2010.

[58] An Opportunity Missed, Defensestudies.org, archived from the original on November 1st, 2014.

[59] US withdraws "pain ray" from Afghan war zone, Daily Mail, London, January 25th, 2010.

cumvented by manipulating the description of the intention behind the weapon. A purely objective analysis of the invention is not feasible because an invention itself does not have an intent. The ways in which the Convention can be circumvented are already allegedly exploited by military officials and arms suppliers by classifying the specific weapons as range-finding devices, target illuminators or anti-sensor systems.[60] Therefore, medical personnel from combat zones around the world have been calling for an amendment to Protocol V. They call for all states to be obliged to undertake feasible precautions to avoid such effects as a result of the devices.

3. Significance of International Treaties

The role of international treaties and conventions regarding the use of weapons is an adequate basis on which to analyze moral concerns. The 1980 CCCW does cover weapons that result in superfluous injury or unnecessary suffering, which laser weapons in a specific configuration can easily produce.[61] Art. 35 No. 2 CCCW addresses weapons that go beyond lethal intentions. While it seems that this establishes a certain standard of morality or humanity in warfare, its practicability and significance are debatable. Several questions are raised by the general nature of the provision. What is a superfluous effect beyond lethal intention since death is considered a legitimate intention? When does suffering become unnecessary?

A more direct and specific approach is taken by the Convention on the Prohibition of the Use, Stockpiling, Production and Transfer of Anti-Personnel Mines and on their Destruction (informally known as the Mine Ban Treaty, Anti-Personnel Mine Ban Convention, or APMBC). As mentioned before, anti-personnel mines are the only example given by the EPO guidelines of a non-patentable invention based on morality concerns. Using these mines as an example hints at the relevance of international treaties because they require a significant amount of common international understanding. The implementation of international treaties also requires considerable effort by the international community. These factors might be considered relevant with regard to identifying a moral standard in patent law. The EPO guidelines clearly state that such mines are to be regarded as immoral in the context of patent law.

Reasons given for the abandonment of anti-personnel mines include the indiscriminate nature of those devices. While conventional weapons make use of an aiming mechanism in some direct or indirect way that is controlled by a human being or was initiated by a human command, these devices function autonomously (ap-

---

[60] *Kaushal*, Applications of Lasers for Tactical Military Operations, IEEE Access, 20737.

[61] Non-lethal weapons misuse: USDOD: Statement and Human Effects Advisory Panel https://www.icrc.org/ihl.nsf/7c4d08d9b287a42141256739003e636b/f6c8b9fee14a77fdc125641e0052b079.

plying a very basic understanding of the word[62]). Other concerns include the nature of the inflicted injuries which usually affect "innocent and defenseless civilians and especially children."[63] They also obstruct economic development and reconstruction, inhibit the repatriation of refugees and internally displaced persons, and have other severe consequences for years after emplacement. The difficulty of removing or controlling them and safe detonation of these mines contributes to these severe consequences. Most countries that are especially affected by the placement of anti-personnel mines usually also lack the resources and equipment or even the governmental oversight and control to effectively identify and locate or restrict access to mine fields.

Given the notions of civilian life, innocence and suffering, the underlying values that shaped the rationale of the Mine Ban Treaty are centered around humanistic values, arguably human dignity.[64] In that way they are similar to the values of modern European constitutions which prominently feature human dignity. Certain similarities with the moral debate regarding advanced biotechnology can be identified on that basis. Human dignity is also a prominent value in those discussions. Consequently, these matters of life and death in biotechnology can be linked to debates around the need to alter human stem cells and thereby arguably human life. In addition, another significant area of debate is around outcomes are societally important enough to outweigh the concerns about the alteration and destruction of cells. Similarly, in the drafting of agreements and treaties such as the CCCW 1980 or the Mine Ban Treaty, it was stated that human suffering must be minimized, even during war time.[65] Consequently, the questions are similar and also subject to debate, given the fact that the U.S. is not part of the Mine Ban Treaty because of diverging opinions on the effects of and need for anti-personnel mines.[66] It is thus clear that the question of morality comes down to balancing opposing interests. The weight of different interests and the values included in the process are subject to the legal culture of a specific legal system.

4. Potential Violations of National Law

The following section therefore primarily focuses on using these examples to ascertain potential aspects of national prohibitive legislation. Thereafter, the analysis addresses the potential effect of violations on patentability, rather than providing an in-depth analysis of the provision in general.

---

[62] In a more common understanding, autonomy refers to a more complex device that uses a certain algorithm to initiate its actions and reactions. However, the function of an anti-personnel mine is governed by a very simple proximity or pressure algorithm that results in the detonation of the charge.

[63] Preamble of the Mine-Ban Convention.

[64] Statement of the UN Secretary General António Guterres, November 25th, 2019.

[65] Preamble of the Mine-Ban Convention.

[66] US Landmine Policy 2020.

II. Potential Moral Considerations with Regard to Modern Weapon Technology 49

Generally, it is not possible to make clear statements about the violation of morality due to the commercial exploitation of an invention by addressing criminal law provisions. However, it showcases how deep an analysis has to go to identify possible morality concerns in technologies that are not as obviously controversial as advanced biotechnology. The reason for this is the interplay between illegality and morality. Prohibitive legislation expresses at its core immoral behavior or at least behavior that is considered to be detrimental to society. The concept, nature and scope of such provisions is marked by the legal culture of the legislative background.

Laser weapon systems use photon radiation, which has the potential to affect the air. Such radiation is also emitted by nuclear decay or other nuclear events. In Germany, several criminal law provisions exist to prevent the use of radiation.

a) Potential Violation of Sect. 311, 309 StGB[67]

In brief, there are specific sections of German law which relate to atomic or nuclear explosions, as well as any related ionizing radiation. Those laws were originally designed to secure a stricter standard in the operation of nuclear power plants. Any events penalized by Sect. 311, 309 StGB are generally either the result of failures in the control of nuclear fission or terrorist attacks. However, terrorist attacks are already penalized under a variety of other sections.[68] It might not be directly obvious how such penalties are related to the patentability of modern military weaponry, however. To illustrate the relevance, it is necessary to give a more in-depth analysis of the scientific terms and function of directed-energy and railgun devices. A more detailed analysis is also necessary, since – as will be shown – the provisions themselves do not establish a clear and concise use of scientific terminology. The scientific inaccuracies might be attributed at least partly to a lack of understanding by the legislator of the time.

For the purpose of the following analysis, it must first be determined whether the use of modern weapon technology is potentially covered by at least parts of the respective sections of law. The consequences for patentability and other restrictions that may apply in German criminal law will be addressed briefly, without being subject of extended criminal law analysis.

b) Applicability

First of all, Sect. 311 StGB requires the violation of an administrative regulation which is defined in Sect. 330d (1) no. 4 StGB. Therefore, the section is technically only applicable to persons who are subject to administrative regulations, more specifically regulations regarding the protection of the environment according to Sect. 330d (1) No. 4 StGB. The administrative regulation can also stem from a

---

[67] Strafgesetzbuch (German Criminal Code).
[68] Such as Sect. 84 et seq.

specific piece of legislation. A restriction of application is only achievable by the interplay of Sect. 311 StGB and Sect. 330d (1) No. 1 StGB. It raises the interesting question of whether the piece of legislation can also be Sect. 311 StGB itself, even though that is in contrast to the intended concept. Even from this initial point, the legal analysis of these provisions encounters several uncertainty issues. Furthermore, since the use of nuclear power in Germany has been decreasing and accidents as well as terrorist attacks are extremely rare, no substantial jurisprudence or legal commentary exists.

Sect 309 StGB which is also applicable to ionizing radiation, does not incorporate the requirement to violate an administrative regulation. Instead, Sect. 309 requires more specific intentions of the perpetrator or certain consequences from the use of ionizing radiation.[69]

Sect. 311 StGB is not applicable to intentional actions only but simply requires the violation of respective administrative regulations and the consequent release of ionizing radiation. Furthermore, the section requires the offender to have a direct intention to act with malicious intent to cause harm or damage to a person, property of high value, environmental surroundings, animals or plants of significant value.

Given all these requirements, the mere use of ionizing radiation is already unlikely to be covered by this part of the German Criminal Code. Ionizing radiation is not part of any officially regulated power production facility or subject to administrative regulation. However, the intentional use of a laser weapon might be covered by Sect. 311 StGB. This makes sense, because intentional use is much narrower than the concept of the regulation itself. Therefore, even though it is unlikely that Sect. 311 StGB will cover all intended usages of directed-energy weapon systems, they are not entirely excluded. Therefore, this section is still applicable, even though there was probably no intention by the legislator to cover it.

Another aspect that restricts the clear identification of moral standards from criminal provisions is the fact that, generally, the usage of weaponry also holds the possibility of justification or exclusions of guilt. Therefore, a potential violation of criminal law provision does not make the use of a weapon system absolutely illegal.

c) Ionizing Radiation

There exists no legal definition of the term "ionizing radiation". It is a difficult subject to define in legal terms, since different molecules and atoms ionize at different energy levels – ranging anywhere from 10 eV to 33 eV. More unstable molecules and atoms are ionized more easily and require less energy. In addition, generally speaking, each photon that hits a molecule or atom needs to transport that amount of energy to ionize. The specific energy per photon required means that radiation can be categorized into different categories which is also what most German

---

[69] Such as loss of life, or significant damage to the environment, etc.

legal scholars suggest.⁷⁰ For example, 10 eV of energy can be converted into a specific spectrum of electromagnetic radiation with the specific capability to ionize air molecules. However, this calculation ignores aspects of multi-proton ionization. Such ionization describes an effect where the energy state of each photon package is irrelevant and the sheer number of photons suffices to initiate ionization. High-powered laser rays are specifically suited to producing high quantities of coherent photons even though the contained package energy is less than sufficient for traditional ionization.⁷¹

d) Potential to Violate Regulations on Ionizing Radiation

The fact that the ionizing capability of the emitted ray is only applicable to the atmosphere significantly restricts the effective range of laser beams. Therefore, any of the relevant weapon technologies are not likely to have atmosphere ionizing capabilities. However, given the effects of multi-proton ionization, it is possible that both railguns and directed-energy weapons have an ionizing effect on skin or other biological matter. A highly powered railgun might also be (theoretically) able to ionize parts of the atmosphere it travels through. These considerations show how difficult it is to identify a violation of a criminal provision.

5. Relationship of Legal Violations and Patentability

It is a fundamental principle of patent law that the illegality of an invention does not automatically render it immoral.⁷² It is therefore necessary to address how the identified violations relate to the requirements for patentability in general. First, the relationship between international treaties and patentability will be reviewed. After that, the analysis will focus on the violation of national legislation and its effect on patentability.

a) International Treaties and Patentability

International treaties usually focus on issues that are subject to general global consensus. It can be observed that existing debates about the morality of technology generally focus on issues of humanity, dignity, humane treatment and societal consensus on tolerable amounts of suffering. These purposes can range from medical treatment to the need⁷³ for war or armed conflict. Public international law on

---

⁷⁰ *Tozer*, Theory of the Ionization of Gases by Laser Beams, Physical Review Journals Archive, American Physical Society, 1965, 139.

⁷¹ Id at 141.

⁷² This is a lead ahead to the following chapters and will be analyzed in more depth. For the purposes of this chapter, it is sufficient to leave it as a superficial overview.

⁷³ Again, this is expressly an observation and not an opinion on this deeply philosophical issue.

weaponized conflict is therefore not inherently different from other issues of morality.

The Geneva Convention, as an example, expresses some international consensus. It consists mainly of general outlines or accepted rules rather than actually enforceable law.[74] Even a clear violation of either treatment is not necessarily reprimanded by the international community in any meaningful way. Hence, there has not been sufficient analysis of how an international treaty might influence patent law or which relevancy it bears in the context of patentability. Herein lies the most significant difference with the debate regarding advanced biotechnology. Restrictions on the patentability of weapon technology or any other technology besides biotechnology have to be assessed under the general provisions of patentability. These provisions usually include terms such as "morality", "public order", etc. The restriction of biotechnology on the other hand is usually incorporated into specific patentability provisions.[75] The incorporation broadens the debate because it is difficult or even borderline impossible to effectively apply such a general provision in the context of patent law.

With that being said, one possible angle to identify a potential effect on patent law is Art. 36 of the additional protocol of the 1980 CCCW. This protocol restricts the production, development, storage and in-field application of any weapon system that is covered by the initial agreement. This wide array of restrictions makes it clear that no meaningful differentiation is possible between actual development or government incentives for such development by third parties. Given the nature of a patent as providing an exclusionary right, it is possible to argue that an invention has to be excluded from patentability on account of the violation of the CCCW. Otherwise, the function of a patent to provide incentives to develop new technologies would go against a state's obligations as formulated by the treaty. A state cannot, on the one hand, forbid any conceivable use or development of a certain technology, while simultaneously granting patents for the same technology.

b) National Law and Patentability

Apart from the more obvious regulatory standards of international treaties which directly focus on certain technologies, a possible violation of national law might also be the basis for morality concerns. Even though the exclusion from patentability cannot legally be based on the mere violation of a single national law, morality and ordre public are commonly reflected in national legislation.[76] However, such provisions allow for the inverted conclusion that an invention may not be excluded from

---

[74] It might be argued that such treaties, primarily or more commonly, serve symbolic functions.

[75] Most notably the EU Biotechnology directive.

[76] Clearly stated by the TRIPS agreement in Art. to prevent states from using national prohibitive law to restrict the international intentions of patent law.

patentability on the grounds of moral concerns if its commercial exploitation is perfectly legal.[77]

Therefore, identifying possible national laws which are violated by a new technology serves as a promising starting point. The examples mentioned relate to instances where such a violation might occur due to the commercial use of the weapon technologies. In the context of these specific regulations, differences between the traditional weapon systems and the recently developed concepts of direct-energy weapons and railguns are further emphasized. This emphasis helps to identify the fundamental nature of those weapon technologies and makes it easier to understand why a different approach to regular weapon technology might seem reasonable. The analysis further underlines how regulations or laws that might be relevant to a specific weapon technology are sometimes vague and insufficient. These shortcomings are usually caused by a lack of necessary scientific understanding.

Without the necessary understanding of the potential uses of a technology, no great debate about the modern technologies can exist. This allows moral concerns to hide even further beneath a legal and technological thicket. As long as a moral concern is not obvious, it is unlikely that it is going have a significant effect on patentability. In spite of this, the examples of national legislation demonstrate how a potential violation can be identified. Additionally, it means that there can be debate about whether a certain violation is relevant to the understanding of morality within patent law.

III. Conclusion

Given the new and highly efficient aspects of relevant weapon technologies, this analysis considers the role morality and public order play in the frame of patentability and whether the current framework is adequate for recent developments. Addressing different varieties of morally concerning inventions, it can be observed that the underlying principles of morality relate to a similar set of values. These introductory remarks indicate how the fundamental considerations of the purpose and idea of patent law and morality are similar.

The global similarity of the considerations poses a question of how major patent jurisdictions address this issue with regard to their own understanding of patent law. In other words, it is of scientific interest to more gain insights about the influence of legal culture.

The combination of both examples of technology indicates that a moral controversy can either be very direct or difficult to identify. An open controversy is subject to emotional debate and heavily influenced by non-legal viewpoints around

---

[77] Otherwise, a state might be able to abuse the provision to protect its economy against foreign patent holders.

morality. This makes it difficult to assess the situation with purely legal tools. Incorporating moral considerations into a legal standard is very complex and is likely to be unable to keep up with the dynamic developments of technology.

On the other hand, identifying moral concerns out of the context of heated social debates brings its own set of challenges. Using international and national legislation as a compass of morality is possible but requires very careful assessment. In addition, it is necessary to be aware of the limitations of legal analysis in the context of patentability and morality.

Achieving a thorough understanding of the legal background of patent law morality requirements is a necessary basis for any further assessment.

C. Moral Considerations in Patentability in European and German Patent Law

As described, this chapter incorporates a black letter analysis of German and European patent law and the most important case law. However, all three patent jurisdictions covered by this thesis are members of the World Trade Organization. All members are subject to the Agreement on Trade-Related Aspects of Intellectual Property Rights (TRIPS). Therefore, Art. 27 TRIPS, which is the basis for morality clauses in patent law regimes, applies to all relevant jurisdictions.

This chapter begins by introducing Art. 27 TRIPS and its fundamental approach to morality clauses in patent law. From this point it moves on to an analysis of European patent law provisions and finally German patent law restrictions (I.). This then serves as a basis for the later research on the U.S. and Chinese patent law regimes.

Secondly, morality and ordre public on a European patent level are analyzed (II.). A major aspect of this analysis is the challenge in determining ordre public on a supranational level – the EPO. Several possible solutions and member-specific approaches are possible and are addressed. The second part focuses on the *Brüstle* case, relevant within the EU. The *Brüstle* case marks the major decision on how moral concerns are applied within the European Patent system. This sub-chapter includes a detailed analysis of the shortcomings of morality approaches.

Moving from the supranational to the German patent system, the chapter then addresses the national level in the hierarchy (III.). Both German and European Patent law have a common theme in that they include specific legislation regarding morality in patent law. Both are also civil law cultures and therefore share the same legal cultural background.

The fourth sub-chapter (IV.) addresses the requirement of "commercial exploitation". Legally, not the invention itself must raise moral concerns but only the commercial exploitation of said invention. This requirement is part of all three levels and is therefore analyzed independently.

Ultimately, the chapter closes with a conclusive summary (V.) of the findings.

I. Art. 27 (2) TRIPS and Respective Regulations

Art. 27 (2) of the TRIPS Agreement is a regulation which also relates to moral and legal order and its connection to the exclusion of patentability. It is therefore possible for any WTO-member to "exclude from patentability inventions, the prevention within their territory of the commercial exploitation of which is necessary to protect ordre public or morality, including to protect human, animal or plant life or health or to avoid serious prejudice to the environment, provided that such exclusion is not made merely because the exploitation is prohibited by their law."[1]

Subsection (3) of Art. 27 allows for further exclusion, however, it only covers methods for the treatment of humans or animals and patents which contain plants, animals or other biological processes. Therefore, this subsection is not directly relevant to the current analysis.

The formulation allows for the identification of two fundamental principles: an invention may only be excluded from patent protection in a case where its commercial exploitation is also prevented.[2] Additionally, exclusion has to be a qualified regulation and intended to protect the legal and or moral order. Those aspects are not defined in a more precise manner. Yet, the numeration of human, animal or plant life and "serious prejudice to the environment" indicate that only assets of similar significance may justify an exclusion from patentability.[3]

1. Relevance of Art. 27 (2) TRIPS for the Interpretation of Subsequent Regulation

Art. 27 (2) TRIPS functions in two notable ways. Firstly, it prohibits the legislative power from barring inventions from patent protection whose commercial exploitation has been explicitly permitted in other national legislation. It also prevents the judicial branch from applying the national patentability exclusion regulations based on Art. 27 (2) TRIPS to inventions whose commercial exploitation is permitted.

The application of any national patentability regulation is subject to a two-tier conformability test respective of Art. 27 (2) TRIPS. In a first step, it is necessary to establish whether the commercial exploitation of a certain invention is prohibited by legislation. In such a case, the second step assesses whether the relevant prohibitive legislation can be considered part of the legal or moral order.[4] However, just because the commercial exploitation of an invention has not yet been regulated does not mean the respective patent has to be granted. Art. 27 (2) TRIPS clearly states that the

---

[1] Art. 27 (2) TRIPS; *Gervais*, TRIPS Agreement: Drafting History and Analysis (3rd edition, Sweet & Maxwell 2008), 210; *Porter*, Human Embryos, Patents and Global Trade: Assessing the Scope and Contents of the TRIPS Morality Exception, in: Embryonic Stem Cell Patents: European Law and Ethics (Aurora Plomer & Paul Torremans eds, Oxford University Press 2009); *Sreenivasulu*, Biotechnology and Patent Law: Patenting Living Beings (1st edition, Manupatra 2008).

[2] *Romandini*, 232; *Spranger*, LMK 2010, 298400.

[3] *Rott*, Patentrecht und Sozialpolitik unter dem TRIPS-Abkommen, 225.

[4] *Romandini*, 232 et seq.; *Vossius/Grund*, Mitt. 1995, 339, 341.

prevention of commercial exploitation has to be a necessity but not already subject to specific legislation. For example, in cases where only contracts regarding the invention are prohibited, it may still be excluded from patentability based on Art. 27 (2) TRIPS.[5]

The terms "morality" and "public order" stem from the TRIPS agreement and therefore have to be interpreted autonomously. Identical terms in different pieces of national legislation are generally irrelevant. For example, in German patent law the definition is very strict. It only applies to the commercial exploitation of the patent but it is hard to subsume a certain case under the definition. Even though German law features identical or similar terms in other civil law provisions,[6] the content or meaning in the PatG differs significantly. Other German legislation with similar morality provisions is, unfortunately, not transferrable.

The nature of legal decisions to work on a case-by-case basis makes a general assessment even more difficult. Identifying a general principle of morality and public order is impeded by the specific circumstances of each individual case.[7]

Consequently, morality in patent law has not been subject to a great variety of legal discussion in recent years. However, as a consequence of the previous considerations, the basis for the approach has to be the fundamental function of the patent law system and its incentives.[8] The TRIPS agreement itself does not provide definite insights on the fundamental function of patent law. Art. 27 (2) TRIPS specifically provides the possibility for member states to realize their own understanding of patent law and morality. The general assumption that patent law is intended to incentivize inventors and thereby increase the public welfare[9] has been referred to, based on a variety of previous aspects. For example, it has been mentioned in German jurisprudence that the disclosure of an invention has to be beneficial or useful to the general public.[10] A mere increase in technical findings is considered insufficient to qualify for patentability. It is necessary for the invention to be applicable in a technical context which is in line with the function of the patent system.[11] Interestingly enough, the very fundamental function of the patent system is not entirely clear. There is consensus about the general advancement of technology. However,

---

[5] *Romandini*, 233; *Straus*, GRUR Int. 2010, 918.

[6] Most prominently in Sec. 242 German Civil Code (BGB – Bürgerliches Gesetzbuch).

[7] EPA, ABl 95, 545 = GRUR Int. 95, 978 – Pflanzenzellen.

[8] *Vorwerk*, GRUR 2009, 375.

[9] BGHZ 88, 209, 277; also: *Kuflik*, in: Weil/Snapper, Owning Scientific and Technical Information, 1989, S. 219 (230); *Kraßer*, § 3 II, who point out the other detail that, in addition to the incentive of inventive action in general, the aspect of disclosing the technical details of an invention further increases technological advancement by making it available to other professionals in the technical field.

[10] BVerwG NJW 1959, 1507, 1509.

[11] BGH GRUR 1966, 312, 316.

only a few opinions exist that actually add a restriction to this function by including a variation related to something being "socially benefitting".[12]

Fundamental considerations of patent law include the analysis of philosophical and political aspects in the context of law. Those elements make it possible to identify the values according to which opposing interests in particular cases have to be balanced.[13] The notion of "balance" further indicates that the core of ethical and moral considerations is a complex application of the principle of proportionality.

In conclusion, Art. 27 (2) TRIPS is the foundation of moral considerations in national patent law regimes on an international level. However, it does not provide any specific insights into how to interpret terms of morality or ordre public.

Points of access for such considerations are the particular national provisions.

2. Regulatory Approaches in the EU and Germany

German and European Patent law include general moral restrictions clauses, which function as a general restriction and include very broad terms. Such clauses are part of the initial requirements for every patent and their very existence is already heavily debated. However, the implementation of a general moral restrictions clause is arguably necessary and falls in line with the fundamental concept of patent law.

The German Patent Code includes the most specific requirements regarding the role of morality in patentability of all the relevant patent jurisdictions. It is the second subject considered in this section. All morally challenging aspects of any technology are subject to an examination according to Sect. 2 (1) PatG. This section describes the regulatory approach to restrict patentability independently from novelty or technical aspects just by addressing the function and intention of the utilization of the invention itself.

This section begins with an analysis of Art. 53 (a) of the European Patent Convention (EPC). The European Patent Organization functions as a supranational institution and is the next level in the hierarchical system of patent law systems.

3. Art. 53 (a) European Patent Convention

According to the Examination Guidelines of the EPO, the intention of Art. 53 (a) EPC is to "deny protection to inventions likely to induce riot or public disorder, or to lead to criminal or other generally offensive behavior".[14] Inciting riots seems to be an

---

[12] For example: BGH GRUR 1966, 312, 316; BGH GRUR 1972, 80, 83 and BGH GRUR 1980, 444, 447.

[13] *Pedrazzini*, Die patentfähige Erfindung, p. 28.

[14] Guidelines for Examination in the European Patent Organization, Part G-II 4.1.

extremely high bar for exclusion; that a patent in its commercial use would actually have the potential to induce a riot seems hardly imaginable.

As mentioned before, the very next sentence of the Examination Guidelines states that "Anti-personnel mines are an obvious example".[15] Providing this example is interesting considering the fact that the commercial use of such mines – albeit morally questionable – is unlikely to cause a riot within the society that intends to use the mines. Furthermore, the aspect of being an obvious example makes it difficult to pinpoint where exactly the bar is set.

In any case, it is necessary to analyze what constitutes obviousness. The guidelines also mention weapon technology specifically. Even it is just a remark within the guidelines and might not bear a significant amount of legal weight, it signals that weapon technology is an area of special consideration. It further indicates that there must also be other examples of weapon technology that might be considered – nonobvious – examples of exclusion.

The background to this statement is likely already to have been discussed at the Convention on the Prohibition of the Use, Stockpiling, Production and Transfer of Anti-Personnel Mines and on their Destruction (Anti-Personnel Mine Ban)[16] from 1997. The treaty was the result of the International Campaign to Ban Landmines (ICBL).

The basis for the campaign and the subsequent treaty included the considerations that an anti-personnel mine works as an indiscriminate weapon meaning it does not distinguish between soldiers, civilians or aid workers. Because of the longevity of mines, they pose a threat to the safety of civilians during conflicts and for years and even decades after a conflict has ended.[17] A cease-fire or peace treaty does not affect the placed landmines since they usually function autonomously without any influence from the military force that originally placed them. The main argument against mines lies in the fact that an anti-personnel mine is inherently indiscriminate and 70 to 85 percent of casualties involve the loss of civilian life.[18]

These aspects supposedly classify such mines as inhumane weapons which violate basic elements of international humanitarian law. In addition to the failure to discriminate, anti-personnel mines are said to inflict disproportionate damage in relation to military objectives which also constitutes a violation of the law of war. According to the ICBL, an anti-personnel mine inflicts "brutal damage to the human body that

---

[15] Guidelines for Examination in the European Patent Organization, Part G-II 4.1; *Viens*, Morality Provisions in Law Concerning the Commercialization of Human Embryos and Stem Cells, in: Embryonic Stem Cell patent: European Law and Ethics (Aurora Plomer & Paul Torremans eds, Oxford University Press 2009).

[16] Ratified by 162 states including Germany which incorporated the convention in various pieces legislation.

[17] Anti-Personnel Landmines: Friend or Foe? A Study of the Military Use and Effectiveness of Anti-Personnel Mines, International Committee of the Red Cross, 2020.

[18] Landmine and Cluster Munition Monitor, 2020.

kills or creates life-long injuries". This fact might be usually attributed to almost all explosive devices. However, it is necessary to note that anti-personnel mines are usually specifically designed to injure, not kill their victims. Injured targets increase the logistical, especially medical, support required by enemy forces that encounter the victims.

The effects of mines are devastating; however, the argument that all types of anti-personnel mines are inherently inhumane has met considerable opposition, mainly in the U.S. The U.S. has argued that the mines developed by their military are not long-lasting and are therefore still a viable military option.[19] The argument of military necessity and feasibility has been the subject of an extensive study by the Red Cross which concluded that "Mines [...] have rarely been used in conformity with international law, and have little to no effect on the outcome of hostilities".[20]

In conclusion, the explanations from the EPO for the interpretation of ordre public are very broad but also oddly specific. Both aspects are not an ideal basis for a consistent and practical application of the morality clause.

4. Sect. 2 (1) PatG in German Law

Sect 2 (1) PatG is similar to Art. 53 (a) EPC but uses different term to "ordre public" and "morality". However, the differences in terms do not translate into a different scope of protection. Sect. 2 (1) PatG excludes inventions from the benefit of patent protection in cases where the utilization of the invention violates principles of morality or public order ("öffentliche Ordnung").[21] The distinction between utilization and other events such as sales, purchases or licensing is crucial, since the exclusion only applies to violations via utilization.[22]

Furthermore, the exclusion only applies to the commercial utilization of the invention.[23] The general reasoning behind the exclusion is based on two main arguments: (a) to avoid the impression that the German Patent and Trademark Office endorses, supports or approves an unlawful or immoral invention and (b) to avoid the publication of such an invention in an official register.[24] In particular, the second reason has been increasingly met with criticism in the German legal literature. Sect. 2 used to include a subsection which applied the exclusion of patent protection to cases

---

[19] US Landmine Policy, 2020.

[20] Anti-Personnel Landmines: Friend or Foe? A Study of the Military Use and Effectiveness of Anti-Personnel Mines, International Committee of the Red Cross, 2020.

[21] The term public order in this context differs from the U.S. concept of national security, i.e. crisis protection of the state and its citizens by the government.

[22] *Melullis*, in: Benkard, PatG Sect. 2 re. 1; *Verlinsky*, Cytoplasmic Cell Fusion: Stembrid Technology for Reprogramming Pluripotentiality, 2 Stem Cell Reviews 297, 301 (2006).

[23] *Melullis*, in: Benkard, PatG Sect. 2 re. 3; *Burdach*, Mitt. 2001, 10.

[24] *Melullis*, in: Benkard, PatG Sect. 2 re. 6; *Bunke*, Mitt. 2009, 169; *Nieder*, Mitt. 2001, 97.

where violations of morality are the result of the patent publication.[25] However, the recent version does not include such a provision. It is argued that the new version thereby indicates the intent of the legislator that relevant violations are limited to commercial utilization. Any dangers of moral violations as a result of the publication are therefore supposedly irrelevant.[26]

However, the change in the provision was made to harmonize the German patent regime with the TRIPS treaty. Additionally, the treaty does not contain any exclusion of patent protection on the basis of an unlawful or immoral publication.[27] Therefore, the question remains whether the change was primarily due to harmonization. If that was the case, the initial argument becomes somewhat unconvincing.

The aspect of "bio-piracy"[28] is generally addressed under aspects of novelty or the violation of pre-existing intellectual property (in German law under Sec. 8 PatG).[29] Addressing "bio-piracy" under these aspects seems like a rational and precise dogmatic approach; however, those aspects do not specifically obstruct bio-piracy, even though the legal literature tends broadly to consent to the idea that bio-piracy has a distinct questionable or worrying feel to it.[30] This leads to the impression that the

---

[25] Sec. 2 (1) older wording: "publication" of the invention was included parallel to the commercial exploitation of the invention.

[26] *Melullis*, in: Benkard, PatG Sect. 2 re. 6.

[27] Begr. RegEntwurf BT-Drucks 14/5642 p. 14.

[28] Bio-piracy is the term used to describe the patenting of indigenous knowledge and resources of so-called "third world countries". A common problem with this practice is that the respective patent might be of detrimental effect to the society or community it stems from, somewhat defeating one the fundamentals of patent law in general (*Melullis*, in: Benkard, PatG Sect. 2 re. 4); with a view on the utility of the European Biotechnology Patent Directive: *Enzthaler/Zech*, GRUR 2006, 529; *Gold/Gallochat*, The European Biotech Directive: Past as Prologue, 7 European Law Journal 331 (2001), 333; *Krauß*, Mitt. 2001, 296, 300; *Porter*, The Drafting History of the European Biotechnology Directive, in: Embryonic Stem Cell Patents: European Law and Ethics (Aurora Plomer & Paul Torremans eds, Oxford University Press 2009); *Spranger*, GRUR 2001, 91.

[29] *Melullis*, in: Benkard, PatG Sect. 2 re. 4 and *Nägele/Jacobs*, Mitt. 2014, 353 et seq.; *Green*, Stem Cell Research: A Target Article Collection Part III – Determining Moral Status, 2 The American Journal of Bioethics 20 (2002), 25; historically: *Leskien*, ZUR 1996, 299; *Porter*, The Patentability of Human Embryonic Stem Cell Patents in Europe, 24 Nature Biotechnology 653, 655 (2006); *Varju/Sandor*, Patenting Stem Cell in Europe: The Challenge of Multiplicity in European Union Law, 49 Common Market Law Review 1007, 1009 (2012).

[30] *Melullis*, in: Benkard, PatG Sect. 2 re. 4, describing the measures in Sect. 34 PatG inadequate to "combat" bio-piracy suggesting it is a potential threat that needs to be addressed; *Hellstadius*, A Comparative Analysis of the National Implementation of the Directive's Morality Clause, in: Embryonic Stem Cell Patents: European Law and Ethics (Aurora Plomer & Paul Torremans eds, Oxford University Press 2009); *Herdegen*, GRUR Int. 2000, 859, 860; *Krauß*, Mitt. 2005, 495; *Mertes*, Understanding the Ethical Concerns that Have Shaped European Regulation of Human Embryonic Stem Cell Research, 1 Proceedings of the Belgian Royal Academies of Medicine 127, 138 (2012); *Overwalle*, Patenting Stem Cell Research in Europe and in the United States, in: Crossing Borders: Cultural Religious and Political Differences Concerning Stem Cell Research (W. Bender et al. eds, Agenda Verlag 2005); *Spranger*, GRUR Int. 1999, 601; *Vazin/Freed*, Human Embryonic Stem Cells: Der-

use of the morality restriction is an unpopular mechanism in patent law. Other parts of the thesis address this impression further.

Both the European and German legislative approaches include patentability restrictions based on moral considerations. The significant terms are either "morality" and "ordre public" or a variation thereof. Understanding of these terms is necessary to assess the relationship of morality and patent law further.

II. Ordre Public and Morality on a European Level

The EPO is a European (but not EU) institution and thereby supranational. It does not grant European Patents but is responsible for the distribution of patents that come into effect in different Contracting States of the EPO. Streamlining the process of patent applications within Europe and working towards granting each individual national patent helps to reach this goal. The patent application process of each Contracting State has to be taken into account, albeit the case that it is parallel and not cumulative. Legal problems arise in case of moral considerations. The understanding of moral concerns in patent law is strongly affected by the respective national law. However, Art. 53 lit. (a) EPC requires the EPO to assess ordre public and morality as well as novelty and other patentability requirements as well.

1. Determining the Meaning of Ordre Public and Morality

First, the question arises of which sources are available to the EPO for determining the content of the terms ordre public or morality. Art. 53 lit. (a) EPC only states that it is insufficient for an exemption of patentability to be solely based on the fact that the commercial exploitation is prohibited "by law or regulation in some or all of the Contracting States". Based on this provision the EPO has drawn the conclusion that even if the commercial exploitation is permitted in all Contracting States, it is still possible to restrict patentability.[31]

However, in legal discussion, this interpretation of Art. 53 lit. (a) EPC has been heavily criticized for several reasons:

1. The wording of the provision includes the status of the legal assessment of the commercial exploitation. The term invention is only included to describe that a prohibition of the commercial exploitation in one or more Contracting States alone is insufficient to draw the conclusion of a violation of morality. The explicit statement only relates to the insufficiency of the legal prohibition of the com-

---

ivation, Culture, and Differentiation: A Review, 28 Restorative Neurology and Neuroscience 589, 592 (2010).

[31] T 356/93, February 21st, 1995, Abl. EPA 1995, 545, Egr. Nr. 7; T 356, EPO, May 23rd, 2000, Egr. Nr. 2.16; EPO, July 24th, 2002 Egr. 2.5.2.

mercial exploitation. It does include the far broader declaration that the legal status of the commercial exploitation is irrelevant to the patentability assessment process.[32] This clarification indicates that the provision intended that not all prohibitive legislation should be based on the significant fundamentals of society and is therefore inadequate to be the basis for an exclusion of patentability. Adding this sentence to the provision would be meaningless, if the EPO could determine the interpretation of the terms independently.[33] The only support that the EPO can derive from the provision is the fact that the provision does not explicitly contradict its interpretation.

2. Contradicting its interpretation, however, is the fact that the EPO board appeal defined ordre public as the deeply rooted and recognized behavioral rules within European cultural society.[34] It is almost inconceivable to assume that such a deeply rooted rule would not be incorporated in legislation or administrative acts.[35] It also goes against most other interpretations of the particular national implementations of the exemptions of patentability based on morality and ordre public. The general interpretation of ordre public assumes that the violated principle has to be part of the legal system. Without being part of the legal system is might fall into the category of morality. Consequently, it cannot be part of ordre public without being part of the legal system.

3. Lastly, this interpretation clearly violates Art. 27 (2) TRIPS. This section evidently states that in order to exempt an invention from patentability, the commercial exploitation of said invention has to be prohibited. That would not be the case, if the commercial exploitation of an invention is permitted in all member states.

It seems that it is necessary to assess an invention according to Art. 53 lit. (a) EPC by analyzing the understanding of morality of a specific Contracting State.[36] This common interpretation of EPC law was also supported by another board within the EPO.[37] It specifically stated that ordre public has to be identified according to the legislation and administrative rules that most Contracting States have in common. Analyzing several Contracting States would allow the moral compass within European countries to be determined more accurately. The board even goes so far as to declare that in cases where such legislation and administrative rules can be identified, it is neither necessary nor reasonable to turn towards other assessment methods. Following this reasoning, the question arises as to what Contracting States are relevant to the discussion of ordre public violations.

---

[32] *Romandini*, 259; *Straus*, GRUR 1996, 10.
[33] *Busche*, GRUR Int 1999, 299, 303.
[34] T 356/93, February 21st, 1995, Abl. EPA 1995, 545, Egr. Nr. 7.
[35] *Romandini*, 260.
[36] *Schatz*, GRUR Int. 1997, 588, 594.
[37] EPO, November 7th, 2001, Abl. EPO 2003, 473, Egr. Nr. 9.3.

2. Relevant Contracting States[38]

Assuming that the EPO Boards of Appeals are going to apply Art. 53 lit. (a) EPC in a comparative way, the question arises as to which Contracting States are relevant for the assessment.[39]

According to one legal opinion, the EPO is supposed to assess the legal systems of all member states. Otherwise, the patentability assessment would not be independent from the state the patent application was filed in.[40] Other scholars support the idea of using an entirely independent standard;[41] however, the same problems and practical limitations as mentioned before arise as well.

Majority support has a different approach: a patent application for a specific member state should only be assessed by the ordre public of that specific member state. This is supposed to apply, even if the application is made via the EPO and is intended to take effect in numerous member states.[42] Arguments for this interpretation are supported by the legal nature of the European Patent distribution process. The concept of the distribution system allows patent applicants to choose in which member state they would like to obtain a patent. In cases where the national patent office grants the patent, it naturally only grants protection in the legal system of that specific state. The main advantage for the patent applicant is the convenience of having a central institution for the patent application process. Hence, it seems adequate to only assess the invention according to the ordre public of the specific member state in which patent protection is actually intended. Using the ordre public of another member state, in which the applicant does not even seek patent protection, seems unnecessary and unreasonable.[43]

The EPO has never directly addressed this legal discussion and merely seems to apply a uniform European standard that is independent from the Contracting State in which the applicant is seeking patent protection. This interpretation of uniform legal requirements is supported by the considerations discussed below.

Once again, we must refer to the wording of Art. 53 lit. (a) EPC. In cases where the prohibitive legislation which contradicts the commercial legislation is part of the ordre public, an exemption from patentability can be based on these provisions. It is said that an exemption of the patentability can be made, regardless of whether the specific Contracting States have been mentioned by the EPO in its decision.[44] Now,

---

[38] It is important to clarify that "contracting states" refers to a member of the EPC and not a member state of the European Union.

[39] *Romandini*, 260 et seq.

[40] *Bossung*, Mitt. 1974, 123.

[41] *Straus*, GRUR Int. 1990, 913, 919.

[42] *Schatz*, GRUR 2006, 879, 886; *Calame*, Öffentliche Ordnung und gute Sitten, 148, with further references.

[43] *Calame*, Öffentliche Ordnung und gute Sitten, 149.

[44] *Romandini*, 261.

whilst that might be true, however, just because it is not explicitly contradicted by the wording of Art. 53 lit. (a) EPC does not mean it is intended to function that way. It seems to be more of a mechanism to prevent the EPO from confusing any kind of prohibitive legislation with the principles relevant to the exemption of patentability. It could also be interpreted as the opposite of what is claimed. The provision states that prohibitive legislation of one or all member states alone is an insufficient reason for the exemption from patentability. It could allow for the interpretation that both legislation in one state and legislation in all states are equally irrelevant. Such an interpretation would not support the idea on a uniform European standard since it is not the prohibitive legislation of all states but the ordre public that is decisive.

Secondly, the interpretation is based on the function of the European Patent system. The intention of the EPO is not to render the national patent offices and patent legislation irrelevant. It intends to compliment them and provide a more convenient and effective mechanism for the application process. On this basis, the following argument is made. The older version of the EPC from 2000[45] allowed for the rejection of a patent application based on existing patents in national patent regimes. This was possible even if the patent application was not seeking patent protection in that specific Contracting State. *Romandini* draws the conclusion that this means that the EPO does not have the function to enable patent protection in all cases where national patents may be granted due to international agreements.[46] Otherwise Art. 53 lit. (a) EPC would have included the capacity to limit patent protection to those national patent regimes in which ordre public does not oppose the commercial exploitation of the invention. In addition, it could have been possible to change the patent claims according to each separate patent regime. Possibilities to adjust the patent application or restrict the grant of the patent to specific member states would clearly support the interpretation of Art. 53 lit. (a) EPC to utilize a uniform European standard for determining the legal and moral order.[47]

The "uniform European standard" conclusion is, unfortunately, not based entirely on a precise premise. It is correct to assume that a provision is more than just an administrative mechanism to distribute and collectively assess patent applications for the European Union; however, the premise has to be analyzed more closely. According to the foregoing explanations, it can be generally assumed that the provision does not provide the EPO with the power to assess ordre public according to their independent interpretation. This applies in particular if the commercial exploitation is permitted in all member states of the European Union. Therefore, ordre public of the member states has to be relevant. The issue of whether it has to be understood as a collective standard or solely the requirements of the specific nations in which the patent application is made, cannot be solved by assuming the specific requirement in Art. 53 lit. (a) EPC is a uniform and over-arching requirement.

---

[45] Art. 54. (III) EPC 2000.
[46] *Romandini*, 262.
[47] Id.

66   C. Moral Considerations in Patentability in European & German Patent Law

Whether or not the patent application can be restricted to each Contracting State that does not determine the commercial exploitation to be a violation of ordre public, is not mentioned. Hence, it might be argued that the provision was designed from the very beginning to relate only to the ordre public of the specific patent regime mentioned in the application. If Art. 53 lit. (a) EPC is interpreted in such way that it requires the EPO to assess the application according to each national standard of ordre public, it would not have been necessary to include the capacity to restrict the patent application to certain member states. The same goes for the capacity to adapt the patent claims in a particular way, since such possibilities would be inherent in the provision without being explicitly mentioned.

In conclusion, the wording of the provision and the systematic approach to the presumed intentions of the specific Art. 53 lit. (a) EPC are, at best, ambiguous. They do not allow for a definitive answer on whether a uniform European standard has to be applied. It might still be possible that the EPO is bound to identify the standard of ordre public according to each specific state mentioned in the patent application.

However, this leads to a different problem: what happens in a case where the understanding of ordre public order differs between the Contracting States?

a) Differences in the Understanding of Ordre Public within the EPC Contracting States

In a case where the commercial exploitation of an invention violates the ordre public of one or more but not all Contracting States, the specific application of Art. 53 lit. (a) EPC is uncertain. According to the discussion above, it is not clear which standard of public order is relevant. Several main lines of argument suggest observing the standard from least to most strict, which can be categorized in the following manner: the EPO has to grant a patent (a) where it does not violate the ordre public in at least one Contracting State, (b) only in a case where the commercial exploitation does not violate the ordre public of the majority of Contracting States or (c) only in a case where the commercial exploitation does not violate the ordre public in all Contracting States (designated in the patent application).

aa) Lowest Standard – Validity of the Patent in One Contracting State

The majority opinion within the German legal discussion,[48] the UK Patent Office,[49] the EPI[50] and an expert opinion issued by the European Commission[51]

---

[48] *Appel*, 169; *Wiebe*, GRUR 1993, 88, 90; *Busche*, GRUR Int., 1999, 299, 304; *Rogge*, GRUR 1998, 303, 308; *Calame*, Öffentliche Ordnung und gute Sitten, p. 149.

[49] UK-IPO, G 2/066 – Wisconsin Alumni Research Foundation, Amicus Curiae Submission of the United Kingdom from October 26th, 2006, p. 4. (with the very interesting restriction that it has to be a "major state" of the European Union which just happens to include the United Kingdom).

decided to apply the smallest common denominator. They agreed that the EPO has to grant the patent, even if it is only admissible in one of the Contracting States. The expert opinion is based on its conclusion of the pluralistic nature of the ethical peculiarities in the different Contracting States. These peculiarities have to be respected by the EPO and the jurisprudence of the ECJ and the ECtHR.[52] Interpretation of Art. 2 (1) ECHR is also subject to the Contracting States, while the ECtHR allowed for a certain degree of leeway in a case where specific ethical characteristics of a member state required a deviation.[53] Additionally, this jurisprudence regarding the discretion in matters of ordre public is also found in the decisions concerning Art. 36 TFEU.

To follow-through on this aspect of deviation, the EPO is obligated to grant the European Patent, even if the commercial exploitation of the invention violates the ordre public in one or more Contracting States.[54] National patent courts are subsequently able to nullify European Patents for their own jurisdiction; in case such patents would face ethical problems in the specific Contracting States. However, the decision concerned the patentability of inventions concerning embryonic stem cells.[55] There is no definitive argument for the transferal to other types of inventions or the identification of a general principle in European Patent law.

Procedural inconsistencies within the EPC were the basis for the interpretation. It is not possible to appeal a decision made by the EPO to exempt an invention from patentability based on Art. 53 lit. (a) EPC before the national patent courts, but it is possible for national patent courts to nullify[56] the domestic part of a European Patent collective. This asymmetry between the grant process of the patent and the nullification procedure before the national courts would lead to practical difficulties. The patent issuing process would be considered definitive while the actual granting of the patent can be contested.[57] Therefore, the patent should be granted even if differences in the standard of ordre public between the Contracting States. Otherwise, the patent protection might be cut short without a specific justification in the relevant Con-

---

[50] The Institute of Professional Representatives before the European Patent Organization – EPI, Amicus Curiae Brief in the Case G2/06 from November 1st, 2006, 19.

[51] *Plomer*, Stem Cell Patents: European Patent Law and Ethics Report, 114.

[52] *Plomer*, Stem Cell Patents: European Patent Law and Ethics Report, 114 et seq.

[53] So called: "margin of discretion".

[54] *Plomer*, Stem Cell Patents: European Patent Law and Ethics Report, 114 et seq.

[55] *Romandini*, 263; *Plomer*, Human Dignity, Human Rights and Article 6(1) of the EU Directive on Biotechnological Inventions, in: Embryonic Stem Cell Patents: European Law and Ethics (Aurora Plomer & Paul Torremans eds, Oxford University Press 2009).

[56] Pending the empowerment of the patent courts by the national legislator according to Art. 138 EPC.

[57] *Romandini*, 263; *Plomer*, Towards Systemic Legal Conflict: Article 6(2)(c) of the EU Directive on Biotechnological Inventions, in: Embryonic Stem Cell Patents: European Law and Ethics (Aurora Plomer & Paul Torremans eds, Oxford University Press 2009).

tracting State. The possible nullification of the patent by a different Contracting State would still be in accordance with its understanding of ordre public.

Romandini disagrees with this explanation. He argues that the Contracting States can allow the transformation of a rejected European Patent application into a national patent application according to Art. 135 (1) lit. (b) EPC. This technically functions as a remedy against the rejection by the EPO at the national level.[58] Such a rejection is especially relevant, because the transformation is still permissible, even if the patent application was denied on the grounds of a violation of Art. 53 lit. (a) EPC. In each case, whether the EPO rejects or approves a patent application, the defeated party still has a national remedy to attempt to enforce its own opinion regarding the patent. Therefore, the system of national remedies and the patent examination process at the EPO level are not suitable in terms of addressing the instant problem of different standards of legal and moral order within the Contracting States.

Romandini further disagrees with the interpretation and reasoning provided by the expert opinion of the European Commission.[59] Referencing the ethical pluralism of the EU and the jurisprudence of the ECtHR would only be admissible, in cases where the decisions of the EPO had binding character for the national patent courts. Only then would the interpretation of the EPO directly influence patentability in all Contracting States and have the potential to exclude an invention from patent protection based on a European standard public order. A patent exclusion by the EPO may then be possible even if the invention is permitted in other Contracting States.[60] However, national patents can still be issued and the EPO patents can still be rejected by Contracting States based on ethical considerations. According to *Romandini*, this leads to an exclusion of the transferability of any reasoning in relation to Art. 2 ECHR.

If the EPO decides that a patent application has to be rejected in its entirety, based on the violation of ordre public in some Contracting States, national patent offices are allowed to grant patent protection in their respective jurisdictions. Consequently, *Romandini* sees no restriction of the pluralistic nature of the European Contracting States.[61] It is understandable that the intention of the EPO and the contracting parties was to secure national peculiarities and ensure their core sovereignty. However, this cannot be achieved by simply relying on the national patent office. This core principle has to be included within the EPO patent process. It also makes no difference for the national patent regimes in general, whether or not the aspect of national ethical peculiarities is included in the considerations of the EPO.

---

[58] *Romandini*, 264.
[59] *Romandini*, 265.
[60] *Romandini*, rf. 964.
[61] *Romandini*, 265.

One problem with this explanation by *Romandini* is the assumption that the capacity to transform a European Patent application into a national patent application is equal to an actual judicial remedy. Such a remedy would be Art. 138 (1) EPC.

First of all, the remedy according to Art. 138 (1) EPC actually provides for the possibility of judicial control. Art. 135 (1) EPC on the other hand only enables the transformation into a new patent application which requires an entirely new assessment by the national patent office. This patent application can be subject to subsequent procedure before the national courts. Secondly, Art. 135 (1) EPC can only be initiated at the request of either the applicant or the proprietor of a European Patent. Thus, competitors who do not hold patents or only national patents are excluded. In contrast, Art. 138 EPC does not include any restrictions relating to the request. This leaves it up to the national court proceedings to determine which entity is entitled to initiate such a procedure.

Regarding the expert opinion issued by the European commission, *Romandini* accuses the documentation of confusing different aspects of the patentability issue. According to *Romandini*, the interpretation of Art. 36 TFEU by the ECJ does not mean to determine collective ordre public across the European Union. The interpretation aims rather to decide whether said provision allows member states to restrict fundamental freedoms of the European Single Market.[62] The boards of appeal of the EPO, on the other hand, have to decide whether the rejection of a patent application can be based on Art. 53 lit. (a) EPC. While the features which characterize both provisions are similar to a certain degree, the intentions of the provisions differ significantly. Therefore, jurisprudence regarding the "margin of discretion" of Art. 36 TFEU is supposedly non-transferable.

Interestingly enough, the ECJ uses a different standard to develop collective fundamental rights based on an overall view of all constitutional documents of the EU member states. It is not necessary for the ECJ to find the smallest common denominator or a principle that is explicitly present in all member states.[63] It is often referred to as a "collective heritage".[64]

Romandini argues that this distinction between ECJ jurisprudence regarding collective fundamental rights, on the one hand, and the interpretation of Art. 53 lit. (a) EPC are inherently different. Addressing the ECJ and its interpretation of collective fundamental rights actually supports an interpretation of Art. 53 lit. (a) EPC which does not include the margin of discretion. Hence, *Romandini* draws the conclusion that the standard of ordre public has to be a collective European interpretation.

---

[62] *Romandini*, 265.
[63] *Turpin*, RTDE 2003, 615, 625 et seq.
[64] *Jarass*, EU-Grundrechte, rf. 28 with further explanations.

(1) Comparison of Art. 53 EPC and Art. 139 EPC

Other authors include an analysis of Art. 139 (2) EPC which regulates the relationship of older national patent rights and newer European Patent rights. Older national patent rights have the same effect as newer European Patents. Accordingly, the older national rights may lead to the annulment of the national part of a European Patent according to the applicable national law. However, the older national patent rights do not oppose the granting of the European Patent in its function as a collective patent bundle. It is argued that Art. 53 lit. (a) EPC is supposed to function in a similar fashion. National restrictions on commercial exploitation that are not existent in all European Contracting States cannot be the basis for an exclusion at the European Patent level. They can only lead to the nullification of a patent at the national level.[65] While *Romandini* agrees with the result, he rejects the comparison of Art. 139 (2) EPC and Art. 53 lit. (a) EPC, since they have inherent differences. Art. 53 lit. (a) EPC constitutes a binding reason for rejection of a patent application which is applied by the examination office of the EPO. In contrast, Art. 139 (2) lit. (b) EPC addresses a reason for nullification which is not subject to the examination process of the EPO.[66] He concludes that it is incorrect to assume that both Art. 139 (2) EPC and Art. 53 lit. (a) EPC include a national and not a European reason for patent rejection.[67] Focusing on a national level is unconvincing for two reasons. First, arguing that the EPO examination process only includes Art. 53 lit. (a) EPC and not Art. 139 (2) EPC fails to address the actual content of the provisions. This argument arguably has too much of a focus on procedural law. The comparison on the content of the provision is still valid and relates to the interplay of national characteristics and the European Patent level.

Secondly, the resulting conclusion that national peculiarities are unfit to be regarded as patentability restrictions on a European level is also misleading and incorrect. It is not the case that a nationally based interpretation of the patentability exclusion of Art. 53 lit. (a) EPC elevates national peculiarities to the European Patent level. Where the EPO identifies a certain violation of ordre public of a member state, it can simply restrict the collective patent bundle to the specific state. By doing so, the EPO maintains the rest of the bundle, assuming that other Contracting States have been selected by the applicant.

(2) Relationship of EPO and National Interpretation

A different argument is formulated when it comes to the practical effects of having the EPO interpret Art. 53 lit. (a) EPC according to the peculiarities of the national Contracting States. It is said that shifting this from the European level of examination to the national level is reasonable and more practical, the reason being that the EPO

---

[65] *Romandini*, 266.

[66] *Romandini*, 267 and further explanations in rf. 967.

[67] *Romandini*, 267.

examiners usually have a more technical background and the national examiners are generally experienced in the legal and moral peculiarities of their own legal system.[68] *Romandini* argues against this, however, by suggesting that a restrictive use of the provision will have the same result. Where the EPO examiner determines that the commercial exploitation of the invention might be violating ordre public, he rejects the application. This in turn enables the national patent offices to assess the patentability of the invention conclusively.[69] The actual practice of the Contracting States and the fact that they do not implement Art. 135 (1) lit. (b) EPC removes the possibility of transforming a European Patent application in a national one. In this context, *Romandini* relies on a variety of factors which are not inherent in the legal system and therefore fails to provide a precise theoretical approach.

(3) Relevance of the Report by the EU Commission

According to the report commissioned by the EU Commission, the grant of a patent bundle where there is a possible violation of ordre public in a single member state is preferable. This conclusion is based on the fact that it enables and forces the national courts in the EU Contracting States to refer to preliminary ruling by the ECJ.[70] *Romandini* disagrees with that interpretation, since the judges of the national courts still have to assess the patents according to Art. 53 lit. (a) EPC and not according to national law.[71]

However, *Romandini* himself misunderstands Art. 53 lit. (a) EPC. By stating that Art. 53 lit. (a) EPC is different from national law, he is prejudging the results of the interpretation of Art. 53 lit. (a) EPC in general. Considering that Art. 53 lit. (a) EPC can very well be interpreted as relating to the interpretation of legal and moral order according to national peculiarities, this conclusion is simply an effect of interpreting the provision differently and does not necessarily provide any insight into the actual interpretation of the provision. The report by the commission also bases its explanations on the assumption that the terms of ordre public and morality are to be interpreted according to national law and customs. Therefore, *Romandini*'s conclusion does not technically qualify as critique of the interpretations within the report. Additionally, *Romandini* argues that the EPC is not subject to the jurisdiction of the ECJ, which excludes an interpretation of the EPC by the ECJ within a preliminary ruling initiated by a national court of a Contracting State.[72] However, such an interpretation is also not necessarily correct. The ECJ used his interpretative competence prominently in the *Brüstle* decision.[73]

---

[68] *Calame*, Öffentliche Ordnung und Gute Sitten, p. 150; also *Romandini*, 267.
[69] *Romandini*, 267.
[70] *Plomer*, Stem Cell patents: European Patent Law and Ethics Report, 113.
[71] *Romandini*, 268.
[72] Id.
[73] EuGH Slg. 2011, I – 9871 rf. 34.

A different solution is presented by *Straus*, who argues that the rejection of a patent application is not permissible, as long as the invention may be commercially exploited within a single Contracting State. According to *Straus*, ordre public[74] in a collective European sense simply cannot exist, unless the invention is considered to be violating ordre public in all Contracting States.[75] Again, *Romandini* argues that this line of reasoning is tautological.[76] According to him, *Straus* interprets Art. 53 lit. (a) EPC in such a way that he assumes a violation of Art. 53 lit. (a) EPC only where all Contracting States prohibit the commercial exploitation of the invention. In doing so, *Romandini* further explains, *Straus* only repeats the standard of interpretation of Art. 53 lit. (a) EPC, which is the very starting point of *Straus*' argumentation.[77] Frist of all, the rhetorical term *Romandini* uses to criticize *Straus*' explanations would be "circular reasoning" instead of "tautological".[78] In addition, *Straus*' argument still bears meaning. He identifies the problem that there is no uniform standard of ordre public within the Contracting States. This is particularly the case where even one country disagrees with the majority opinion. According to his reasoning, this is a natural consequence of determining the European standard to be the sum of all legal and moral considerations within the Contracting States.

The actual problem with the explanation by *Straus* is the blurring of lines between the identification of an interpretative standard of Art. 53 lit. (a) EPC and the separate problem of how to address differences between the concepts of ordre public between Contracting States. This has been correctly pointed out by *Calame* as well.[79] Other authors point out that the grant of a patent bundle by the EPO seems to be less of an approval than the grant of a patent by a national patent office.[80] Still, the explanation of *Straus* bears significance, considering that the line between the standard of Art. 53 lit. (a) EPC and the concepts of the Contracting States is not razor-sharp. Addressing the differences in the concepts of ordre public within the different Contracting States is the very basis for the discussion regarding the interpretation of Art. 53 lit. (a) EPC. Without differences in such concepts, the different methods of interpreting Art. 53 lit. (a) EPC would always lead to the same result.[81]

---

[74] *Straus* uses the broader "ordre public", GRUR Int. 1990, 917.

[75] *Straus*, GRUR Int. 1990, 918.

[76] *Romandini*, 268.

[77] *Romandini*, 268.

[78] A tautology requires two separate statements which are formally identical.

[79] *Calame*, Öffentliche Ordnung und gute Sitten, p. 147.

[80] *Rogge*, GRUR 1998, 303, 308.

[81] Assuming that the EPO would not create a separate understanding, even if the member states agree unanimously.

bb) Medium Standard – Validity in the Designated State of the Application

Another approach sets the standard related to the majority of ethical considerations of the Contracting States. Only if the exploitation of the invention violates the ordre public of the majority of the Contracting States, does the EPO have to reject the patent application.[82] This focus on the majority of Contracting States can be observed within the Boards of Appeal of the EPO. The Boards of Appeal are obliged to apply the generally accepted principles of process in all Contracting States, where the EPC does not specify a proceeding.[83] Yet, the Boards of Appeal do not have to prove the existence of the principle in all Contracting States to accept it as a general rule.[84] In an earlier statement, the Examining Division of the EPO gave the following explanations:[85]

> "In applying Art. 53 lit. (a) EPC the examining division intends to be guided by laws and regulations of the majority of its contracting states on a given subject. The underlying idea is that the EPO should not create its own morality standards but rather should look at and be guided by the legal situation of the contracting states because these laws and regulations reflect the morality standards of the societies in these states. In doing so the EPO will be in line with the thinking of a majority of population in those countries for which a patent may be eventually granted."

In the objection, proceeding from which these explanations stem, a decision was made to deny a "euthanasia"-patent the right to include the application claim "to be used on humans". However, active euthanasia is permitted in the Netherlands and Belgium.[86] A similar, general statement was made in 2001 regarding the "Krebsmaus" patent. In this case the objection division stated that ordre public according to Art. 53 lit. (a) EPC has to be identified by determining the laws and administrative regulations which are common in most of the European Contracting States. Such a process would enable the EPO to come closest to a standard which determines "right" and "wrong" within European legal culture.[87]

This definition and method are justified by referencing the jurisprudence of the ECJ.[88] A similar standard was applied by the ECJ when it came to the question of how to define the fundamental rights of the European Union. Art. 6 (3) TEU determines the fundamental rights "as they result from the constitutional traditions common to the Member States, as general principles of Community law" alongside the European Convention for the Protection of Human Rights and Fundamental Freedoms. The analysis of the fundamental rights contribute to an identification of European

---

[82] *Rogge*, GRUR 1993, 303, 308.
[83] According to Art. 125 EPC.
[84] Case law of the Boards of Appeal of the European Patent Organization, 6, p. 566.
[85] EPO, statement from November 19th, 1999, re the patent application 96928587.
[86] Quote regarding the national legislation from the specific period.
[87] Abl, EPA 2003, 472, Egr. Nr. 9.3. – "Krebsmaus/HARVARD".
[88] As pointed out by *Romandini*, 271.

morality (or ordre public). In his analysis, the ECJ stated that the process of identifying the "constitutional traditions common to the Member States" is not based on the smallest common denominator but rather an overarching principle which may be the result of common traditions. Common traditions do not necessarily have to be present in all member states.

Transferring the jurisprudence of the ECJ in matters of fundamental rights of the European Union therefore seems suitable. However, the system of fundamental freedoms and the exemptions of patentability follow different regulatory approaches. In addition, the EPO is not part of EU law and the terms "ordre public" and "morality" are therefore not fully interpreted according to the EU requirements. Referencing ECJ jurisprudence is consequently not sufficiently convincing to adopt this method of interpreting Art. 53 lit. (a) EPC.

cc) Strictest Standard – Validity in All Contracting States

Ultimately, some authors interpret Art. 53 lit. (a) EPC as allowing for a rejection of a patent application where the commercial exploitation of the invention violates the ordre public in a single Contracting State.[89] This strict principle was applied in the EU directive 40/93 regarding the European Community Trademark.[90] It may seem like a strict and potentially technology-adverse approach; however, the crucial member state in which the invention is considered to violate ordre public, has to be one of the designated Contracting States mentioned in the patent application. Therefore, technically speaking, this approach is not actually "stricter" than the first standard, it is just different.

Focusing on the moral and public order principles of a single Contracting State allows the patent applicant to strategically design their application. They may designate only those Contracting States in which the standards of legal or moral order do not pose a threat to the patentability of his invention. Yet, even if the patent applicant fails to exclude potentially adverse Contracting States, the patent can be partially granted without violating Art. 118 EPC and the principle of unity of the European Patent application.[91] Art. 118 (2) EPC simply requires a uniform version of the patent application for all designated Contracting States, where numerous applicants exist and are not the same in respect of different designated Contracting States.

Consequently, the applicants are regarded as joint applicants before the EPO. Additionally, the unity of the application in these proceedings will not be affected and equally the text of the application or patent will be considered uniform for all designated Contracting States. The last consequence in particular is regarded as being

---

[89] *Schatz*, GRUR Int. 1997, 588, 595; *Guglelmetti*, NLCC 2008 396, 400 Rc. 23.

[90] EU-directive from December 20th, 1993. Art. 7 (1) lit. f and Art. 7 (2).

[91] *Schatz*, GRUR Int. 2006, 879, 886; *Torremans*, A Transnational Institution Confronted with a Single Jurisdiction Model: Guidance for the EPO's Implementation of the Directive from a Private International Perspective, 272, 301.

solely applicable to the procedural requirements, since the end of Art. 118 EPC states "unless this Convention provides otherwise".[92] It is argued that Art. 118 EPC does not create the unity of the application but rather defines it as given as long as it exists according to the EPC.[93] Foundation of the European Patent is the unity of the material European Patent law according to which the European Patent is granted. Yet, since the ordre public of the Contracting States according to Art. 53 lit. (a) EPC is the standard of the patent grant, the European Patent cannot be granted uniformly, if the law of the Contracting States differs substantially and is relevant to the decision.[94]

Romandini argues against this interpretation based on the following points:

While the described aspects may seem to provide a solution for the problem of having different standards of ordre public, the EPC requires a uniform patent application and allows for no exceptions.[95] In addition, Art. 105a EPC provides for the applicant to apply for a limitation of his patent with retroactive effect. However, such a limitation has to affect the European Patent in all Contracting States in which it was granted. An application to limit the patent only in some of the Contracting States which granted the patent is not permitted.[96] Accordingly, where a patent violates the legal or moral order of a certain Contracting State, it has to be inadmissible to apply for a limitation in only those certain Contracting States.[97] This line of reasoning is based on the premise that Art. 118 EPC actually requires a unity of the European Patent application.[98] Furthermore, the exemption from the assumed unity of the patent application is criticized for being based on different material law. The examiners of the EPO consistently apply the provision of Art. 53 lit. (a) EPC, regardless of the designated Contracting States.[99] The terms ordre public and morality in the general clause need further interpretation to be applied. However, the application by the examiner is not necessarily directly in accordance with the national law which is part of the ordre public.[100] National provisions and legislation are only the base for the interpretation and help to identify a European standard.[101]

In addition, it is argued, that the concept of the European Patent is not that of a substitution for the national patent systems. This line of reasoning can be partly observed given that it is possible to transform a European application into a national one according to Art. 135 (1) lit. (b) EPC. Additionally, such a European standard would force the EPO specifically to assess the invention regarding ordre public for

---

[92] *Schatz*, GRUR Int. 2006, 879, 886.
[93] Id at 888.
[94] Id at 886.
[95] *Teschemacher*, GRUR Int. 2002, 636, 637.
[96] *Wichmann/Naumann*, Mitt. 2008, 1, 3.
[97] *Romandini*, 272.
[98] Id.
[99] Id.
[100] *Engelbrecht*, Institutional and Jurisdictional Aspects, 227, 261.
[101] *Romandini*, 272.

every designated Contracting State. This obligation stems from the principle that the EPO has to assess the requirements for the application of Art. 53 lit. (a) EPC independently and regardless of the legal or factual nature of the obstacles preventing patentability. Consequently, the examiners either have to identify the factual circumstances in each member state according to Art. 114 EPC or interpret the legal system pursuant to the principle of *iura novit curia*.[102]

While it does not constitute a legal issue, it seems to be a practical one. However, it is unclear how an examiner is supposed to act, where the applicant remains silent once they have been notified that the invention might be violating the ordre public of one of the designated Contracting States. Technically, the examiner might be *ex officio* obligated to limit the application to those Contracting States, in which no exemption from patentability exists. It might also be possible that the examiner simply notifies the patent applicant and remains inactive until the applicant responds. Without a solution, this approach provides no simple answers but these are required for the sake of simplicity and practicality in the European Patent system, according to *Romandini*.[103]

b) Discussion of the Legal Arguments

However, *Romandini*'s arguments fail to precisely address the difficulties and benefits of this approach. The issue of the silent applicant is simply a consideration regarding practicality and is therefore only of limited supportive argumentative strength in a theoretical and dogmatic legal discussion. The other aspects of a European morality standard address the premises and assumptions mentioned before and are prone to the above-mentioned circular argument.

It is true that Art. 105a EPC allows for a request for limitation or revocation of the proprietor. Either the European Patent may be revoked or be limited by an amendment of the claims. This request is only applicable retroactively, after the patent has already been granted by the national patent offices. Hence, it is difficult to abstract an over-arching principle from these considerations. While Art. 105a (1) EPC grants possibilities to change already existing patents, the actual question concerns the uniformity of patent applications.

Any considerations of Art. 105a (1) EPC have to be assessed in the context of an already existing patent with a definitive examination by the EPO and the national patent offices. Establishing a principle based on Art. 105a (1) EPC by transferring its requirements is also limited content-wise, since the provision actually offers very little in the form of specific requirements. Art. 105a (2) EPC only restricts the admissibility of the request when no opposition proceedings are filed in respect of the European Patent. The direct formulation of the Art. 105a EPC is therefore not a solid

---

[102] *Romandini*, 273 with further references.
[103] *Romandini*, 274.

II. Ordre Public and Morality on a European Level 77

foundation for identifying an over-arching principle regarding the uniformity of a European Patent application.

The second argument revolves around the method an EPO examiner applies when it comes to assessing the requirements of Art. 53 lit. (a) EPC. Even if that was a correct assessment of the practice of EPO examiners, it does not constitute a valid theoretical argument. It definitely supports the idea of the greater European community standard for legal or moral order, but it does not provide a specific reason. It is the case that the practice of the EPO can still very well be considered to be incorrect or have been falsely applied. At best, this "observation" is merely an indicator within the debate and the effect is not very convincing.[104]

Ultimately, the most compelling argument concerns the practical implications of the possibility of restricting the examining process to the countries designated for the application. While it would force the examiners to assess national peculiarities and the legal system, it is still the most viable solution. The idea that this would be impractical for an EPO officer is incorrect, as a simple comparison demonstrates. Where an application involves difficulties or doubts regarding the legal or moral order of one or more Contracting States, the examiner has to assess the situation: in scenario A, applying a European community standard, he has to identify that standard and apply it to the new situation, whereas in scenario B, the examiner only has to identify the standard of each designated state and apply it accordingly.

It seems like scenario B has the potential to be more expensive and costly, since the identification of a European community standard for public order would involve a one-time-effort. However, as has been established before, it is difficult to determine the legal or moral order even in a single Contracting State. Due to the volatility of morals and the lack of an established standard, the issue remains very complex. In addition, new and emerging technologies are usually not easily categorized under the stiff and vague definitions that already exist. It can be observed that new technologies develop their own definitions and characteristics with regard to the legal and moral order of a national state. It seems to be more efficient to use the existing jurisprudence and legal discussions of each national member state to address the morality of a new technology, rather than relying on a European one, especially since the attempts to establish such a standard usually fall back even further on constitutional principles without recognizing that such a definition is practically worthless and does not provide a suitable solution. Accordingly, an approach involving a broad general European community standard would constantly need to be updated. Such an update process would likely be highly costly and time-consuming and would require a thorough understanding of each national principle regarding legal and moral order.

So, in conclusion, even if an examiner had to identify and apply the principles of ordre public of each individual Contracting State, it is highly likely that this approach would regularly still be more practical than developing and relying on a European

---

[104] *Romandini*, 272; *Engelbrecht*, Institutional and Jurisdictional Aspects, 227, 261.

community standard. Applying the standards of each Contracting State is also supported by the interpretative standard applied to the EU Biotech Directive, which includes vague terms such an "embryo" and "human life". It is generally agreed upon that those terms are not interpreted according to a European standard, which can be assessed by the ECJ.[105] Rather, it seems more likely that the use of the terms was intended as a reference to national law and the respective ordre public.[106] Further analyzing the reasoning of the EU Biotech Directive and identifying the differences between civil law and patent law exceeds the scope of this analysis by far and such an analysis is therefore not included. Consequently, this argument serves merely as an example that EU legislation can properly function by referring to each national legal system and its own interpretative method of legal terms.

c) Conclusion

Having a supranational organization poses complex challenges even before the content of morality and ordre public can be addressed. In addition, the problem only arises because legal culture is heavily influenced by a national understanding. This fact is the basic assumption of the entire previous discussion. It indicates that it is necessary to understand how legal cultures differ, even if the supranational EPO is based on a common understanding.

Yet, there exist certain aspects of patentability within the European Union that have required a uniform interpretation and have been subject to significant judicial proceedings.

3. Jurisprudence

The most notable past decisions and legal discussion regarding morality in patent law stems from biotechnological advancement and embryonic stem cell research. Both in the U.S. and in Germany this topic has been the subject of heated debate.[107]

---

[105] *Romandini* 296, rf. 1042; with regard to biotechnology: *O'Sullivan*, International Stem Cell Corp v. Comptroller General of Patents: the Debate Regarding the Definition of the Human Embryo Continues, 36 European Intellectual Property Review 155 (2014).

[106] *Romandini* 296, who draws a parallel to the "employee" jurisprudence of the ECJ in which the national understanding was also considered to be solely relevant (ECJ judgement regarding EU directive 77/187).

[107] *Kock/Prozig/Willnegger*, GRUR Int. 2005, 183 et seq.; *Golan-Mashiach*, Design Principle of Gene Expression Used by Human Stem Cells: Implication for Pluripotency, 19 The FASEB Journal 147 (2005), 150; *Koenig/Müller*, GRUR Int. 2000, 295; *Rao/Condic*, Alternative Sources of Pluripotent Stem Cells: Scientific Solutions to an Ethical Dilemma, 17 Stem Cells and Development 1, 21 (2008); *Takahashi/Yamanaka*, Induction of Pluripotent Stem Cells from Mouse Embryonic and Adult Fibroblast Cultures by Defined Factors, 126 Cell 663, 669 (2006); *Teschemacher*, The Practice of the European Patent Organization Regarding the Grant of Patents for Biotechnological Inventions, IIC 1988, 18, 20; *Torremans*, The Construction of the Directive's Moral Exclusions Under the EPC, in: Embryonic Stem Cell Pa-

Even though it has quietened down in recent years, the decisions remain significant for interpreting the scope of application in the provision. Most notably, the EU harmonization which took place in the late 1990s and early 2000s included a provision on biogenetic research and its implementation in the patent law of EU Contracting States.[108]

For example, German Sect. 2 Subs. 2 PatG refers to aspects of living nature and organisms and implementations of the afore-mentioned EU legislation. However, these areas of technology are highly complex and require an interdisciplinary approach. They also include philosophical, religious and ethical arguments. The latter, in particular, come from a metaphysical background which further increases the difficulty of a rational and dogmatically precise discussion. The same applies for aspects of human dignity which, for some major legal definitions, also includes a metaphysical element.[109]

This initial position gives some indication of why most interest groups usually lack a deeper understanding of the scientific background and even more so of the legal background and therefore are rarely interested in a dogmatically precise and unbiased application of the law.

a) Brüstle *Case*

One of the more recent and important decisions is known as the *Brüstle* Case. It started in 1997, when *Oliver Brüstle*[110] – pharmaceutical inventor and chemist – submitted a patent application to the German Patent Office. The patent application DE 197 56 864 C 1 had three main claims which related to isolating and purifying neuronal precursor cells.[111] The claims covered the procedure to produce these

---

tents: European Law and Ethics (Aurora Plomer & Paul Torremans eds, Oxford University Press 2009).

[108] See above.

[109] *Ahrens*, GRUR 2003, 89, 91 et seq.; *Pralong*, Cell Fusion For Reprogramming Pluripotency: toward Elimination of the Pluripotent Genome, 2 Stem Cell Reviews 331, 340 (2006); *Shamblott*, Derivation of Pluripotent from Cultured Human Primordial Germ Cells: 95 Proceedings of the National Academy of Sciences 13726 (1998).

[110] *Staunton*, Brüstle v Greenpeace, Embryonic Stem Cell Research and the European Court of Justice's New Found Morality, 21 Medical Law Review 310, 313 (2013); *Stazi*, Biotechnological Inventions and Patentability of Life: The US and European Experience (Edward Elgar 2015); *Turovets*, Derivation of Human Parthenogenetic Stem Cell Lines, in: Human Pluripotent Stem Cells: Methods and Protocols (Philip Schwartz & Robin L. Wesselschmidt eds., Springer 2011).

[111] Scientific background: The scientific precursor cells are stem cells which are able to differentiate into other body cells; however, since they are neuronal precursor cells, they can only develop into other neuronal cells but not other body cells such as skin cells, muscle or other organ cells; *Fuchs*, Mitt. 2000 1; *Shroff/Hopf*, Use of Human Embryonic Stem Cells in the Treatment of Parkinson's Disease: A Case Report, 17 International Journal of Emergency Mental Health and Human Resilience 661 (2015).

specific cells, the cells themselves which originated from the specific procedure and finally the use of those cells to treat neuronal defects.[112] There are numerous other decision in German patent law which also address aspects of moral considerations. Yet, the *Brüstle* Case is a prime example of the difficulties faced by trying to identify the moral background and significance of Sect. 2 PatG and its subsections. Although it does not directly address the aspects of Sect. 2 Subs. 1 PatG, it illustrates the different legal approaches to the concept of ordre public.

aa) Factual and Legal Background

The human cells in the patent application were not limited to adult precursor cells, which are multi-potent, but also included stem cells from the embryonic phase. These cells include so-called pluri-potent cells which can develop into any kind of body cells. Lastly, cells from the embryonic phase include toti-potent cells which are from the very early embryonic phase and have the ability to develop – under the right circumstances – into a human being.[113]

Pluri-potent cells were not part of any patent claim but were the base material in the process of isolating the multi-potent neuronal precursor cells.[114] Of legal interest was Sec. 2 (3) s. 3 PatG (former version).[115] The process which was the subject of the patent claim itself did not include any embryonic stem cells but embryonic stem cells were obtained in a prior process. The formulation of Sec. 2 (3) s. 3 PatG in its former version specified that a patent could not be granted where the patent application requires the use of embryonic cells.

---

[112] DE 197 56 864 C 1 p. 2, 17 et seq.

[113] *Henning*, Reproduktionsmedizin 2003, 282 et seq.; *Amit/Itskovitz-Eldor*, 200 Journal of Anatomy 225 (2002), 226 et seq.; *Chalmers*, European Union Law: Cases and Materials (Cambridge University Press 2010), 124; *Haase*, Generation of Induced Pluripotent Stem Cells from Human Cord Blood, 5 Cell Stem Cell 434 (2009), 444; *Hartmann*, GRUR Int. 2006, 199; *Laurie*, Patenting Stem Cells of Human Origin, 26 European Intellectual Property Review 59 (2004); *Levenberg*, Endothelial Cells Derived from Human Embryonic Stem Cell, 99 Proceedings of the National Academy of Sciences 4391, 4401 (2002); *Levron*, Male and Female Genomes Associated in A Single Pronucleus in Human Zygotes, 52 Biology of Reproduction 653 (1995); *Sterckx*, European Patent Law and Biotechnological Inventions, in: Biotechnology, Patents and Morality (Sigrid Sterckx ed., Ashgate Publishing 1997); *Sterckx/Cockbain*, Exclusions from Patentability: How Far Has the European Patent Organization Eroded Boundaries? (Cambridge University Press 2012); *Zhao*, Immunogenicity of Induced Pluripotent Stem Cells, 474 Nature 212, 220 (2011).

[114] DE 197 56 864 C 1 p. 2, 17 et seq.; with a critical scientific view: *Byrnes*, The Flawed Scientific Basis of the Altered Nuclear Transfer-oocyte Assisted Reprogramming (ANT-OAR) Proposal, 3 Stem Cell Reviews 60 (2007), 62; *Hansen*, Mitt. 2001, 477 et seq; *Sandel*, The Case Against Perfection: Ethics in the Age of Genetic Engineering (Belknap Press of Harvard University Press 2007); *Schwartz*, Human Embryonic Stem Cell-derived Rentinal Pigment Epithelium in Patients with Age-related Macular Degeneration and Stargardt's Macular Dystrophy: Follow-Up of Two Open-label Phase ½ Studies, 385 The Lancet 509, 512 (2015); *Tronder*, DRiZ 2000, 288; *Trüstedt*, GRUR 1986, 644.

[115] The current equivalent is Sec. 2 Subs. 2 s. 1 No. 3 PatG.

The basis for the debate and the ethic controversy was the fact that for the prior process of obtaining pluri-potent stem cells, a human embryo had to be destroyed. The destruction of cells with the (albeit purely theoretical) potential of creating human life sparked the following legal procedure.

bb) Legal Procedure

The German Patent Office decided that all conventional patentability requirements such as novelty, inventive step and commercial application were fulfilled.[116] Only an action for annulment by the German branch of Greenpeace brought the subject matter before the German Federal Patent Court (FPC). The FCP then decided that the procedure in question did not directly violate Sect. 2 (III) s. 3 PatG (former version). However, it required a previous procedure which necessarily destroyed embryonic cells and therefore indirectly used the specific cells. Such an indirect violation of Sect. 2 (III) s. 3 PatG (former version) was considered to be sufficient for the exclusion from patentability. The main argument revolved around the supposed protective nature of the Embryo Protection Act (Embryonenschutzgesetz) Additionally, the TRIPS agreement supposedly demanded a broad interpretation of the provision.[117]

Auxiliary arguments were found in the constitutional protection of human dignity and life which were supposedly violated if the patent was granted.[118] The definition for a violation of Sect. 2 (III) s. 3 PatG (former version) required that all possible uses of the invention constitute a violation. Therefore, the court assumed that embryonic stem cells were destroyed in any case.

Brüstle decided to appeal the decision and it became a matter for the German Federal Court of Justice (FCJ).[119] The FCJ agreed with the FPC that the patent application did not necessarily require the use of embryonic stem cells in its prior process. However, since the application only identified the process that included the use of embryonic stem cells as a preferable process,[120] the FCJ disagreed with the broader interpretation of the provision.[121] Yet, the FCJ also ruled that the EU Biotech

---

[116] *Batista*, GRUR Int. 2013, 514; with additional considerations: *Baumbach/Rasch*, Mitt. 1992, 210; *Grund/Keller*, Mitt. 2004, 49 et seq.; *Ohly*, EuZW 2011, 914; *Simon/Scott*, Unsettled Expectations: How Recent Patent Decisions Affect Biotech, 29 Nature Biotechnology 229 (2011).

[117] *Jacobs*, Gene Patents: A Different Approach, 23 European Intellectual Property Review 505, 508 (2001); *Schwartz*, Embryonic Stem Cell Trials for Macular Degeneration: A Preliminary Report, 379 The Lancet 713, 714 (2012); *Strorz*, The Limits of Patentability: Stem Cells, in: Limits of Patentability: Plant Sciences, Stem Cells and Nucleic Acids (Andreas Hübel et al. eds, Springer 2013).

[118] BPatGE 50, 45.

[119] BGHE 51, 298 et seq.; reasoning in GRUR 2010, 212 et seq.

[120] DE 197 56 864 C 1, 1 et seq.

[121] BGH GRUR 2010, 214 et seq.

Directive which the provision was based on, was relevant for the interpretation of the provision itself. In addition, the relevant questions of the case exceeded the scope of national interpretation of the provision.[122]

(1) Role of the European Court of Justice

Based on these considerations, the FCJ addressed the European Court of Justice (ECJ) to provide answers on the questions relating to the interpretation of the terms of the EU Biotech Directive. Specifically, the term "human embryo", the scope of the term "use" and whether scientific research is within the area of application of "industrial or commercial" purposes required further clarification.[123]

In a first step the ECJ agreed that the terms of the EU Biotech Directive indeed required a consistent interpretation within the EU Member States. A consistent understanding is necessary to secure the seamless functioning of the European internal domestic market.[124] Focusing on a consistent interpretation seems unusual since the ECJ usually grants more individual leeway to the Member States in cases where ethics and cultural considerations are involved.[125]

The answers provided by the ECJ all contained the same elements of teleological interpretation necessary to provide sufficient protection for any violations of human dignity.[126] Therefore, where human embryonic stem cells are involved, the potential for the development of life is solely relevant, which only includes toti-potent embryonic cells. However, any indirect use of an embryonic cell in its toti-potent phase is sufficient for a violation. This still applies even if the patent itself does not extend the claim to process steps that actually include toti-potent cells. The ECJ agreed thus far with the broader interpretation. The main argument again, related to the protection of and respect for human dignity. Auxiliary arguments considered that a narrow interpretation of the provision would enable the circumvention of the protection by formulating patent applications in a specific manner. Even though that is correct, it is only a mechanism and does not include a new argument. This mechanism rather describes the range of consequences of the exclusion of patentability in the first place. This distinction was also made by the FCJ. The decision mentioned the aspect of abusive circumvention. It was also recognized, however, that this issue relates to

---

[122] BGHE 51, 298 et seq.

[123] BGHE 51, 298 et seq.; *Grund/Burda*, Mitt. 2010, 214.

[124] EuGH Slg. 2001, I – 7079.

[125] *Groh*, EuZW 2011, 911; *Cameron*, Pandora's Progeny: Ethical Issues in Assisted Human Reproduction, 39 Family law quarterly 745 (2005), 747; *Schacht*, Commencement or Completion: What Constitutes a "Human Embryo" Within the Meaning of the EU Biotechnology-Directive? 26 European Intellectual Property Review 66, 75 (2014); *Taupitz*, GRUR 2012, 4; *Taymor*, The Paths around Stem Cell Intellectual Property, 24 Nature Biotechnology 411, 413 (2006).

[126] EuGH Slg. 2011, I – 9871 rf. 34.

the ethical judgement of patentability and does not constitute a stronger argument for the exclusion of patentability on the basis of ethical considerations.

Regarding the distinction between research and industrial and commercial use, the ECJ noted that since a patent grants an exclusionary right, it is not possible to distinguish between the use for research projects and commercial and industrial uses.[127] This decision and reasoning was widely criticized in the legal literature but since it does not specifically relate to the aspects of morality and ordre public, it is not relevant to this analysis.[128]

Regarding legal arguments and consistent standards, the ECJ response was disappointing, since it provided only a very general and in no way detailed analysis and reasoning for its decision.

(2) Referring the Case back to the German Federal Court of Justice

Once those questions had been answered, the case came back to the German FCJ which had to apply the standard defined by the ECJ. The definition of human embryo posed no new ground for any violation by the patent application. However, the original neuralgic point was whether any indirect use of sensitive material such as an embryonic cell was sufficient for the exclusion of patentability. The FCJ had no choice but to reject the patent since the patent application used restricted cells in a process prior to the patented process. Of certain value for the broader analysis is the phrasing of the FCJ explaining why the prior stem cell destruction process is non-patentable: were the application to be granted, it would create the semblance that a process in which embryos are treated in a way which violates human dignity is approved by a governmental body of public law.[129]

The rejection of government approval is not specifically related to the technology. It does include the main argument of human dignity, however, as well as a referral to the fundamental considerations of the provisions of the EU Biotech Directive and the German Patent Act. It shows that the court does not agree with the opinion in the legal literature that a patent has to be regarded without concern for moral consideration. The court rejected the argument that a registered patent in no way conveys governmental approval or endorsement.[130]

---

[127] EuGH Slg. 2011, I – 9873 rf. 41.

[128] *Groh*, EuZW 2011, 912; *Straus*, GRUR Int. 2011, 1049; opposing: *Feldges*, GRUR 2011, 1104; *Batista*, GRUR Int. 2013, 515; *Laimböck/Dederer*, GRUR Int. 2011, 661; *Mahalatchimy*, Exclusion of Patentability of Embryonic Stem Cells in Europe: Another Restriction by the European Patent Organization, 37 European Intellectual Property Review 25, 39 (2015); *Schuster*, The Court of Justice of the European Union's Ruling on the Patentability of Human Embryonic Stem-Cell-Related Inventions (Case C-34/10), 43 International Review of Intellectual Property and Competition Law 626, 641 (2012).

[129] BGHZ 195, 370.

[130] *Dederer*, Europarecht, 2012, 336 et seq.; *Malpas/Lickiss*, Perspectives on Human Dignity: A Conversation (Springer 2007); *Thomson*, Embryonic Stem Cell Lines Derived from Human Blastocysts, 282 Science 1145, 1151 (1998).

b) Analysis of the Reasoning

In a more dogmatic and precise analysis, it is unfortunate to see the courts engaging in a more ethically charged declaration and appraisal of human dignity. This universal argument dissolves the distinction between legally, dogmatically and systematically precise structures and intangible ethical and philosophical arguments. Even more dissatisfying is the fact that the ECJ missed the chance to include the relevancy of the TRIPS agreement. The agreement allows the exclusion of patentability in the case of moral or public order considerations in Art. 27 Subs. 2 TRIPS. The definition in this article is clearly optional and even the EU Biotech Directive clarifies that the TRIPS provisions remain applicable in parallel to the obligations set out in the EU Biotech Directive itself.[131]

aa) Dogmatic Criticism of the Decision

The FCJ showed a certain amount of skepticism about whether the EU Biotech Directive necessarily required a broader interpretation while still upholding the obligations of the TRIPS agreement, even though the agreement included the optional character of the exclusions.[132] It seemed that the formulation of the exclusion as a possibility swayed the decision into a narrow interpretation. It suggests a basis of rule and exception wherein the exclusion of denying patentability is clearly the exception. Even though the FCJ specifically included those considerations in its procedural questions before the ECJ, no clarification was given.[133] This concept of "rule vs. exception" is one of the fundamental beliefs in the patent law community. Patentability requirements are conceived of as "rules" which have to be interpreted widely, whereas exemptions are technically "exceptions" which are to be interpreted narrowly. This disregards the fact that patents themselves are exceptions to competition, which in turn would require a narrow interpretation of the patent scope.

The decision by the ECJ was primarily based on the considerations of human dignity. In the decision, however, no definite statement was made about whether a human embryo directly benefits from human dignity or the process of destroying human embryos violates human dignity as a form of "class dignity".[134] The arguments in both courts even lacked a direct reference to the appropriate constitutional articles which protect human dignity in Art. 1 Sub. 1 GG[135] and Art. 6 Sub. 3 EUV.[136]

---

[131] Art. 1 Subs. 2 EU-directive; generally regarding the necessity: *Dörries*, Mitt. 2001, 16.

[132] BGH GRUR 2010, 218.

[133] The reasons are unknown. However, the FCJ noted in his final and subsequent decision that the ECJ had not ignored or missed that question but rather silently applied the TRIPS standards and considerations in his reasoning. BGHZ 195, 375.

[134] *Groh*, EuZW 2012, 911; *Dederer*, GRUR 2013, 354; *Trips-Hebert/Grund*, PharmR 2007, 397, 401.

[135] German Constitution ("Grundgesetz" – GG).

[136] The Treaty on European Union.

Given the importance of human dignity in both decisions, it can only be assumed that the omission of these provisions was intentional to avoid making any commitments to the highly debated aspects of human dignity and the beginning of life.[137]

Somewhat spectacularly for the whole case is the detail that the respective provisions of ordre public only apply to the commercial use of the patent. The various defined examples are specific utilizations of such a morally questionable commercial use. However, neither the ECJ nor the FCJ considered the fact that the commercial use of stem cells is – at least in Germany – allowed under the provision of the Embryo Protection Act.[138] Therefore, the patent application included possible uses which would not violate moral principle or other aspects of ordre public. Certain uses of the invention were perfectly legal. The general provision is usually interpreted in such a way that every conceivable potential commercial use has to constitute a violation.[139] This interpretation is very narrow and only applicable in a few cases; it would have been highly interesting to see how the high courts in Europe and Germany would resolve this contrast in interpretative approaches.

In addition, only the FCJ indicated that a decision could have been made based on the distinction of the possible different processes to obtain embryonic stem cells.[140] The patent application itself describes processes that only used embryonic stem cells once in a prior process. Another process which involved the destruction of stem cells in every single new application of the stem cell production process might have been the subject of a different legal and ethical assessment. Such a distinction in the severity or intensity of different processes used in a patent involving embryonic stem cells and their destruction thereof was also part of a different approach by the German court.

---

[137] *Curley*, Patenting Biotechnology in Europe: The Ethical Debate Moves on, 24 European Intellectual Property Review 565 (2002); *Condic/Condic*, The Appropriate Limits of Science in the Formation of Public Policy, 17 Notre Dame Journal of Law, Ethics and Public Policy 157 (2003), 160; *Thomson/Odorico*, Human Embryonic Stem and Embryonic Germ Cell Lines, 18 Trends in Biotechnology 53, 57 (2000).

[138] *Hübel*, Mitt. 2011, 494; *Straus*, GRUR 2001, 1018.

[139] *Nordberg/Minssen*, A "Ray of Hope" for European Stem Cell Patents or "Out of the Smog into the Fog"? An Analysis of Recent European Case Law and How it Compares to the US, 47 International Review of Intellectual Property and Competition Law 138, 153 (2016); *Straus*, GRUR Int. 2010, 1105.

[140] *Feldges*, GRUR 2011, 1108; a different approach to not include pluripotent cells in stem cell research was already in development: *Condic*, Alternative Sources of Pluripotent Stem Cells: Altered Nuclear Transfer, 41 Cell Proliferation 7 (2008), 14; with further research: *Daughtry/Mitalipov*, Concise Review: Parthenote Stem Cells for Regenerative Medicine: Genetic, Epigenetic, and Developmental Features, 3 Stem Cells Translational Medicine 290 (2014), 301; *Novak*, Enhanced Reprogramming and Cardiac Differentiation of Human Keratinocytes Derived from Plucked Hair Follicles, Using a Single Excisable Lentivirus, 12 Cellular Reprogramming 665, 681 (2010); *Plomer*, After Brüstle: EU Accession to the ECHR and the Future of European Patent Law, 2 Queen Mary Journal of Intellectual Property 110 (2012); *Straus*, GRUR Int. 2011, 1049.

The FCJ used a comparison to the "fruit of the forbidden tree"-doctrine to describe the issue of potentially violating processes prior to the actual process of the patent application.[141] It also observed that the issue of legally allowed actions and a seemingly contrary patentability exclusion might be subject to a distinction between a legal approach and ethical arguments.[142] According to the "fruit of the forbidden tree"-doctrine, a forbidden action or process and the results or obtainments thereof do, necessarily, have to be legally treated the same way.

It might have been possible to transfer some of these ideas to the case. In the invention, the prior procedure, which usually destroyed embryonic cells, could be considered the "tree" and the subsequent process within the patent application as a "fruit". Again, the ECJ, unfortunately, did not consider this specific line of argument. Other than the dogmatic criticism described here, the decision by the ECJ was subject to more general criticism.

bb) General Criticism of the EU Biotech Directive

The significant part of any legal discussion generally rejects the exclusion of patentability on the basis of moral considerations. It was argued that the only legal consequence of the decision was that no exclusionary right was granted for the procedure of using embryonic stem cells in a process to produce different stem cells. Theoretically, this would allow anybody with the necessary equipment and technical know-how to perform such a process themselves. Stem cell research itself was not forbidden in certain Contracting States of the EPO. It is possible that the denial of the respective patent therefore increased the actual intensity and number of such procedures and ultimately increased the potential violations of human dignity.[143] Such a result might be labeled absurd and outright counter-productive. The legal action brought forth by Greenpeace was actually intended to stop or decrease stem cell research and might be considered questionable or short-sighted, as well.

However, the specific argument of the ECJ was relying on the effect a granted patent conveys to the general public. The specific criticism does not apply to a possible endorsement or appreciation. Without an intellectual property right covering the process involving the destruction of human embryonic cells, there is no link to any endorsement by a patent office. Yet, the patent office is only one comparably small governmental body and stem cell research was restricted but still legal and therefore a field of research endorsed by the government. It seemed that the aspect of excluding patentability was almost a minor battleground in the debate on human dignity and the beginning of life.

---

[141] ECJ C-34/10.
[142] BGH GRUR 2010, 217.
[143] *Taupitz*, GRUR 2012, 4.

4. Conclusive Summary and Relevance

The decisions disappointed by failing to deliver a certain standard or catalogue of criteria of what specifically constitutes a violation of moral considerations in European Patent law. However, the criticism of the decision, by pointing out the consistency of the legal system and the irrelevance of the patent as a governmental expression of endorsement or approval, might be effectively countered by addressing the argument carefully. First, the value of a patent is inherently different from simply not prohibiting a certain research activity; this is supported by a distinction at the constitutional level. A patent right is considered property under the German constitution. Secondly, the argument relies on the accusation of inconsistency which, however, is an *ad hominem* since it does not address the issue at hand.

Ultimately, *Brüstle* was able to successfully change the application and obtain his patent. The patent was achieved by including a paragraph which guaranteed that the cells used for the procedure would not be obtained in a process which required the destruction of embryonic stem cells with the ability to develop into human beings.[144]

An interesting take on the aspect of legal order is based on the consideration that Art. 6 (2) of the EU Biotech Directive references specific cases of the general clause of Art. 53 lit. (a) ECP. That would mean that according to the previously analyzed interpretative approaches, the case groups of Art. 6 (2) BioTech Directive are necessarily against the ordre public of each member state. The directive had to be implemented into national law. If the ordre public of a member state were to differ, the legislation based on the EU directive would prevail.[145] However, this is not the case, since the EU directive, as well as Art. 53 lit. (a) EPC only exclude patentability but not commercial exploitation. Contracting States could theoretically allow commercial exploitation while still excluding the invention from patentability and act in accordance with EU law.[146] Furthermore, as mentioned before, the interpretation of the terms "embryo" and "human life" in Art. 6 (2) BioPat Directive is subject to the interpretation of national peculiarities. A national interpretation can result in a much narrower understanding of the terms in one member state than in the rest; additionally, the interpretation does not have to be based in scientific research or the recital of the EU directive. The interpretation is heavily influenced by morality. Consequently, an EPO examiner can only raise an objection to a patent application, where he is under the assumption that the case groups of Art. 6 (2) EU Biotech Directive are applicable, but he cannot definitely exclude the patent application from patentability. Instead, he has to grant the applicant the chance to prove that the patent does not violate the ordre public of the designated Contracting State.[147] The applicant may provide proof in the form of national legislation or administrative provisions

---

[144] *Dederer*, GRUR 2013, 353.

[145] *Romandini*, 300.

[146] Such a legislative act would violate the TRIPS Agreement.

[147] *Romandini*, 301.

which indicate that the interpretation of the national legal system differs and therefore renders the application admissible. That can be the case if no violation of the legal or moral order due to commercial exploitation of the invention is to be expected.

a) Fundamental Principles of Ordre Public or Morality

Ultimately, even the specific case groups of the EU Biotech Directive provide no specific information regarding an overarching principle relating to legal or moral order for the EU scope or specific Member States. However, the broad concept of human life, embryonic stem cells and cloning as represented in jurisprudence has always been based on human dignity. Human dignity therefore seems to be a central motive of the EU and national legislation which is usually of constitutional significance. In addition, it is regularly the most important value attributed to humans and their societal role. This role increases the difficulty of abstracting from this principle to identify a greater scheme in formulating a more specific standard.

b) Characteristics of Human Dignity in Biotechnological Inventions

To identify any features of human dignity that might have the potential to be transferred to other areas of technology, it is necessary to analyze the various aspects of the ethical considerations that were present in the legal discussion surrounding the patent.

Discussions regarding the patentability of living tissue have entered the public stage at the very latest with the *Chakrabarty* decision of the Supreme Court of the United States from 1980. The number of specific publications increased significantly, even though the topic is usually only of interest to a very narrow circle of researchers.[148] Even tabloid papers have taken a stance by morally judging the patent system, describing the patentability of living tissue as the "the worst monstrosity of technological disdain for human life".[149]

In the *Brüstle* Case, the variety of directly or indirectly involved parties surpassed the usual legal or economic interest groups and extended to religious interest groups, animal protection institutions and environmental and ethical interest groups.[150] While it is certainly important to cover a variety of societal and ethical views on the subject

---

[148] See Patenting Life Forms In Europe, Proceedings of an International Conference at the European Parliament Brussels, 7. – 8.2.1989; Patenting Life – Special Report, OTA 1989; Human Genetic Information: Science, Law And Ethics, 1990; Genetic Engineering – The New Challenge, Conference Proceedings and Essay Competition 1993.

[149] Monster aus dem Patentamt?, Süddeutsche Zeitung – Stadtanzeiger vom January 18th, 1990.

[150] The public interest in such discussion can be very well observed by the list of the opponents regarding the Krebsmaus/HARVARD patent EP-B1 0 168 672 – also mentioned in *Jaenichen/Schrell*, GRUR Int. 1993, 451 et seq.

of emerging technology, it also bears the risk that fundamental considerations of patent law might be misinterpreted or omitted from the legal discussion entirely.[151] In light of the polarizing and deeply emotional discussions in the general public regarding the – then – newly emerging question of patentability of human body parts, the lack of a precise and reasonable application of the fundamentals of patent law might distort the function and impression of the national patent system.[152]

The concerns regarding the ethical assessment of human-biological inventions can be categorized and assessed for their significance of a greater fundamental consideration in the following way:

(1) Critique Regarding Technology and Patent Law

First, the very concept of providing patent protection to inventions which might develop into living beings was criticized for promoting the free commercialization of genetic technology. Genetic technology has been – and in some interest groups still is – regarded as incompatible with the ethical beliefs of the general public. Therefore, any means – legal or factual – which have the potential to promote, advance or subsidize genetic research have to be equally unethical.[153] Even though not all genetic technological inventions might be considered purely ethical,[154] a blanket statement that all genetic technology has to be excluded from patentability fails to recognize the distinction between technology and its respective patentability.[155] The judgment of technology and patentability as an inseparable entity has to be discarded. Instead, the peculiarities of patent law have to be considered independently.

(2) Religious Concerns

Several religious interest groups view genetically produced or genetically engineered beings as incompatible with respect for a god or gods, since man would thereby presume to be a creator of life himself.[156] This opposition is commonly known as "playing god".[157] Not only does this argument fail to distinguish between the technologies itself and the role patent law has to play, but it also fails

---

[151] *Appel*, 84.

[152] *Straus*, GRUR 1992, 252.

[153] PBC Amicus Letter, PTCJ E-4, E-6; Brief for Government, PTCJ (BNA), Jan. 1980, at D-1, D-6.

[154] Such as the idea of "Splicing Life", The Social and Ethical Issues of Genetic Engineering with Human Beings 57 (1982); Enquete Kommission des Deutschen Bundestags "Chancen und Risiken der Gentechnologie" 1987.

[155] *Crespi*, Intellectual Property in Business 1989, 17, 19.

[156] Wir Menschen als Schöpfer, Kirchenbote, Zürich, February 16th, 1990; *Rajotte*, Some Theological and Ethical Points of Concern on the Issue of Patenting Genetically Engineered Living Organisms in: Patenting Life Forms in Europe, p. 50: "To claims a patent on a life form is a direct and total denial of God as creator, sustainer, breath of life, immanent spirit within of all beings."

[157] *Appel*, 86.

to convince content-wise. Assuming that a human might presume a god-like position by patenting a gene-editing invention is a misunderstanding of patent law, since patent law does not grant the right to commercially exploit or even use a certain technology. It simply provides a right to exclude third parties. Interpreting such an exclusive right as an affront to divinity and the creation of man overestimates the power and function of patents significantly.[158] Some authors even question the theological weight of the argument by addressing the role of man as "ruler of the creation" according to biblical standards.[159] Theological debate and religious dogmata are not part of this legal analysis; therefore, it suffices to exclude such an argument based on its relation to and understanding of patent law.

(3) Disregard for Nature

Following the theological debate, this time without a direct metaphysical approach, patentability of living tissue is often regarded as the final breach of the balance between man and the rest of nature.[160] Part of the criticism stems from religious interest groups which target the relationship of man and animals.[161] This view of the balance of nature and man stems from the understanding of man as an "advocate", "patron" or "protector" of nature and his "voiceless environment".[162] According to this philosophical understanding, nature is not primarily subject to manipulation and exploitation, but also subject to human responsibility and respect.[163] The basis for the respect and the responsibility of man stem again from the metaphysical premise of a divine creator and thereby blur this argument and the foregoing religious concerns.

This argument bears a significant amount of convincing power, even if only for the sake of the self-preservation of man in a changing environment. By describing the balance of nature and man, it also describes the very problem of patentability of inventions. Every manipulation or change of nature, is the result of a weighting between the benefit for man and human societies and the impact on nature and environmental conditions. The *Krebsmaus* technology is nothing more than the result of such a weighting and is therefore in line with the philosophical approach of balancing the interests of man and values of nature.

---

[158] Id at 87.

[159] Id.

[160] See *Rajotte*, as above, Wir Menschen als Schöpfer?.

[161] Informationsbrief Kirche und Gesellschaft July 10th, 1988; also *King*, in: Genetic Engineering – The New Challenge, 61 et seq.

[162] *Reiter*, Darf der Forscher alles, was er kann?, 31; *Altner*, Ökologisierung der Technik? 4, EKD-Synode, 3; *Jonas*, Technik, Medizin und Ethik, 47; OTA-Report, Patenting Life, 132.

[163] *Eibach*, Grenzen und Ziele der Gentechnologie aus theologisch-ethischer Sicht, in: Genforschung und Widerstreit, 1989, 32.

II. Ordre Public and Morality on a European Level 91

Aspects of proportionality or reasonableness are key to ethical considerations in this regard.[164]

(4) Opposing the Commercialization

Additionally, the patentability of more complex life forms is often categorized as the beginning of commercializing life.[165] Some authors even go as far as to suggest complete exclusion of the patentability of biotechnological inventions in order to prevent the degrading of life to marketable products.[166] Patenting of life forms is, in that context, often referred to as a "sellout of creation".[167]

Again, such an assessment of the patent systems is based on the misunderstanding of the function and significance of patents. Similar to the religious and theological considerations, this view of patent law overestimates the effect of patents.[168] Thousands of years of domestication and animal breeding have crucially shaped and developed the relationship between animals and humans without any form of patent law.[169]

Without offering a full assessment, historically, animals were almost always regarded as property or subject to property laws.[170] Whether such as categorization is still valid in the modern understanding of the animal and man relationship is not the subject of this analysis; however, it is undeniable that animals are subject to property laws.[171]

It is therefore not convincing to argue that the legal categorization of animal or plant life is significantly worsened by allowing temporary exclusive rights of commercial exploitation, while simultaneously regarding or treating animals legally as property.[172] A similar conclusion is drawn by the Office of Technology

---

[164] Similar *Brody*, An Evaluation of the Ethical Arguments Commonly Raised against the Patenting of Transgenic Animals, in: Animal Patens, 145, who makes a case against the useless research with animal subjects.

[165] New Animals Forms Will be Patented, The New York Times, April 17th, 1987, 9.

[166] *Idel/Tappeser*, 12, 14; Wenn Lebewesen zur Ware werden, Süddeutsche Zeitung, September 9th, 1989, 26; Gentechnologie bringt Macht, in: Vaterland, Luzern, October 20th, 1989.

[167] Zuerst das Geschäft, dann die Regel, Tagesanzeiger, Zürich, February 24th, 1990 and more recently with regard to vegetable varieties: Patente auf Gemüsesorten: Ein "Ausverkauf der Schöpfung?", Frankfurter Allgemeine Zeitung, July 21st, 2010.

[168] *Appel*, 88.

[169] Report of the Committee on the Judiciary, in: Animal Patents, 247.

[170] Even if Sect. 90a German Civil Code negates the equality of animals and objects, the same property laws apply.

[171] *Lorz*, MDR 1989, 204; *Pütz*, ZRP 1989, 174.

[172] "In comparison with the treatment of animals up until now, their patentability seems relatively harmless", Testimony of Dr. Walters of Georgetown University, Animal Patents, p. 247.

Assessment (OTA) which evaluates ethical arguments against the patentability of animals.[173]

Some authors argue that just because the treatment of animals in another part of a legal system is allegedly inherently unethical, does not justify the unethical practice of patentability – an argument by comparison is supposedly invalid. Regarding this opposition, it is important to clarify that the argument is not assessing the morality of the treatment but rather the consistency of ethical considerations within the legal system. Without such consistency, a claim for adjusting the patent system is inadmissible, because the standard for ethics and morality has to be consistent across the entire legal system.

(5) Concern based on philosophical considerations

Philosophical concerns revolve around the concept that allowing patentability for living matter would contribute to the institutionalization of reductionism.[174] This argument follows the *Chakrabarty* decision of the Supreme Court of the United States which explained that the patentability requirements covering "(...) any new and useful process, machine, manufacture, or composition of matter" also extend to cover living matter or life forms. Criticism was sparked by the supposed lack of consideration of deep philosophical questions regarding the nature and significance of life. In particular, the term "composition of matter" as a blanket description was regarded as unethically equalizing complex forms of human life and reducing them to merely technical terms.[175]

Adding a philosophical dimension to the discussion makes it significantly more difficult, if not impossible, to come to a reasonable solution. Yet, these considerations alone are insufficient to justify a general exclusion of living matter from patentability. The debate between vitalism and materialism has been decided by science and law clearly in favor of materialism.[176] In U.S. law, it has been pointed out that "(...) there is no legally significant difference between active chemicals which are classified as 'dead' and organisms used for their chemical reactions which take place because they are 'alive'. Life is largely chemistry."[177] A similar observation was made by the German Federal Court of

---

[173] "It is unclear that patenting per se would substantially redirect the way society uses or relates to animals", Special Report, OTA, Patenting Life, 137.

[174] PBC Amicus Brief, PTCJ at E-9; *Hermitte*, Patenting Life Forms: The Legal Environment, 15.

[175] *Kass*, Patenting Life, Toward a More Natural Science (New York, NY, Free Press 1985) by stating: "Consider first the implicit of our wise men, that a living organism is no more than a composition of matter, not different from the latest perfume or insecticide. What about other living organisms – goldfish, bald eagles, horses? What about human beings? Just compositions of matter?", also *Crawford*, Vol. 237 Science 480 (1987).

[176] *Cooper*, Rutgers Journal, Vol. 8 (1980), p. 1 (38 et seq); dissenting and explaining that nature is not entirely dissectible and observable by scientific methods alone: *Chargaff*, p. 223.

[177] C.C.P.A. 569 F. 2d 952 = 201 USPQ 352–395.

Justice.¹⁷⁸ Patent law is mainly science and technology-based; a focus on the metaphysical properties and value of life is impractical, since patent law needs objective or verifiable standards to assess patentability. Yet, shifting the focus to objective and observable characteristics does not mean that patent law fails to recognize other characteristics of living matter; they are just not included in the examination.¹⁷⁹ It is thus observable that ethical considerations usually result in a weighting of opposing interests and are part of legal and ethical considerations.¹⁸⁰

The most important factors in these arguments are: most philosophical and metaphysical arguments are not supported by the exclusionary nature of patent law. And, even though human dignity is supposed to be an absolute value, most arguments include the concept of proportionality.

Apart from these argument concerning human dignity, other arguments are aimed at the relationship between ethics and biotechnology.

c) Specific Arguments Concerning Ethics in Biotechnological Inventions

The fundamental relationship between morality and biotechnology has been the subject of an ongoing discussion that was further advanced by the *Brüstle* decision. The most relevant arguments are:

1. Patentability of Life leads to an Ethical Wasteland

   Famous critics of patent law argue that the historic development of patent law illustrates that by allowing patents for biotechnological inventions, future development will naturally and automatically include the patentability of human life as well.¹⁸¹ This concern is based on the assumption that neither a scientifically precise nor legally definitive definition of life exists. Consequently, it is impossible to accurately distinguish between highly and less highly developed life forms. This lack of definitions will, supposedly, ultimately lead to the patentability of highly developed life forms.¹⁸²

   Such a development seems to be observable in the U.S. In particular, the famous quote of the Supreme Court of the United States extending patentability to "all under the sun that is made by man" is suggestive of this broad and unrestricted

---

[178] BGH, in: GRUR 1969, 672, 673, see also *Savignon*, GRUR Int. 1985, 83, 84.

[179] *Murray*, in: Patenting Life, p. 131; *Keegan*, 10, 13.

[180] *Appel*, 89.

[181] *Fowler/Lachkovics/Mooney/Shand*, From Cabbages to Kings?, in: development dialogue, 1988: 1–2. P 237; PBC Amicus Brief, PTCJ E-7, E-9; and the statement of a member of the Senate (?), in: Clash Looming on Patenting of Animals, The New York Times, June 23rd, 1987, p. 10: "We've approved the patenting of plants in 1930, seeds in 1970, microbes in 1980 and now we've moved to considering patenting animals– next is human beings."

[182] PBC Amicus Brief, PRCJ E-7.

approach. Innovations are likely to become more complex in the field of genetic research and are likely to be relevant to human life. Since this "slippery slope" argument was originally made with regard to potentially patentable animal life, the prediction became verified by the actual development in patent law.[183]

However, for the prediction that human life will eventually become subject of patent law to be verified, it is necessary to note that no significant legal or scientific differences between animal and human life exist. While, scientifically speaking, the genetic information of human beings and animals is similar in their set-up,[184] communities such as the EU and the EPO have agreed upon a general exclusion of patentability regarding human life and even embryonic stem cell research in the EU Biotech Directive. However, in the context of international patents, human cells, tissue, bodily fluids and organs are categorized in the same category as materials from mammals or birds, class A 61 K 35/00, subgroup 35/12.[185] In addition, as was the case in the *Brüstle* Case, main patent claims are usually specified in sub claims to cover human beings as well. Even the exceptions to patentability in Art. 53 lit. (c) EPC are formulated in such a way that methods for surgery or therapy and diagnostic methods are excluded from patentability for both the human and animal body without making any distinction between the value of the two.[186]

It is necessary to accept and recognize that the development of genetic technology raises numerous morally-ethical, philosophical and theological issues. In patent law, the human still stands on top of the hierarchy of values and might be affected by a shift in the ethical assessment of life forms and their patentability. From an overall perspective, it remains uncertain, though not impossible that patentability might extend to human life forms as well. However, such a development is certainly not inherent to nor does it solely affect the patent systems but rather reflects a general argument in the ethical debate.[187]

2. "Slippery Slope" Argument

Patenting parts of the human body is already possible and therefore, the necessary next step will lead to patentability of the human body in its entirety. Once the level of the human body is no longer taboo, no arguments referring relating to the role of the human or his distinguishing characteristics may hinder the advancement of patentability.[188] Patent law seems to approach the patentability of the human itself

---

[183] German patent law does not include a supreme decision which causes *Moufang* to describe the existence of an absence of authority, GRUR Int. 1990, 60.

[184] *Appel*, 90.

[185] *Appel*, 90, also *Vossius/Jaenichen*, GRUR 1989, 708, 709.

[186] Referring back to the natural argument, it seems that patent law provides a stronger protection and appreciation of animal life than the rest of the legal system.

[187] *Appel*, 91; *Hoffmaster*, The Ethics of Patenting Higher Life Forms, 34 – dissenting *Keefan*, 10, 14.

[188] *Badish*, Patenting Human Material: What Form of Political Responsibility?, 55.

with each advancement in patenting human genetic material. *Appel* argues that this tendency is rooted in the lack of an exact and generally agreed upon definition of the genetic identity of humans[189] and the ever-advancing research and increasing feasibility of the human genome. Failing to define the genetic identity of humans precisely leads to an increase in practical problems. As long as it is undefined or insufficiently defined what genetically determines a human being, a solid, safe protection for the genetic identity of human beings cannot be achieved.[190]

This problem is intensified by the external pressure experienced by patent offices around the world. Genetic research (foremost the Human Genome Project) is immensely costly[191] and it is expected that those investments will be justified by obtaining protection for the research results – potentially via patent law.[192]

3. The Human Body as a Product

Finally, the commercialization of the human body is anticipated and regarded as a threat.[193] However, commercial interests regarding the human body are not a new phenomenon and can be observed as a necessary result of medical-technical advancement, since such advancement is usually regulated by an economic and political framework. Deciding whether patentability may lead to an unbearable commercialization of the human body and therefore be excluded from patentability is a highly complex issue which has to take into account a wide variety of different aspects. The process of reaching a result in such a complex decision is shaped again by weighing opposing values and interests.[194]

These major arguments show that the discussion is very tightly linked to the topic of biotechnology itself. It seems hardly possible to identify a general abstract standard that these arguments are based on.

d) Identifying Abstract Characteristics

The foregoing analysis indicates that most ethical, philosophical and even religious considerations fail to be completely convincing. Their shortcomings are not due to their lack of intellectual value but rather based on the misinterpretation and overestimation of patent law and its effects. The arguments are not to be discarded, because they illuminate the ethical dimension of patent law, especially when it comes

---

[189] *Kastenmeier* during the draft of the Transgenic Animal Patent Reform Act, PTCJ (Vol. 36) 1988, 499 (502), "I turn, I think Congress must have better definition of how much genetic material constitutes the legal definition of what constitutes a human being".

[190] *Appel*, 92.

[191] Mapping Our Genes – Genome Projects: How Big, How Fast?, OTA-Report, 180 et seq.

[192] *Appel*, 92.

[193] *Moufang*, GRUR Int. 1993, 439, 450.

[194] *Appel*, 92.

to human and animal life. It can be concluded that, at the very core of the considerations, lies a weighting of values and interests. A solution is often found by placing the values and interests in relation and identifying a status that considers each side or value proportionally. This indicates that the ethical considerations of patent law, i.e. the ordre public or morality, are not a set of solid values but rather a complex concept that follows the principle of proportionality.[195] Applying the principle of proportionality to identify a more practical and reasonable standard of legal and moral order might prove useful.

III. Fundamental Considerations of Morality in German Legal Literature

As a specification, several inventions regarding human life or animal genetic identity and animal well-being have been incorporated in Sect. 2 Subs. 2 No. 1 through 4 PatG back in 2005.[196] As mentioned before, these exclusions do not directly apply to the technologies in question but will rather be used as one of several starting points to identify similar fundamental concepts of morality and public order in German patent law.

1. Factual and Legal Background of the German Provision

Since the implementation of Sect. 2 Subs. 2 PatG is based on the EU Biotech Directive[197] the analysis of the German provisions necessarily has to be based on the preceding considerations at the European level.

Before the European Biotech Directive came into effect the protection of animate nature was considered to be insufficient. While this might be the case, it leaves the question of why the area of animate nature needs an exclusion from patent law unanswered. A variety of authors consider the existence of this dispute to be only partly justified for a variety of reasons, similar to the general objections already mentioned in the introduction to Sect. 2 PatG. An additional argument addresses the practical relevance of patentability in the realm of animate nature.[198] Patent protection of a new lifeform seems improbable under given technological circumstances

---

[195] *Pedrazzini*, Die patentfähige Erfindung, 28.

[196] G v. 21.1.2005 (BGBl. I S. 146).

[197] ABl. EG Nr. L 213, 30.07.1998. The implementation by Germany was considerably delayed and was eventually part of a contract violation proceeding before the ECJ which decided to the disadvantage of Germany.

[198] *Melullis*, in: Benkard, PatG Sect. 2 re. 14.

and any genetic manipulation of animals does not change the animal type but rather its characteristics.[199]

The discussion originated during the beginning of advances in the field of genetic manipulation.[200] As many EU Member States began to react to the changing beliefs of the population and adjusted their national patent regime, the European Commission mainly intended to harmonize the changing patent regulations.[201] A variety of more or less specific considerations was given: the altered view within society regarding genetic manipulation, protection of the environment, the status and protection of animals and the protection of the integrity of nature to prevent detrimental changes to affected animals and their physical well-being.[202]

2. General Considerations Regarding the Morality Provision

The very existence of the regulation in Sect. 2 No. 1 PatG has been subject to criticism. The reason for this lies in the different understanding of the fundamental considerations regarding the functions and objectives of patent law.

a) Fundamental Objections to the Provision

A strong opinion argues that, since a patent does not provide a positive right of use which can be enforced against the state or within the legal system, no moral considerations apply at all.[203] It is true that a patent only provides a limited right to exclude others from using the patented invention. Since any legal or natural person is free to apply and use new technology apart from the prohibitive legislation or intellectual property rights of third parties, the exclusion from patentability is therefore unable to prevent the use of the technology in question. Without a patent, the market lacks the obstacle of a third-party right and is therefore free in its use of the technological invention in the context of any competition. It seems that the concept of excluding patentability on the grounds of legal or moral order is counter-productive.[204]

Furthermore, this opinion ties the functionality of the patent office closely to the legal nature of a patent. Since a patent does not protect the right of use, the patent

---

[199] *Melullis*, in: Benkard, PatG Sect. 2 re. 14, giving a comprehensive overview regarding other problems in patent law stemming from the protection of genetically manipulated seeds and the natural spread thereof.

[200] *MGK, Moufang*, Art. 53 EPC re. 50 et seq.; *Melullis*, in: Benkard, PatG Sect. 2 re. 14.

[201] *Melullis*, in: Benkard, PatG Sect. 2 re. 14.

[202] *König/Müller*, GRUR Int. 1999, 595; *Melullis*, in: Benkard, PatG Sect. 2 re. 15.

[203] *Melullis*, in: Benkard, PatG Sect. 2 re. 16; in contrast to the original medieval right of privileges which actually granted a positive right of use; *Pilenko*, Das Recht des Erfinders, S. 53 et seq. and *Beier*, GRUR Int 1978, 123, 124.

[204] BGH NJW 1973, 1412. IUP – dissenting: *Vorwerk*, GRUR 2009, 375.

office is in no position to decide how the protected invention is allowed to be used.[205] In addition, the classic counter-argument that the grant of a patent is equivalent to governmental endorsement or recognition is met with the consideration that a patent is legally granted even if the invention is not advantageous to the society.

A particular assessment would overstrain the patent office and is therefore impractical; any statement regarding the significance, adequacy or sense of purpose cannot be made and is thus not to be expected.[206] Furthermore, a classic counter-argument is that the patent office should not be forced to participate in the preparation of inventions which violate public or moral principles.[207] The need for public institutions to uphold such principles is famously apparent in the decisions of the German Federal Supreme Court.[208] It is also necessary to consider the reasoning that granting a patent, to some extent, displays an official recognition and appreciation, since official participation of a state institution is required.[209] The terms "social disorientation" and "levelling effect on moral principles" which are sometimes used to descried these phenomena[210] seem to be a bit excessive but describe the basic understanding. Even the EPO accepted this interpretation of the particular Article and its versions in national patent legislation by explaining: "Art. 53 lit. (a) EPC is merely intended to prevent an invention, the publication or exploitation of which would infringe the fundamental principles of 'ordre public' or morality being given an appearance of approval through a patent issued by an international authority."[211]

Other national legislations prior to European harmonization included similar statutes, especially targeting medications, and they justified those regulations by directly addressing the problem of utilizing the grant of patent as an advertising measure.[212]

It is also the case that the German legal system is influenced by the goal of being established on the basis of a set of uniform and consistent principles.[213] Aspects of legal and moral order are almost omnipresent in German legislation and usually function as an ultimate corrective to uphold the uniform principle of the German legal system. The general limits of every piece of legislation set by legal and moral order

---

[205] *Fuchs*, Mitt. 2000, 1, 3; *Haedicke*, JuS 2002, 113, 116; *Melullis*, in: Benkard, PatG Sect. 2 re. 16.

[206] *Melullis*, in: Benkard, PatG Sect. 2 re. 16.

[207] *Melullis*, in: Benkard, PatG Sect. 2 re .18.

[208] BPatG, GRUR 73, 585, 586 – IUP; EPA, GRUR Int. 1993, 865.

[209] *Paver*, Patent World, March 1992, 12; *Beyleveld/Brownsword*, Mice, Morality and Patents, 44.

[210] *Rogge*, GRUR 1998, 303, 304; *Calame*, Öffentliche Ordnung und gute Sitten, 121; *Schatz*, GRUR Int. 1997, 588, 593.

[211] T 0866/01 dated 11 May 2005, Egr. 9.7 – Euthanasia Compositions/Michigan State University.

[212] *Romandini*, 227 et seq. with further references.

[213] BVerfGE 98, 106, 118.

III. Fundamental Considerations of Morality in German Legal Literature   99

should also apply to patent law.[214] However, it is often noted within the legal discussion that this principle is not universally applied in every piece of legislation and contradictions in certain areas of law are accepted to some extent.[215] German copyright law allows for the establishment of copyright regarding works which violate legal or moral principles.[216] Additionally, in German civil law, it is possible to legally own objects which can only be used in illicit acts.[217] Why it should not be possible to also patent the inventions which precede such objects is not entirely clear and certainly not a necessity of the uniform principle.[218]

This line of reasoning seems to be conclusive; however, it fails to identify the crucial differences between patent law on the one hand and property law and copyright law on the other hand. While the latter requires only the existence of the work or the object for it to be respected by the legal system, patent law requires a formal act of official recognition. It is even more surprising considering the results of limiting legislation in each case. The lack of patent protection of an invention violating the legal or moral order results simply in the lack of a patent, or plainly put – nothing. The lack of recognition of ownership of objects with only illicit uses results in an object without a legal owner and without a person responsible for a possibly dangerous item. The need for legal assignment is entirely different in both cases, therefore defeating an argument based on comparison.

However, in a case in which the violation of moral or public principles due to the use of the invention is obvious, the patent office is entitled to dismiss the application. Sect. 42 Subs. 2 PatG mentions limited scope of assessment.[219] In addition to the obviousness of the violation, it has to be severe in a sense that its use is especially harmful for the general public or even despicable.[220] The EPO supposedly shares this very high assessment standard;[221] however, what exactly applies to this somewhat ambiguous definition is not entirely clear and is extensively discussed.

Additional considerations, within the reasoning of the opinion, are focused on the dynamic nature of public and moral principles.[222] Where the principles change over time, the protection of an invention originally deemed unfit for patent protection might be morally sound in a future assessment. The dynamic nature of this development is said to be counter-productive to the function of patenting.[223] Even the possibility of a later re-application is no suitable solution. The application in an

---

[214] *Teschemacher*, GRUR 1992, 134; *Pedrazzini/Blum*, GRUR Int 1960, 151.
[215] *Calame*, Öffentliche Ordnung und Gute Sitten, 119 et seq.; *Schack*, GRUR 1983, 56, 60.
[216] BGH I ZR 12/08.
[217] BGH, 3 StR 295/05.
[218] *Romandini*, 226.
[219] *Melullis*, in: Benkard, PatG Sect. 2 re. 16.
[220] *Melullis*, in: Benkard, PatG Sect. 2 re. 18.
[221] EPA GRUR Int. 93, 865.
[222] *Melullis*, in: Benkard, PatG Sect. 2 re. 17.
[223] *Haeckicke*, JuS 2002, 113, 116; *Melullis*, in: Benkard, PatG Sect. 2 re. 17.

indefinite future bears the risk of the invention losing its novelty or losing the race to a faster competitor who has filed the patent application under more favorable circumstances.[224] Historically, these considerations carry a certain weight. Measures regarding birth control were originally deemed to be a violation of moral principles and were therefore denied patentability by the German courts.[225] Nowadays, however, the use of condoms to prevent the spread of diseases and overpopulation are the subject of governmental endorsement.[226] Other popular examples include observations in fields of potency- and virility-enhancing pharmaceuticals and various birth control medications.

Finally, it is argued that even if patent law includes the objective to regulate the use of morally questionable inventions, the mechanisms of its legal framework are inadequate for doing so.[227] Addressing the legal framework refers back to the legal nature of the immaterial right a patent is granting. A patent merely provides a right of exclusion of others and therefore has little to no significant impact on the use of an invention. The decision to refrain from granting a patent only has the consequence that no right of exclusion is granted; a prohibition of use of any kind is therefore not included. Consequently, it is claimed that the use of inventions in violation of moral or public principles can – and therefore should – only be the subject of specific prohibitive legislation.[228]

The in-depth analysis of the opposition to the provision reveals that it is not entirely convincing. Therefore, it is necessary to make the case that the provision is actually necessary and reasonable.

b) Arguing in favor of the Morality Provision

A patent exclusion indirectly affects the financing of inventions and is therefore likely to affect the development and production of an invention.[229] This chain of thought is countered with the alleged limited objectives of patent law, which again do not include the task to regulate the development and production.[230]

A major argument to address the concerns raised by the previous aspects lies in a deeper analysis of the function of patent law itself. It is almost universally agreed upon that patents serve – at least additionally – as an incentive to encourage technological advancement. The advancement of a technology can only be justified when

---

[224] *Melullis*, in: Benkard, PatG Sect. 2 re. 17; 6. ÜG Bl. 61, 140; *Schulte*, § 2 re. 14, 22; *Kranz*, GRUR 62, 389, 390 f.; *Roederer*, Applied Chemistry 34, 616.

[225] RGBl. 08, 292.

[226] *Melullis*, in: Benkard, PatG Sect. 2 re. 17.

[227] *Rogge*, GRUR 1998, 303, 306; *Melullis*, in: Benkard, PatG Sect. 2 re. 17.

[228] *Melullis*, in: Benkard, PatG Sect. 2 re. 17.

[229] *Melullis*, in: Benkard, PatG Sect. 2 re. 16 – see *Schatz*, GRUR Int. 97, 588, 597; *Rogge*, GRUR 98, 303, 306.

[230] *Melullis*, in: Benkard, PatG Sect. 2 re. 17.

those advancements are positive for the well-being of the society. Therefore, patent law can only function properly if it includes a mechanism which prohibits the endorsement of technological advancements which negatively affect social well-being. A norm excluding inventions the exploitation of which violates ordre public prevents investments in such inventions. It also incentivizes research to develop a product which does not violate said principles but still manages to fulfill market requirements in order to satisfy a potential demand in the market for such a product.[231] In addition, the argument that the morality clause has to be interpreted narrowly fails to convince. As mentioned before, this argument is based on the assumption that the exception to a rule has to be interpreted narrowly. However, not only does this not reflect legal reasoning but it is also entirely ambiguous. The "rule" and the "exception" can be formulated freely. As mentioned in the previous sub-chapter, patent law itself can be considered an "exception" to the general rule of competition.

Additionally, patent exclusion prevents special interests groups from lobbying to change prohibitive legislation, where they have already obtained a patent and are trying to economically exploit their right.[232]

Following the opinion that the provision is indeed justified, the next section addresses the subject of the assessment of the morality concerns.

3. Subject of the Examination Process

It might be rather difficult for an examiner to identify the certain aspect of an invention which might violate the moral or legal order. It is easier to understand the different possibilities by arranging a set of examples:

It might be possible that the development of the invention itself is characterized by procedures which are considered to be ethically questionable. The *Krebsmaus* decision falls into this category, since the procedure necessary to obtain the matter relevant to the invention included the painful treatment and killing of mice.[233] Furthermore, it is also possible that the application of the invention violates the ordre public of the relevant patent system. It can be difficult and ambiguous to give a specific example, but usual examples range from torturing methods,[234] methods of executing the death penalty[235] to the development of anti-personnel mines.[236] These

---

[231] *Romandini*, 228 et seq.

[232] A further look with an example of how an appeal to WTO regulations can be relevant can be found at: *Romandini*, 229, 230 for an additional argument regarding the protection of competitors who have a serious disadvantage in a hypothetical scenario where a violating invention is granted and later the technology becomes non-violating.

[233] EPO – T 0315/03 – Krebsmaus.

[234] *Romandini*, 240.

[235] *Romandini*, 242 – at least in European countries, where the death penalty is no longer part of the legal system.

[236] Guidelines for Examination in the European Patent Organization, Part G-II 4.1.

seem like obvious examples which fulfill the definition; however, upon closer analysis, the identification of a standard which provides a guideline to assess specific inventions and their application becomes increasingly difficult.

A third group of examples describes the conflict of a patent and its respective right of exclusion based on highly valued principles of the legal system. A method for life-saving treatments provides such a high benefit for the well-being of society that its application must not be hindered or prevented by intellectual property rights.[237] The existence of patents which might interfere with exclusively official state obligations such as issuing passports or producing legal tender must also be prevented since such patents would hold no economic value to non-state institutions. Interference with official state obligations does not provide technological advancement beneficial to society and is therefore not covered by the intentions of the patent regime. The final example of this group relates to constitutional self-determination rights which might be infringed upon by an exclusionary right. This constitutional approach is rather experimental and is described as relevant when it comes to methods of in vitro fertilization or medical procedures which require the temporary removal of limbs.[238] The latter in particular is highly hypothetical and it is difficult to imagine a scenario where such a medical procedure is actually influenced by constitutional rights. In vitro fertilization might be a more relevant topic and the desire to have children seems more relatable when it comes to constitutional rights, but it is still difficult to imagine the specific scenario.

Once the subject of the morality assessment has been identified, the questions about which moment and location for invention are relevant. This assessment includes considerations at the European level as well.

a) Relevant Moment and Geographic Scope

It would seem plausible that the standard for evaluating moral considerations and public order policies surrounding a certain patent application are at least subject to the ordre public of the location of production of the patented inventions. However, the ECJ decided that instead, the circumstances in the whole territory of the European Community[239] have to be taken into account.[240] However, the patented invention itself is not the subject of the moral evaluation but rather the aspect of subsequent commercial use of said invention. As national patent legislation within Europe has to

---

[237] *Deutsch*, Medizinrecht Rn. 854; *Beyleveld/Brownsword*, Mice, Morality and Patents, 34 et seq.

[238] *Romandini*, p. 241.

[239] Now European Union, the decision was made at time when the term was still European Community.

[240] EuGH GRUR 2011, 1104; *Melullis*, in: Benkard, PatG Sect. 2 re. 24.

adhere to European Patent legislation, this standard on the European tier has to be applied by each national patent office on a national tier.[241]

However, even though it seems *prima facie* to be coherent and standardizing the relevant circumstances to establish the appropriate moral and legal guidelines, it only applies to European legislation which takes effect in all EU Member States. If no such relevant legislation exists on a European level, it becomes much more difficult to establish a moral and legal order which is equally relevant in all Member States.

In other prominent parts of ECJ jurisprudence, considerable leeway has been granted to the individual EU Member States, especially in aspects of prohibitive legislation based on moral and ethical grounds.[242] Therefore, the legal and moral aspects of individual Member States remain relevant for national patent procedures as long as no specific European legislation regulating the invention in question exists.

This relationship of EU and national state law leads to other problematic aspects:

(1) What quality of regulation is relevant to patent law? Is only prohibitive legislation sufficient?

(2) Can this legislation be in line with the German provision Sec. 2 Subs. 1 PatG which specifically states that a violation caused by the commercial use of an invention being subject to prohibitive legislation or administrative regulation does not constitute an exclusion of patentability alone?

The ECJ decision in *Brüstle* still holds, since it was taken in consideration of Sec. 2 Subs. 2 No. 3 PatG which relates to a specific case of legal and moral order and does not include such a restriction. However, since Subs. 1 and Subs. 2 are inherently different in that regard, it seems far-fetched to argue for a transferal of the reasoning regarding the aspect of geographical limitations and standardized scope of application.

This is interesting insofar as the commercial exploitation of an invention might violate the legal or moral order of a specific member state. The prohibitive legislation, however, of the member state is not based on fundamental considerations of the European community and is more of a national peculiarity. According to one legal approach, a national patent court or a patent office is barred from applying a stricter national standard with regard to legal or moral order, in case the commercial exploitation is admissible in other European country and no consensus exists within the European Member States.[243] Additionally, the intention of the consistent patent principles within the European Union was to create incentives to invest in the Eu-

---

[241] *Melullis*, in: Benkard, PatG Sect. 2 re. 24.

[242] With an overview: *Wicks*, Human Rights Law Review, 556 et seq.

[243] *Wolters*, Die Patentierung des Menschen, 199 et seq.; *Rogge*, GRUR 1999, 303, 305; *Kewitz*, Der gemeinschaftliche Patentschutz für biotechnologische Erfindungen, 137; *Ahrens*, GRUR 2003, 89, 95 with some restrictions as to what the European "requirements" on patentability are.

ropean domestic market; this intention would be contradicted where the requirements for patentability differ between the Member States.[244]

While it is true that the historic intention of European standardization was to achieve a more streamlined patent regime within the European domestic market, it is incorrect to assume that only a European consensus for ordre public may be relevant and applicable to national patent applications.

The requirement to interpret European directive-based national legislation consistently only affects actual substantive law that has been agreed upon in the legislative process.[245] The terms "legal and moral order" refer to national provisions or requirements that restrict the commercial exploitation of an invention. Neither the TRIPS agreement nor the European legislation have standardized those terms. Therefore, terms that are outside of patent law are not part of the harmonization endeavor. The only aspect relevant to the consistent interpretation is the significance of provisions and requirements that constitute ordre public. The focus on national law is related to the principle that the terms are required to be interpreted autonomously and this is specific to the characteristic features of patent law. It is necessary that this principle is not confused with a requirement to interpret the terms consistently throughout the various European Patent legislations. Such a requirement does not exist. The meaning of ordre public has to be interpreted according to the national legal system which is assessed according to the national patent offices and the patent courts.

The commercial exploitation of inventions is regulated by national law and cultural peculiarities. A consistent interpretation of public order in each national patent regime would not change the differences in the European economic market. Whether the division of the market begins with the aspects of patentability or the commercial exploitation of an invention is irrelevant from an economic point of view. The irrelevance leads to the possibility that an invention may be exempt from patent protection, even if the basis for the rejection is not a uniform concept within the European Union.[246] Such an interpretation is also indirectly confirmed by the ECJ.[247]

b) European Union vs European Unity

Other, more practical, considerations concern the concept of identifying an understanding of ordre public that is actually based on the consensus of every EU member state. It is already difficult to identify a solid standard within a single member state, so identifying 28 individual ones comparing similarities seems im-

---

[244] *Wolters*, Die Patentierung des Menschen, 199.

[245] *Romandini*, 257.

[246] *Romandini*, 258 and *Guglielmetti*, NLCC 2008, 396, 400 rf. 23 with further references.

[247] ECJ, October 9th, 2001, Rs. C-377/90, Slg. 2001, I-07079, Egr. Nr. 38 et seq. with further explanations on the relevance and significance given by *Romandini*, 258.

practical, if not almost impossible. This legal challenge is similar to the previous discussion on the EPO.

In addition, the European Union is based on the principle of respecting national sovereignty, which specifically includes aspects of cultural peculiarities of a certain significance which may not be overruled by European legislation. The respect for these aspects restricts a unification of elements that are inaccessible to a unification process.

Restricting the unification process makes it even clearer that the interpretation of the terms "legal and moral order" has to be subject to each member state and its own identification process for the patent offices and patent courts. Requiring a certain level of significance for the incorporated provisions and specifications of the national attempts to assess the content of "legal and moral order", is sufficient to achieve the intended harmonization of the patent regimes within the European Union.

4. Understanding Ordre Public in Morality in German Legal Culture

With the broader understanding of the reasoning behind the provision in mind, it is included in the wording of the provision in Subs. 1 that a violation of moral or legal principles does not actually have to occur.[248] This is attributed to the use of the conjunctive "would" constitute a violation.[249] The mere possibility is not sufficient; it has to be a significant and specific threat to the moral or legal order.[250]

A certain opinion within the German legal discussion states that prohibitive legislation or prohibitive administrative acts are usually insufficient to exclude a patent application from patentability. This argument is based on the consideration that most legislative or administrative provisions are not the expression of "eternal moral wrong".[251] Furthermore, this opinion resorts to use of the term "supremely important legal consideration".[252] It is noted that such elements of important legal assets cannot be subject to restricted interpretation.[253] The approach of rendering the sole function of the patent office to simply provide a technological assessment is not

---

[248] VGH München, GRUR-RR 2003, 297 – Aufreißdeckel; *Melullis*, in: Benkard, PatG Sect. 2 re. 25.

[249] Another interpretation might also be possible albeit less convincing: any commercial use of an invention usually renders the invention as disclosed which in turn excludes it from patentability. Therefore, any commercial use has to take place in the future. The use of un-patented inventions is not subject to the legislation; therefore, any relevant commercial use of an invention that, as a result of a violation will not be patented, is entirely hypothetical.

[250] *Singer/Stauder*, Art. 53 EPC re. 13; *Melullis*, in: Benkard, PatG Sect. 2 re. 26.

[251] *Vorwerk*, GRUR 2009, 375, with further references to: the early mention by *Kranz*, GRUR 1962, 389, 390f. who was in favor of revising the provision and the mention by *Roederer*, Applied Chemistry, 1934, 616 et seq.

[252] *Vorwerk*, GRUR 2009, 375, 376; with reference to BGH, GRUR 1993, 88, 90 and BGH, GRUR 1998, 303, 304.

[253] *Vorwerk*, GRUR 2009, 377.

universally accepted. It is said that a technologically focused examiner will always grant patent protection to military weapons regardless of function or destructive capabilities.[254] These considerations and discussions are rare in the patent law discussion and jurisprudence. For the analysis they are very useful since they are referring explicitly to weapon technology: two examples given are an anti-tank projectile which is described as having "optimal destruction probability" and a flamethrower whose main advantage and technological progression lies in its "devastating effect".[255] This formulation is especially interesting since the term "devastating effect" in any other context would be exclusively and significantly negative.

In this general argument, the "moral accountability" of the state in all official acts is important, and this includes in the granting of patents.[256] Constitutional jurisprudence in Germany for instance is especially clear when it comes to the aspect of human dignity and its recognition and protection by the state.[257] It is often argued, however, that within the patent law application process, the patent office has to establish whether the invention as a whole breaks the confines of morality. This argument leads to the very broad assessment standard. Consequently, patentability is still possible where just one hypothetical use of the invention exists that does not violate any principles of morality or ordre public.[258]

Furthermore, it is the obligation of the inventor to prove that a non-violating application of the invention exists. It is difficult to identify the definition in cases where the patent application is formulated by the inventor without a clear distinction of potential uses. It is left to the examiner to determine whether the specific use of the invention violates the principles of morality or ordre public.[259] Patent offices usually require a disclaimer in this case to exclude moral violations from patent protection.[260]

Vorwerk argues furthermore that even though morality is dynamic and might even change on a day-to-day basis, such a dynamic development is not a sufficient basis to justify a narrow interpretation of Sect. 2 PatG.[261] He continues by claiming that wherein a case the patent office examiner identifies a patent application which violates morality or public order, the patent cannot be granted regardless, based on the assumption that the moral principles might change in the applicant's favor in the near

---

[254] *Horn*, GRUR 1977, 329.

[255] Patent application in *Horn*, GRUR 1977, 329.

[256] *Vorwerk*, GRUR 2009, 376.

[257] BVerfGE 39, 1, 41; BVerfGE 46, 160, 164; BVerfGE 49, 89.

[258] *Vorwerk*, GRUR 2009, 377.

[259] *Fuchs*, JZ 1999, 597; EPA GRUR Int 1994, 959, 963; *Vorwerk*, GRUR 2009, 377.

[260] *Vorwerk*, GRUR 2009, 377, 378.

[261] *Vorwerk*, GRUR 2009, 375, 378 – also *Benkard/Melullis* and *Moufang*, in: MünchGemeinschaftskomm-EPÜ Art. 53 No. 44 who states that even though aspects of morality are under constant and dynamic change, fundamentals are not affected as severely.

future. The relevant moment in time to evaluate the relevant moral principles must always be the moment of the patent application and the moment of the assessment.[262]

Even this line of argument does not identify or suggest a suitable standard for the assessment but rather addresses the scope and relevant moment in time. The truly difficult aspect is to mold considerations of morality and ordre public into a practical standard. Without a fundamental approach to ethics in patent law, future decisions are highly likely to be subject to arbitrary considerations. The discussion about morality regarding the patentability of weapon technology, for example, and its beneficial nature to society are not an entirely new subject of as a legal grey area.

It is therefore necessary to attempt to incorporate key fundamental ethical considerations into the legal framework regarding the patentability of morally challenging technology. Of equal importance is its relationship to prohibitive legislation and administrative provisions.

a) Ordre Public and Morality as Ethical Considerations

As with all philosophical approaches when there is an attempt to transfer them into legal reasoning, they are bound to be subject to a variety of inherent restrictions. It is therefore useful to breakdown the fundamentals of the key philosophical approaches and identify abstract teachings which might be suitable for an adaptation into legal considerations. The relationship between ethics and the law haves been subject to numerous analyses. Both law and morality are complex cultural concepts which are hard to define or summarize.[263] In this context, the term law is limited to positive law and morality relates to social morality.[264] Ethics are usually defined as the justification of norms and regulations which incorporate morality into binding law.[265] While similar, the terms ethics and morality are not synonymous. Broadly speaking, ethics describes the process of justifying moral behavior in a variety of ways. An ethical approach in the context of this analysis is therefore limited to its functional aspect. To further understand the relationship between law and morality, it is helpful to identify similarities and differences:

(1) Similarities and Differences between Law and Morality

    Historically speaking, law and morality are based on the same accepted customs. Customs can be classified as a state of indifference from which law and morality may be derived. Those customs as cultural phenomena were later differentiated

---

[262] *Vorwerk*, GRUR 2009, 375, 378.

[263] *Coing*, 131 et seq.; *Rehbinder*, 6 et seq.; *Radbruch*, Rechtsphilosophie, 143 – regarding the difficulty see *Henkel*, 14 et seq.

[264] Other spheres of morality include autonomous morality, the ethical systems of religious and metaphysical systems and the humane moral (*Appel*, 98).

[265] *Leist*, Eine Frage des Lebens, 1990, 67, who describes the objective of ethics to justify morality in a certain scenario and requires an understanding of the "how" and "why" of moral action.

into the separate aspects of morality, law and customs in a more specific sense. Morality and law are usually described as a Venn-diagram, where the two centers are functioning as poles with a strong effect of attraction, repulsion and complementarity.[266]

Generally speaking, the abstract similarity of law and morality is that both are a set or series of standards or regulations. Such series of standards are characterized by four distinct features: the content of the standards, the commitment and scope of the standards, the degree of enforceability and their scope of validity.[267]

(a) Content-wise, both morality and law include standards which determine behavior in the form of instructions and prohibitions. Such a set of rules is binding for the society in which the law and morality exist. Both sets of standards make use of imperatives.[268] Standards in the form of a legal system mainly or almost exclusively focus on outward behavior or even the effect on the outward world, while standards of morality predominantly focus on the inner motives that lead or supposedly lead to the outward behavior.[269]

(b) Both morality and law are directed at the behavior of humans. Typically, law is generally binding on all or most members of a society. Morality on the other hand, has a more distinguished variety of levels of commitment.[270] Social morality covers a social group of individuals with a consistent standard of commitment for each member.[271] Since morality functions as a framework for the coherence of the group, it is of existential significance for the permanence of the group. Therefore, the group can extend the binding effect of the moral standards to those group members who reject certain behavior regulations based on different understandings of customs.[272] Historically, the biggest impact on the development of individual and social morality in Europe has been the Christian religion.[273] The occidental culture and civilization has based its most significant foundations on the Christian morality system, even though it only has a direct binding effect on Christians.[274] Law uses a hierarchical structure of different

---

[266] *Kaufmann*, Recht und Sittlichkeit, 9.

[267] Using the same features: *Appel*, 100.

[268] *Rehbinder*, 58 et seq.; *Zippelius*, Wesen des Rechts, 33 et seq.; *Smid*, 39 et seq. and *Henkel*, 25, 42.

[269] *Appel*, 100; see also *Radbruch* who summarizes the analysis in with the phrases "inwardness of morality" and "outwardness of law", Rechtsphilosophie, 143.

[270] *Henkel*, p. 68 et seq.

[271] *Bergson*, Les deux sources de la morale et de la religion, 18th edition, 1937, making similar observations to *Henkel*, 73 and *Appel*, 100, who speaks of a moral close.

[272] *Henkel*, 73.

[273] Generally, for other major religions around the world see *Japser*, in: Sokrates, Buddha, Konfuzius und Jesus, Die großen Philosophen, Bd. I (1957).

[274] *Henkel*, 71 and *Appel*, 101.

III. Fundamental Considerations of Morality in German Legal Literature   109

levels of significance for certain sets of law, where the superior law overrides inferior regulations (*"lex superior derogate legi interferiori"*). Such a system does not exist in morality, since morality includes no *"lex superior"*.[275] In summary, the claim of law to be generally binding is different in morality. A general claim may only be observed by the shaping of constitutional values.[276]

(c) Law requires a refined and efficient mechanism of enforceability to be meaningful and significant.[277] It seems that this aspect constitutes the greatest difference between morality and law. Since morality describes inward behavior and motivation, it is considered to be a facet of individual freedom.[278] A moral act cannot be subject to enforcement in the same sense that law requires enforceability. However, morality does not lack any form of enforceability, since it might even be able to override and change legal regulations in time. The major difference lies in the guarantee that all law is enforceable and will be enforced.

(d) Of equal importance for law and morality is the aspect of recognition and compliance. Those aspects depend on the acceptance of the target group. Where either series of standards is incorporated in a societal group structure, it becomes part of the social reality and is therefore valid. Validity in law as well as morality is always a factual issue.[279] Law includes an additional level of validity. It must be formally created and implemented by a responsible institution at the same times as being complied with higher ranking standards, such as constitutional values or international treaties.[280] When a legal regulation is also based on moral considerations and adheres to the principle of justice, it is considered to be morally valid.[281] Such moral validation is desirable but technically not necessary for the legal efficiency of law.

Apart from those formal similarities, *Radbruch* describes a deeper and content-related connection between the two terms. He uses the term "Wertidee" which can be translated as "idea of value".[282] It formulates the concept that law and morality are centered on values and may be evaluated in relation to values. Placing all values and their relationships on a common basis, it leads to the existence of a set of general human fundamental values, which are essential for a well-ordered human community.[283] In a dynamic and pluralistic society, values experience a permanent sta-

---

[275] *Appel*, 101.

[276] Id.

[277] See *Zippelius*, Das Wesen des Rechts, 42; who explains that enforceability alone is insufficient; law also requires the guarantee that the regulations will be enforced.

[278] *Radbruch*, 141.

[279] *Coing*, 298.

[280] *Appel*, 102; *Karpen*, JuS 1987, 593.

[281] *Rehbinder*, 150 et seq.; *Coing*, 192, 202, 215; *Henkel*, 391; *Zippelius*, Rechtsphilosophie, Kap. 4, 75 et seq.; *Kaufmann*, Recht und Sittlichkeit, p. 41 et seq.

[282] *Radbruch*, 142.

[283] *Henkel*, 333.

tus.[284] The set of permanent values constitutes the social order of values and is similar to social morality. Since it is desirable to raise essential values above the dynamic of society, those values are fitted with the normative enforceability of law and integrated into the legal system.[285] Another popular formulation is to describe the aspect as the "reception of the social order of values by legal regulation".[286] The predominant social morality is therefore identical to the dominant legal morality. The relationship between morality and law has shifted throughout history and the predominant aspect could usually be identified by determining the series of standards that prevails in case of a confrontation. In modern society, the principle of "rule of law" is generally accepted, even though the dominance of law is usually backed by moral maxims.[287] In most modern democratic and constitutional states, the levels of law and morality are combined in a higher framework of legal regulations. The rule of law is qualified by incorporating essential principles of morality and justice. Such a moral charge of law and constitutional provisions leads to the embedding of an ethical standard.[288]

The German Constitutional Court stated that the law is intended to mirror the ethical (or rather moral) beliefs of the legislator, which are, in turn, determined and limited by the constitutional framework.[289] This dichotomy is most easily identifiable in Art. 1 to 20 of the German Constitution where moral standards are incorporated into law.[290] Other European countries usually include a constitutional set of principles which grant specific rights to the citizens.[291] Those are supported or amended by the ECHR which is also intended to protect human rights and fundamental freedoms in Europe. In the U.S., a similar concept was realized by the Bill of Rights of 1789/91 which became part of the U.S. Constitution in the form of the first ten amendments and added specific guarantees of personal freedoms and rights.

In conclusion, even though morality and law are independent and autonomous terms, they share a tight relationship and heavily influence each other. In terms of their overlap, certain values are created, which are equally important to and protected by law and morality.[292] The German legal discussion tends to argue for a protection of such values of minimal extent to prevent a so-called "dictatorship of values" which in turn could lead to a "moralization of law"[293] and "juridification of morality".[294]

---

[284] *Appel*, 104.

[285] *Appel*, 104, *Henkel*, 348 and *Zippelius*, Wertungsprobleme im System der Grundrechte, p. 131, 151.

[286] *Henkel*, 348; dissenting *Smid*, 56 et seq.

[287] *Appel*, 104.

[288] *Appel*, 105; dissenting *Maus*, Rechtstheorie 20 (1989), 191, 194 and *Smid*, p. 53 et seq.

[289] BVerfGE 39, 1, 44.

[290] *Appel*, 105.

[291] Specifically, the Bill of Rights 1689 in England, which listed a number of fundamental rights and liberties.

[292] *Appel*, 105.

[293] For German law: *Appel*, 105; *von Olshausen*, NJW 1982, 2221 et seq.

German court decisions have been more prone to morality in legal assessments, than even decisions by the Federal Administrative Court.[295]

b) Ordre Public and Morality across the German Legal System

German jurisprudence has made it clear that the relevant standard for morals relies on a median perception of morality.[296] By referring to the median perception, it is indicated that the standard has to be based on an empirical rather than an ethical foundation.[297] Interestingly enough, one of the most general clauses within German civil law is also interpreted to be as close to the values of the German Constitution as possible.[298] While it seems like a solid and legally certain approach, it clashes with the term "order of morality" in Art. 2 (1) of the German Constitution. Some authors also identify this issue but merely refer to the structural concept of incorporating the morality law of Art. 2 (1) of the German Constitution entirely within the constitutional order itself.[299] As has been established above, this concept falls short because it does not consider the function and independence of all elements within Art. 2 of the German Constitution, especially considering the intent of the legal structure to cover non-constitutional and non-legal sources of policy or rules.[300]

From a legal dogmatic perspective this approach provides certain challenges. While it is generally accepted that it is difficult to identify a median moral standard, especially when it comes to the commercialization of sexuality,[301] by referencing the constitutional values, which are also insufficient to address every possible moral issue, the standard moves away from the original dynamic. Such a dynamic with changing values in a changing, pluralistic society was, however, identified by the German Federal Court of Justice.[302] Legal authors argue that such a change is legally irrelevant where constitutional values are involved. While this seems like a standard approach to constitutional law, it addresses a different question. In case a certain civil law issue violates constitutional law, it is no longer part of ethical considerations in the narrow sense that Sect. 138 BGB refers to. This issue arises inadvertently when the connection to a constitutional order is too static as it does not allow for the dynamic of moral considerations within a society, especially in the present case

---

[294] *Maus*, Rechtstheorie 20 (1989), 191 et seq.

[295] BVerwG, NJW 1982, 664 et seq.

[296] BGHZ 179, 218 ref. RGZ 48, 124.

[297] *Jauernig*, BGB § 138, re. 6, also v. Tuhr II 2 § 70 I.

[298] Specified by the German Federal Constitutional Court, BVerfGE 81, 256 and the Federal Court of Justice.

[299] MD Art. 2 I, re. 45, 46; *Jarass/Pieroth*, Art. 2 re. 15 with more references. Also BVerfGE 6, 433 et seq.

[300] Id.

[301] *Jauernig*, BGB § 138, re. 7 with several examples.

[302] BGH NJW 2008, 141.

where the ethical considerations are supposedly based on empirical observations, as difficult as that may be.

For the ongoing analysis it is also important to note the interplay of Sect. 138 BGB with Sect. 134 BGB. The latter is intended to address any legal concerns a civil law issue might result in. Both sections therefore address legal and moral concerns, respectively. In order of applicability, Sect. 134 BGB has a er range of application and is therefore primarily applied. Sect. 134 BGB renders a civil legal transaction void, where it violates any German law – with certain restrictions regarding the specific type and circumstances of the violation.[303] Relevant for the ongoing research question is, especially, that this interplay and ranking system of Sect. 134 BGB and Sect. 138 BGB determine that any illegal transaction is not subject to a subsequent assessment according to moral standards. It might be the case that a legal transaction might be subject to moral concerns, however, only in the case that the legal transaction is not subject to specific regulation. If a legal transaction is explicitly legally allowed, it may not be considered immoral according to Sect. 138 BGB, unless based on circumstances not subject to the regulation. With that insight, it is easy to categorize legal matters and their relevant assessment. Matters that are non-regulated are subject to potential moral considerations and subsequent restrictions; additionally, since they are non-regulated, they are not subject to any decisions about legal order. Regulated matters, on the other hand, go both ways: either they are explicitly allowed or forbidden. Anything that is allowed cannot – based on the same reasons at least – be subject to relevant moral considerations.[304] Explicitly forbidden matters are in violation of the legal order and are therefore not subject to any legally relevant moral assessment, since the legal order is primary in this regard.[305]

As already discussed, the concept of moral order within patent law is subject to a variety of considerations with varying degree of superficiality. Regarding the previously identified significant differences between other parts of the law and patent law, it is remarkable that authors still argue that since the term moral order is also found in other parts of civil law, the relevant jurisprudence can be utilized for the interpretation of moral order within patent law.[306] However, how such mechanisms actually work is not included in the discussion but represents a more general concept of a specific weighting process that does not actually take account of the specific requirements of patent law. It starts by opposing certain aspects of "utility of the

---

[303] *Mansel*, in: Jauernig, BGB 2018, § 134 re. 8 et seq. Not all violations automatically render a legal transaction void; it is necessary that the violated law addresses the content of the legal transactions and not merely the surrounding circumstances. For the purposes of this analysis, a more detailed discussion of the specifics is not necessary.

[304] Highly discussed in German law regarding sexual services. However, this does not technically address the core issue but is more of a discussion about the range and effect of the German Prostitution Protection Act, which arguably legalizes parts of sexual services – anything not covered is therefore still subject to possible moral concerns.

[305] *Mansel*, in: Jauernig, BGB 2018, § 134 re. 8.

[306] *Fitzner*, in: BeckOK Patentrecht, re. 6 ref. to *Sprau*, in: Palandt, BGB § 826 re. 4, 5.

invention" and the "damaging effects or dangers for people and the environment".[307] Relying on such terms would indicate that no absolute values of morality exist or are, at least, negotiable. It also poses the question of how the "utility of an invention" should be assessed. It merely relates to technological utility or social utility – identifying a standard for moral utility is identical to identifying a standard of morality in the first place, making this approach circular at best. Beyond that, it is suggested that an exclusion to patentability can be given where the invention is regarded as "especially despicable" by the general population.[308] Firstly, this approach introduces another standard that uses one of the interchangeable array of adjectives without providing anything that is considerably or significantly legally applicable. More interesting, however, is the reference to the "general population" indicating that the approach to morality in patent law is supposed to be based on empirical data, which again raises questions of practicability and legal uncertainty.

Given the amount of vague terminology, the discussion usually focuses on the obligation of the patent applicant. He is supposedly obligated to formulate the patent claims and the patent description in such a manner that they do not include "violations of the moral or public order".[309] It is logical and necessary to transform the morality standard within patent law into an obligation of the patent applicant. This approach makes it difficult to reconnect the distinction between the morality of the commercial exploitation of the invention and the invention itself. This distinction is explicitly stated in Sect. 2 PatG and also the European equivalents, where morality is considered to be a legal concept.

c) Morality as a Social Concept Instead of a Legal Concept

Other voices reject the notion of morality as a legal concept altogether.[310] The norm of Sect. 138 BGB is usually interpreted to address heteronomous morality rather than autonomous morality. Since the law requires an objective standard which applies to all subjects of state equally, the standard cannot be individually established by the subject itself.[311] Furthermore, it relies on the common moral considerations within the German legal domain, excluding smaller population groups such as foreigners or immigrants with deviating moral considerations.[312]

---

[307] *Fitzner*, in: BeckOK Patentrecht, re. 7.

[308] *Fitzner*, BeckOK PatG § 2 re. 7.

[309] *Fitzner*, BeckOK PatG § 2 re. 8.

[310] *Jakl*, in: Gsell/Krüger/Lorenz/Reymann, BGB Großkommentar, § 138 re. 40.

[311] *Jakl*, in: Gsell/Krüger/Lorenz/Reymann, BGB Großkommentar, § 138 re. 35 with further references.

[312] OLG Hamm NJW-RR 2011, 1197 (1199); *Armbrüster*, in: MüKo BGB § 138 re. 17; *Staudinger/Sack/Fischinger*, 2017, re. 66.

One might argue against these stipulations, mainly based on the aspect that such an approach would violate the democratic principle of Art. 20 (1) GG.[313] A heteronomous approach to morality would mean that parts of the population are affected by the moral considerations of a majority. The proposed solution is an interpretation of Sect. 138 BGB based on legal positivism which considers laws to be the relevant criteria by which to interpret morality within a democratic society.[314] While this solution is certainly tethered to the concept of democracy, it falls short with regard to legal flexibility of the norm and would make Sect. 138 BGB, as well as the constitutional explanations, superfluous.

In the area of company law, the aspect of morality and public order directly references the general civil law provision of Sect. 138 and Sect. 134 BGB, even though the specific company legislation does not make the connection.[315] When looking at Sect. 4 GmbHG[316] which regulates the admissible firm names in company law, morality and public order is one of several restrictions when choosing a firm name. Applying the standards of Sect. 138 and Sect. 134 BGB does not work directly since it requires more refined consideration of firm regulations and jurisprudence which has been developed for other regulatory approaches.[317] Regulations with similarly oriented aspects such as Sect. 8 (2) No. 5 MarkenG,[318] which restricts trademark registration in case of morality or public order violations, naturally offer suitable comparison. However, the legal discussion also addresses aspects such as Sect. 2 No. 1 PatG which is the very subject of this analysis and not really suited as the reference point for any other concept of morality or public order in other areas of the law. Therefore, it is remarkable that it is still referenced in the legal discussion.

Moving on from civil law regulations and IP-related references, morality and public order also play a significant role in competition law in Germany. Sect. 3 UWG[319] is the general clause of the Anti Unfair Competition Act in Germany and basically forbids any act that violates public order or morality. In counterdistinction to the approach of German company law, the interpretation of Sect. 3 UWG is generally considered to be specifically interpreted according to its own standards,[320] thereby indicating that other areas of law that also include a specific clause or general clause regarding morality or public order are irrelevant for the interpretation. Those terms may not be subject to uniform legal assessment.[321]

---

[313] *Jakl*, in: Gsell/Krüger/Lorenz/Reymann, BGB Großkommentar, § 138 re. 40.

[314] *Jakl*, in: Gsell/Krüger/Lorenz/Reymann, BGB Großkommentar, § 138 re. 42.

[315] *Heinze*, in: MüKo GmbHG § 4 re. 108.

[316] German Act on the Limited Liability Company.

[317] *Heinze*, in: MüKo GmbHG § 4 re. 108.

[318] German Trademark Act.

[319] German Anti Unfair Competition Act.

[320] *Fezer*, in: Fezer/Büscher/Obergfell, Lauterkeitsrecht: UWG § 3 re. 332.

[321] *Fezer*, in: Fezer/Büscher/Obergfell, Lauterkeitsrecht: UWG § 3 re. 332.

III. Fundamental Considerations of Morality in German Legal Literature

Those two fundamental considerations shape our understanding of law and ethics across the entire U.S. and the German legal systems. While the first aspect might still be applicable in patent law, since morality might cover aspects outside of legal provisions, the second aspect proves highly problematic in patent law. This is due to the fact that the relationship between immorality and illegality in patent law is different from all other areas of law.

d) The Unique Relationship of Immorality and Illegality in Patent Law

The TRIPS agreement, the EPC and each national counterpart clearly define that illegality does not necessarily lead to immorality of the invention. Anything legal in the specific national legal landscape cannot be considered immoral in terms of patent law. Therefore, the relationship between law and morality is practically reversed in patent law.

To further explain and analyze these results, it is helpful to determine the following starting points:

1. Illegality refers to the legal provisions of a certain legally sovereign entity. Therefore, certain areas within that legal system have to have the same understanding of legality.
2. In all aspects of European and U.S. law, morality is considered to be either broader than legality while still including the legal provisions or as an entirely separate set of rules.
3. Additionally, for all aspects of European and U.S. law, anything that is illegal cannot be considered morally sound.
4. Moral considerations are either broader than or subsidiary to legal provisions.

Having identified these starting points, it becomes even clearer, that the terms "morality" and "public order" of Art. 53 EPC or the German equivalent have to be interpreted as "patent law specific" as so many others point out.[322] However, as identified above, those attempts at interpretation do not withstand critical analyses and are consequently insufficient. It is necessary to reject the notion of "distinct interpretation" because it still too closely attributes aspects to the overall concept of morality and law across the entire legal system. The terms have to be developed independently within the patent law system. Both terms have to be regarded as entirely different concepts, since they have nothing in common with the general understanding of the interplay of law and morality.[323]

---

[322] With further references: *Melullis*, in: Benkard, PatG Sect. 2 re. 1 et seq.

[323] It might be argued that a sufficiently independent and patent law-specific interpretation of the terms serves the same purpose; however, It is not just a question of semantics, since – from a dogmatic point of view – law-specific interpretation and law-specific terms are different in their legal application and understanding.

This understanding of the interplay of law and morality changes the background of the research question regarding the standard of morality and public order in patent law. The original approach which involves addressing the problem as an issue of interpretation of morality and public order as is addressed in other areas of the law without identifying the significant difference in the concept of the terms in patent law, results in the wrong legal background for determining the fundamental functions of the specific provisions in EU and German patent law.

It also simultaneously increases and decreases the difficulty of the analysis. The increase in difficulty arises from the new definition of the research goal and method which now has to focus solely on patent law itself and the general – not legal – interpretation of the aspects of morality and public order. The increased difficulty also stems from the use of the terms themselves, which are very usual in German and also European legislation. This usage suggests that the legislator had the general legal meaning in all other areas of law in mind when the legislation was drafted, possibly trying to ensure a uniform control mechanism throughout the whole legal system.

This presumed intention raises the fundamental consideration of whether the use of the terms is even necessary if it is a patent-specific problem that has to be tackled. The use of such well-known and well-defined or discussed terms easily leads to confusion within the legal debate. With that being said, the intention and function of the provision itself must not be contested. As has been established in previous chapters, it is necessary and part of the legislative intention to exclude inventions from patentability based on aspects other than the standard patentability requirements such as novelty, technical feasibility, etc. This intention is also grounded in the fundamental functions of patent law and is not easily dismissed by the prominent legal discussion surrounding the provisions.

Having established the need for the restrictions in Art. 53 EPC and Sect. 2 PatG, but having also identified the shortcomings and general inadequacy of the use of the specific terms morality and public order within the legal provisions leads to the possibility of establishing a new approach. This method also allows the countless difficulties in interpreting the provisions to be dismissed – not only the most relevant terms of "morality" and "public order" but also almost everything else, foremost the term of commercial exploitation and the standard of application.

As well-intended as the provision and its requirements might have been, the practical application has proven that most aspects are either extremely difficult or entirely impossible when it comes to their legal certainty. In addition, most legal discussions tend to ignore the specific set-up of the requirements by simply focusing on the aspects of morality and public order.

e) Interim Result

Given the established relationship of illegality and morality in the context of patent law, it becomes apparent that "morality" in the patent law realm is vastly different from the use of morality in the general sense and even the use in all other areas of law.

f) Identifying Elements of Morality and Ordre Public in Patent Law

It is almost unanimously accepted that the term ordre public has to be interpreted specifically according to the characteristics of patent law.[324] The variety of very detailed definitions in other parts of German public law, especially police law, are therefore only of very limited help.[325] Once again, the existence of prohibitive legislation alone is insufficient.[326]

The commonly used term "ordre public" differs from the legal order in its intention incorporated in Sec. 2 PatG. Usually, while various legislation is usually covered by both terms, a violation of legal order is only relevant when the legal system as a whole, as an expression of the opinion of the general public, is distorted in a severe way. Hence, "ordre public" is broader as it includes other legislation that is deemed to be of general importance to the general public.

As established before, only prohibitive legislation that includes an absolute prohibition without exceptions qualifies as a suitable piece of legislation relevant to Sect. 2 PatG. However, since the general definition is fundamentally very narrow, a further limitation is introduced which restricts the relevant provisions to those which incorporate significant fundamentals of the legal and moral order which are generally regarded to be fundamental and binding.[327]

Therefore, only provisions which are of essential significance may be considered for the ordre public of Sec. 2 PatG.[328] The terms fundamental and essential seem to be interchangeable in that regard and are very open to interpretation. Some specifications have been given by the Federal German Patent Court which laid out that such provisions were relevant which "the legislator made based on the fundamentals of a question relating to the state or economic life based on state political, social or economic beliefs, not only on useful or suitable consideration".[329] It seems that this

---

[324] *Melullis*, in: Benkard, PatG Sect. 2 re. 34; *Rogge*, GRUR 1998, 303.

[325] BGH, GRUR 1973, 585 – IUO; *Melullis*, in: Benkard, PatG Sect. 2 re. 34; *Warren-Jones*, A Mouse in Sheep's Clothing: the Challenge to Patent Morality Criterion Posed by "Dolly", 20 European Intellectual Property Review 445, 456 (1998).

[326] BGH, GRUR 1973, 585.

[327] BPatGE, 46, 170 – Verkehrszeichen; *Melullis*, in: Benkard, PatG Sect. 2 re. 36; *Rowlandson*, WARF/Stem Cells (G2/06): The Ordre Public and Morality Exception and Its Impact on the Patentability of Human Embryonic Stem Cells, 32 European Intellectual Property Review 67, 71 (2010).

[328] *Melullis*, in: Benkard, PatG Sect. 2 re. 36; *Singer/Lunzer*, rf. 53; *Rogge*, GRUR 98, 203, 205; *Mes*, § 2 PatG No. 8; *Seville*, EU Intellectual Property Law and Policy (Edward Elgar 2009).

[329] BPatG GRUR 2003, 142; *Mayer*, AcP 194, 105.

lengthy definition would provide a more refined standard. However, on further analysis, the specifications given are also vague and open to interpretation.

aa) Essential Constitutional Principles as a Significant Element?

According to the German Federal Court of Justice, these considerations also include the essential constitutional principles which are an immovable basis for German public or social life.[330] One relevant constitutional principle is the democratic principle.[331] Again, the Federal Court of Justice agrees with the German Federal Patent Court and focuses especially on human dignity and human rights, such as the rights to personal freedom, physical integrity and life.[332] It is, however, not necessary for the provision to be constitutional.

In general, provisions which are generally believed to fulfill these requirements by addressing the essential fundamentals of human cohabitation within community are particularly those provisions which protect human or fundamental rights.[333] Expression of such universal rights is found in the UN Universal Declaration of Human Rights and the European Convention on Human Rights.[334] Thus, it is argued that a violation of those rights necessarily leads to a direct rejection of a patent application since every state institution is directly bound by those provisions.[335] Sect. 2 PatG is supposed only to offer clarification in those cases. The definition for a violation of Sect. 2 PatG is very narrow and the threshold for a violation particularly high. Taking a closer look, the scenario in which an invention violates a fundamental right of said provisions in such a manner that the patent office is directly obligated to reject the application is difficult to imagine. First, the grant of a patent would have to be characterized as an act of public authority. The patent office is a public authority and the granting of an immaterial right is easily identifiable as such an act. Secondly, this specific act has to be in violation of the UN or EU provisions. The perspective therefore shifts from the granting of the patent to the invention itself and the original question arises again: when does a patent infringe a certain right? The assessment can only be based on the possible use of the invention.

One might argue that the research itself, which is incentivized by the patent system in general, can be a basis for the assessment of a possible violation. However, the research is only indirectly affected by the granting of a patent. To assume governmental interference in a human right by indirectly incentivizing potentially vio-

---

[330] BGHZ 42, 7, 13.

[331] BGHZ 94, 248, 250.

[332] BGHZ 48, 327, 330.

[333] *Busche*, GRUR Int. 1999, 299, 305; *Melullis*, in: Benkard, PatG Sect. 2 re. 37.

[334] UN Universal Declaration of Human Rights Art. 1; Preamble to Protocol No. 13 to the Convention for the Protection of Human Rights and Fundamental Freedoms concerning the abolition of the death penalty in all circumstances.

[335] BGHZ 1994, 248, 249; *Melullis*, in: Benkard, PatG Sect. 2 re. 37.

III. Fundamental Considerations of Morality in German Legal Literature 119

lating research seems too much of a stretch. In constitutional law, acts of public authority are categorized as interceptive and interfering administrative acts and state service or performance acts.[336] The granting of a patent is clearly part of the latter category, even if the patent is subsequently used by a private entity as a matter of interference. According to German general constitutional law, the granting of a right cannot therefore directly constitute a direct violation of an international treaty or agreement.

If the assessment is based on the later commercial use of the invention, the already well-known problems of determining sufficient severity of the violation arise. The standard here has to be similar to the general standard in Sect. 2 PatG – at the very least it cannot be sufficient for a patent rejection if the only conceivable method of use is violating a human right. Otherwise, almost any invention could possibly be rejected on the basis of endangerment of a human right.

This consideration of an obligation to reject a patent application stemming directly from the EU Convention on Human Rights or the UN Charta has to be rejected wholesale. It seems much more suitable to use the already existing Sect. 2 PatG which was specifically created to address such aspects and operates in a patent law-specific way.

Of course, since the patent regulatory system focuses on the field of technological advancement, the relevant rights of the legal order are those which can be affected by a technological application of scientific fundamentals.[337] Examples of such rights are included in the provisions of: genetic engineering, embryonic research, stem cell research and potentially, animal protection laws.[338] Additionally, rights included by the German Federal Court of Justice exceeding the relevance of individuals[339] and the constitutional protection of marriage and the family in Art. 6 GG is considered to be part of the legal order relevant to Sect. 2 PatG.[340] Also included are provisions relating to the protection of the environment.[341] Here, the standard for rejection of an application is set as a serious endangerment to environmental protection.[342] The endangerment has to be concrete and has to have the potential to lead to permanent damage to the environment; the mere possibility of an endangerment is supposed to be insufficient.[343]

---

[336] BVerfGE 85, 386, 398.

[337] BGHZ 42, 7, 13; *Melullis*, in: Benkard, PatG Sect. 2 re. 37.

[338] *Melullis*, in: Benkard, PatG Sect. 2 re. 37.

[339] BGHZ 94, 248, 249.

[340] *Busche*, GRUR Int. 1999, 299, 305.

[341] BGH, GRUR 1995, 397, 399; *Busche*, GRUR Int. 1999, 299, 305.

[342] *Plassmann*, ZAkDR 37, 54 et seq.; *Melullis*, in: Benkard, PatG Sect. 2 re. 39.

[343] BGH, GRUR 1995, 397, 399 – Außenspiegelanordnung; *Melullis*, in: Benkard, PatG Sect. 2 re. 39.

bb) Approaches to Define Ordre Public in German Legal Literature

Apart from these rights and provisions which are already vague to some extent, other aspects which are considered to be of relevance for the legal order of Sect. 2 PatG are public peace and peaceful and orderly living conditions.[344] Further requirements for a violation of these specific considerations, however, include that the use of the invention in question is expected to disturb or seriously endanger those public interests.[345] *Melullis* seemingly paraphrases this principle by saying that any invention which intends to violate safety regulations or provisions protecting the physical integrity of human life does not qualify for patent protection.[346] It is a very interesting proposition because "safety regulations protecting physical integrity" are very broad and interpretive terms. In addition, this notion moves from the original standard of the very narrow definition which includes "every conceivable method of application" to the "intention" of the inventor or applicant. This apparent shift in the assessment process is highly significant and leads to a whole different set of discoveries when assessing the patentability of an invention. If such different standards were to actually exist in German patent regulation, the process would almost become arbitrary. So far the standard has moved from being so strict and narrow that it is practically irrelevant to a mechanism which can possibly cover a wider variety of inventions, in which the main basis for assessment is the subjective element of intention.

Moving from the very broad definitions of constitutional rights to specific safety regulations, it is assumed that regulations protecting honesty and orderly conduct in business transactions are also eligible to be regarded as part of the legal order relevant to Sect. 2 PatG.[347] It seems strange that terms such as "honesty" and "orderly conduct" are part of the legal order and not the broader moral order. Such terms barely fit the very strict and narrow part of the definition relating to violation generally accepted in Sect. 2 PatG.[348]

However, in line with the nature of provisions relevant to Sect. 2 PatG, any safety regulation that allows for an exception is not relevant for Sect. 2 PatG.[349] This seems to be in line with the theme of determining every conceivable application of the invention in a commercial use, and therefore showing a limited consistency in the considerations regarding legal order.

Naturally, since the definition is generally very strict and narrow and only certain inventions and their respective use violate the legal order with sufficient severity for an exclusion from patentability, the inversion of the argument cannot be made: any

---

[344] EPA, GRUR Int. 199, 305; *Melullis*, in: Benkard, PatG Sect. 2 re. 38,
[345] *Melullis*, in: Benkard, PatG Sect. 2 re. 38; EPA, GRUR Int. 1995, 978 – plant cells.
[346] *Melullis*, in: Benkard, PatG Sect. 2 re. 38.
[347] *Melullis*, in: Benkard, PatG Sect. 2 re. 40; *Plassmann*, ZAkDR 37, 54 et seq.
[348] Id.
[349] Id.

use of an invention that is not expressly forbidden by regulations or provisions does not automatically lead to accordance with the legal order in its entirety.[350] It goes without saying that the explicit approval of a commercial use of an invention negates the possibility that said invention is in violation of the legal order.[351]

In conclusion, all the approaches and definitions provided are insufficient. Even if several different theories of what constitutes a qualified provision are provided, they rely on very strict and narrow definitions. These impractical definitions make it almost impossible for the legal theories to be actually relevant. Content-wise, human rights and constitutional rights and principles are the most promising approach because they are the least likely to be subject to change.

Since the relevant aspect of the invention is its commercial exploitation, it seems necessary to express the possibility that even if the invention might be admissible as part of fundamental research, its commercial exploitation can still be considered to be violating the legal order. This dichotomy relates more to freedom of trade which is also partially outlined as a constitutional right in German law.[352]

Another aspect that poses a theoretical challenge is the relationship of "morality" and "ordre public" as separate legal terms.

5. Meaningful Distinction of Morality and Ordre Public?

The aspect of morality is technically independent of the term ordre public. Any violations can therefore appear alone or cumulatively.[353] However, if a violation of ordre public is considered to be insufficient in its severity, it cannot be considered a violation of morality for the same reason; ordre public is more specific and blocks further ground for rejection.[354]

a) Attempts to Distinguish between the two Terms

Morality is therefore considered to be a different approach in a more dynamic field where legislation has been unable to catch up due to rapid technological or scientific advancements.[355] Naturally, aspects of morality are usually incorporated in legislation at some point, which means that ordre public and morality overlap to a certain degree. Evidently, since the violation of provisions and regulations is covered by

---

[350] *Rogge*, GRUR 1998, 33; *Melullis*, in: Benkard, PatG Sect. 2 re. 41.
[351] *Rogge*, GRUR 1998, 33, 35; to some extent: *Straus*, GRUR 96, 10, 14 et seq.
[352] *Romandini*, 254.
[353] *Melullis*, in: Benkard, PatG Sect. 2 re. 45; *Romandini*, 254.
[354] *Melullis*, in: Benkard, PatG Sect. 2 re. 45.
[355] *Melullis*, in: Benkard, PatG Sect. 2 re. 45; *Busse/Keukenschrijver*, § 2 re. 20.

ordre public, the content of morality has to be defined by requirements outside of legal specifications.[356]

The term moral order stems from the fundamental considerations of categorizing "good" and "bad" behavior.[357] This is acknowledged by the EPO[358] as well as the German Federal Court of Justice.[359] Some compare the term to the identical term in the German Civil Code, even though its interpretation in civil law is vastly different, as seen above.[360] The general basis of the concept for moral order is significantly broader than legal order which gives even greater leeway for interpretation by the German Patent Office than the interpretation of the aspects of legal order.[361] In any case the interpretation is restricted by the specifications and characteristics of patent law which limits the leeway and room for interpretation in a significant way.[362]

Hence, the interpretation of the moral order in Sect. 2 PatG is not identical to the dynamic current majority opinion within society. Individual circumstances are also relevant to the assessment of patent law cases; however, the effect of any patent law decision may have relevance for the whole scope of application of patent law. This scope could cover the whole of Germany or even the entire EPO area, so that no consideration can be given to local or regional characteristics.[363] The term moral order has to be consistent within the entire scope of application of the PatG.

Still, the definition of morality has to be crafted with even more precision and care than the definition of ordre public, since moral order is usually characterized by a great variety of considerations and involves assessing which aspect might outweigh the others. Therefore, the interest of the patent system has to be weighed against other concerns.[364] Commonly, patent law is regarded as a mechanism for incentivizing technological advancement,[365] even though that might not be entirely correct, in the sense that it is possible to identify various different aspects that are affected by patent law and it might also be possible to restrict the assumption that technological advancement is inherently beneficial for society.

---

[356] *Romandini*, 255.

[357] The other common distinction in "good" and "evil" is inherently different since "evil" is usually based on intention and intention requires a conscience which limits assessment of other aspects of life not linked to the behavior of a conscience being.

[358] EPA, Abl. 2006, 15.

[359] EPO Guidelines for Examination, Chapter 8.1 Morality or "ordre public".

[360] EPA, Abl. 2006, 15; *Melullis*, in: Benkard, PatG Sect. 2 re. 46, refers to the classic (almost antique) definition of German civil law: "the perception of all people just and fair", still so in BGHZ 10, 228, 232.

[361] Not necessarily a bad thing since the dynamic nature is necessary to adjust to rapidly developing aspects of society.

[362] *Melullis*, in: Benkard, PatG Sect. 2 re. 47.

[363] Id.

[364] *Melullis*, in: Benkard, PatG Sect. 2 re. 48.

[365] Id.

III. Fundamental Considerations of Morality in German Legal Literature 123

Regarding the aspects which could theoretically outweigh the benefit of technological advancement, the disadvantages in the form of dangers to humans and the environment have to be considered.[366] One aspect could be the distribution of genetically modified animals or plants which could endanger animal and plant wildlife, a specific animal or plant species or evolution.[367] Only where the benefits for society, i.e. if, for example, the preservation of genetic resources outweighs the disadvantages for humans and the environment, is a patent supposed to be granted. However, not all modifications of living matter are necessarily excluded from patentability.[368] Originally, any patents in that field of research were regarded as the beginning of monopolizing genetic resources and therefore a privatization of the collective livelihood of humanity which would ultimately endanger the environment.[369] The premise of this train of thought is, unfortunately, flawed, since a patent can only be granted on the field of technological advancements and is excluded per definition where it applies to natural lifeforms.[370] Hence, modifications of the human genome or any genome for that matter are also not universally excluded from patentability.[371]

Even though classical animal breeding is distinguished from genetic modifications by the targeted intervention directed at the genome involving genetic modification, classical breeding relies on natural reproduction and naturally occurring mutations and mixing.[372] However, classical breeding is also capable of causing such a modification within the genome.[373] Modifications are usually considered to be established when a certain new breed of animal or plant is supposed to permanently display a certain characteristic.[374] To achieve a concurrent assessment of both methods of genetic modification is it necessary to refrain from excluding patentability for genetic modifications in general. It is necessary for an exclusion to be based on a more specific endangerment of the environment or wildlife within a specific environment.[375] Since this is part of the moral order, is has to be assumed that

---

[366] EPA, Abl. 2006, 15; *Melullis*, in: Benkard, PatG Sect. 2 re. 51, ref. EPA, Abl. 92, 589.

[367] It is hard to pinpoint how evolution could be endangered in a certain sense since the concept of evolution is a scientific theory which should be above the aspects of endangerment.

[368] *Rogge*, GRUR 1998, 304; *Spranger*, GRUR Int. 199, 595; *Busche*, GRUR 2003, 846; *Melullis*, in: Benkard, PatG Sect. 2 re. 50; EPA, GRUR Int. 1995, 978.

[369] *Melullis*, in: Benkard, PatG Sect. 2 re. 52.

[370] BGH, GRUR 1975, 430; *Melullis*, in: Benkard, PatG Sect. 2 re. 52.

[371] EPA, GRUR Int. 1995, 978; *Melullis*, in: Benkard, PatG Sect. 2 re. 53, EPA, GRUR Int. 95, 978 – Pflanzenzellen zu 17.1; *Busche*, GRUR Int. 99, 299.

[372] *Hansen*, How genetic engineering differs from conventional breeding, hybridization, wide crosses and horizontal gene transfer, Consumer Union, Consumer Policy Institute, 2000, 2.

[373] *Hansen*, 4.

[374] *Melullis*, in: Benkard, PatG Sect. 2 re. 53.

[375] Usually, the endangerment of a specific form of wildlife spirals into an imbalance of the whole ecosystem, thereby endangering the environment in general.

it is the duty of the patent office to assess the danger and act accordingly. However, authors tend to shift the responsibility to the legislator when it comes to decisions on moral restrictions.[376] Such a shift further blurs the distinction between ordre public and morality and is justified by referencing the need for technological advancement and the unhindered process thereof.[377]

b) Concepts of Proportionality in Ordre Public and Morality

An example of how the benefits and disadvantages have been weighted against one another was given by the EPO in 1990[378] when it had to be decided whether the genetic manipulation of mammals was restricted in patentability on the basis of moral considerations. The effects on a specific breed of mice, which were affected by genetic modification in a way which made them unusually susceptible to carcinogenic substances which in turn advantaged the development of painful tumors, were considered disadvantageous.[379] This decision was made before the EU Biotech Directive which has since specifically regulated the patentability of genetic modifications in living organisms. Interestingly for this issue is the nature of the specific element which supposedly outweighed the benefit of technological advancement for humanity. It might be identified as an endangerment of the environment, even though the neuralgic point was fact that inevitable pain was caused to laboratory mice. The discussion therefore was shaped according to emotional arguments rather than neutral legal discussion.[380] This is understandable since the subject of animal suffering is naturally very emotional and ethically challenging, especially in the case of mammals which are common domestic pets.

Still, regarding the individual elements of moral order and the various attempts to identify a practical standard, it is interesting to observe that all those attempts included variations of the terms "essential", "fundamental", "significant" or "universally binding or accepted". Examples for specific norms were usually limited to constitutional rights, constitutional principles and foremost human dignity. All these aspects tend to revolve around the human being with the environment being auxiliary. To discuss the potential suffering of animals in a patent application process is clearly not at the central to these constitutional elements. The aspect of animal well-being and animal protection are only part of a very new (in terms of constitutional amendments) provision within the constitution; the protection of the environment and the natural livelihood in Art. 20a GG from 1994. Animal protection was only

---

[376] *Busche*, GRUR Int. 1999, 299; *Melullis*, in: Benkard, PatG Sect. 2 re. 53.
[377] *Melullis*, in: Benkard, PatG Sect. 2 re. 53.
[378] EPO – T 0315/03 – Krebsmaus.
[379] Abl. 90, 476, 490 – Krebsmaus/Harvard; *Melullis*, in: Benkard, PatG Sect. 2 re. 54.
[380] EPO – T 0315/03.

included in 2002 as – in common perception – a symbolic piece of legislation[381] and has since then had a rather insignificant existence. Given the constitutional background, it is difficult to understand the original discussion around the EPO Harvard/*Krebsmaus* case when trying to apply the various standards in legal literature.

Ultimately, it is exemplary of what function moral considerations within the patent application process serve and how elements of legal order are simply insufficient to act on accordingly, since most prohibitive legislation is reactive or preventive. A patent application process, however, starts with the incentive nature of patents and is therefore a preemptive measure. The treatment of animals is widely considered to be a display of humanity and usually involves an intricate emotional assessment of human behavior.[382] A suffering mammal, especially a domesticated one, is an exemplary display of helplessness and the intentional causation of such suffering is almost universally regarded as morally wrong. Yet, prohibitive legislation is very rudimentary and it does not follow the approach of ranking criminal acts according to their severity or affected protected right. When it comes to the damage done to humans, the violation of life, e.g. killing, is regarded as a more severe crime than the violation of physical integrity, e.g. physical harm. The German Animal Protection Act, however, has a different system whereby killing is regularly permissible while inducing suffering is generally forbidden.[383]

This distinction indicates the emotional connection associated with animal well-being. Therefore, it is necessary to consider moral order and its emotional rather than logical approach in legislation, as has been done in the Animal Protection Act. The same necessity exists in patent law where a typical legal approach is insufficient for protecting moral considerations. Regarding the potential suffering of carcinogenic overburdened mice, it is even more remarkable that the suffering was possible and – while accepted as an inevitable but tolerable "evil" – still unintentional, but the discussion provoked was still of significant magnitude.[384]

A decision which addressed human characteristics regarded a method of identifying a seemingly dead person.[385] The Federal Patent Court decided that such an economic approach to a human body would represent great disrespect for human dignity, since the morally dubious exploitation of a dead body would lead to psychological distress among the grieving dependents. This decision has been widely regarded as over-stepping the realms of fundamental moral considerations.[386]

---

[381] It might seem to be part of an animal friendly political issue; however, it was rather included to prevent religiously correct butchering, i.e. Islamic ritual butchering – it was unsuccessful, as announced by the Federal Constitutional Court.

[382] Animal treatment as display of human morality.

[383] Sect. 3 and 4 TierSchG.

[384] EPO – T 0315/03 Krebsmaus.

[385] BPatGE 29, 39, 42f.

[386] BGHZ 1988, 209, 227; BPatG, GRUR 1985, 276, 277; BGH, GRUR 1973, 585, 586; *Melullis*, in: Benkard, PatG Sect. 2 re. 56.

c) Technicality of Patents in Relation to Morality as an Independent Approach

The technical teaching within an invention cannot be regarded as violating the moral order when it is permitted by legislation, even, if a majority of the population ethically opposes the invention on the basis of significant considerations – such a formulation only makes identifying a standard much more difficult since it contradicts the previous findings. On the other hand, an invention whose application and use violate the public order by requiring an illegal step definitely also violate the moral order. This dependence suggests that the public order is completely encompassed by the moral order with no independence and therefore every conceivable configuration of the two elements mentioned in Sect. 2 PatG remain possible, except a complete separation which seems highly hypothetical.[387]

Given the dynamic and vague nature of moral order and the intention of the patent legislation in Germany, it is generally agreed upon that the standard for a violation of the moral order has to be substantially higher than in other parts of German legislation.[388] Some authors therefore formulate the requirement that a violation is only sufficient where essential and permanent considerations are concerned. The fact that a certain view is currently a majority opinion within society but might change in the course of time is assumed to be insufficient to qualify for a limit of patentability.[389] This distinction seems necessary to restrict the influence of moral considerations to an acceptable level while still retaining fundamental aspects of human morality in the legislation.

d) Limitations of the Proposed Differences between Morality and Public Order

However, on closer analysis, the elements used in the different definitions are barely suitable to form a clear distinction. First, the criteria for terms of sufficiently significant considerations are "essential" and "permanent". Essential is in itself already highly open to interpretation and intolerably vague. Permanent, on the other hand is a very clear term. However, it is hard to pinpoint which moral consideration has been permanent within a society in the past and – more importantly – it is completely impossible to know which moral opinions might last permanently or rather if they will last at all. It is therefore impractical to assume that any moral opinion has a permanent hold in a society. Not even laws or constitutional rights have the characteristic of lasting forever and therefore being permanent. This is also contradictory in terms of the very reason why moral considerations have been included in the patent assessment process in the first place – to capture the dynamic

---

[387] *Rogge*, GRUR 1998, 303; *Fuchs*, Mitt. 2000, 8; *Melullis*, in: Benkard, PatG Sect. 2 re. 57.

[388] *Melullis*, in: Benkard, PatG Sect. 2 re. 48.

[389] Id.

nature of moral standards within a society. By including the requirement for a permanent element, the standard is not only impossible but also stricter than the legal order, even though it was intended to cover a broader aspect of society. This part of the distinction already defeats the purpose of the definition.

The second part of the definition, relating to aspects insufficient to constitute a significant moral barrier, include the term "majority opinion" and "permanent". While the terms permanent and non-permanent are clear opposites, the aspect relating to a majority opinion only helps to distinguish the meaning of the term "essential" in the first part in a minimal way by revealing that a majority opinion within society regarding morals does not equal an essential moral consideration.

Regarding the aspect of non-permanence, the particular problem of including moral considerations which are, by nature, dynamic while also requiring those considerations to be permanent to be relevant, arises again and renders the distinction inapplicable. Almost nothing is immune to change over the course of time, especially abstract constructs such as morals which can theoretically exist indefinitely as an idea.[390] Another more practical approach has to be identified. It might be argued that the relevant scope of time is set to the duration of the granted right which would be twenty years. While twenty years are certainly more manageable than infinity it is still the case that it is impossible to assess a moment in time in the future precisely. It also raises the question of what the result would be, if moral considerations were to change numerous times within the twenty-year period.

These questions illustrate how any appeal to permanence is doomed to fail. A plausible solution might be a prognosis on the basis of past and current moral tendencies. This would still be difficult in terms of the practical application but manageable and usual in the field of law.

Regarding the supposedly inherent benefit of technological advancement, *Melullis* even goes so far as to refer to the incentive given by the patent as an immaterial right in the interests of the whole of humanity[391] which means that any ethical considerations which might oppose the granting of a patent have to be significant and obvious.[392] Supposedly, patent law does not include the function to control technological advancement based on social standards.[393] The definition of relevant moral considerations is therefore changed again by linking it to ethically substantiated norms of central significance.[394] Additionally, such norms have to be generally ac-

---

[390] The philosophical problems with characterizing an idea and how it can exist without conscientious beings having said idea is not part of this analysis, albeit an interesting topic.

[391] *Spranger*, GRUR Int. 1999, 597; *Melullis*, in: Benkard, PatG Sect. 2 re. 49.

[392] BVerfGE 7, 206; *Melullis*, in: Benkard, PatG Sect. 2 re. 49; *Fuchs*, Mitt. 2001, 4, 8.

[393] BPatGE 29, 39, 42; *Melullis*, in: Benkard, PatG Sect. 2 re. 49.

[394] *Melullis*, in: Benkard, PatG Sect. 2 re. 49; *Moufang*, Art. 53, Rn. 37; *Singer/Stauder/Schatz*, Art. 53, Rn. 17.

cepted as binding as well as being regarded as irrefutable given their fundamental significance.[395]

These specifications also imply a variety of uncertainties. Firstly, the aspect of being generally regarded as binding seems to be identical to the attempt to specify the relevant provisions within ordre public. This presumption is verified by the specifications given by *Melullis* about which ethical norms are exemplary for the definition given: the moral order is embedded within the moral foundation of the legal order which is again based on concepts of human dignity, human basic rights and constitutional rights.[396]

Such a specification would render the distinction between legal and moral order meaningless. The conjunction within Sect. 2 PatG "or" makes it very clear that the two terms have to be exclusive to some extent, even if there might be some overlap. This interpretation is explicitly confirmed by the EPO which states in its decision from July 6th, 2004 that "these definitions confirms *(sic)* the view, which appears from the words of Article 53 (a) EPC itself, that 'ordre public' and morality may form the basis of two separate objections either or both of which can be raised in a particular case."[397]

The same aspect of separation is also expressed by Art. 27 (2) TRIPS which describes the possibility of exempting inventions from patentability even if they comply with the legal order but their commercial exploitation would violate the moral order. It also contradicts the original assumption that moral and legal order may only overlap to some extent; however, this connection suggests that the material content of both terms is identical or at least that moral order is part of the legal order with no independent aspects left. The function of moral order-based restrictions was to include the dynamic of morality within a society; an intent for which ordre public is simply unsuitable.[398] Not only does this definition of moral order defeat the purpose of having two separate elements in Sect. 2 Subs. 1 PatG but it also fails to make use of the opportunity to use the separate elements to support a definition of each aspect by distinguishing it from the other one. Such a distinction would be of significant help with the practical application of two separate elements, each of which are very general and therefore in dire need of specification to avoid ambiguous interpretation and ultimately legal uncertainty.

Additionally, applying the standard of moral order has to be undertaken in a very careful and restrained way, since the intention is not to put the Patent Office in a position whereby it can independently exercise technology politics. Any references

---

[395] *Melullis*, in: Benkard, PatG Sect. 2 re. 49; also: *Rogge* GRUR 98, 303, 305.

[396] *Melullis*, in: Benkard, PatG Sect. 2 re. 49, ref. refers to Federal Constitutional Court jurisprudence, which seems difficult to apply in general: BVerfGE 7, 206; 24, 251; BGH NJW 72, 1414; BPatGE 29, 39, 42; Art. 20, 28 GG, BVerfGE 8, 329.

[397] T 315/03, Abl. EPA 2006, 15, Egr. Nr. 10.2, also T 0866/01, May 11th, 2005, Egr. Nr. 6.9.

[398] *Rogge*, GRUR 1998, 304.

III. Fundamental Considerations of Morality in German Legal Literature 129

to moral order in a decision by the Patent Office have to refer to an actually existing norm within the relevant cultural area. The standard has to be noticed and recognized by the Patent Office and courts but they are not in a position to actually determine or specify the standard. Once again, such a distinction results in the principle that an invention cannot be exempt from patentability whose commercial exploitation is specifically permitted by another piece of legislation. This reasoning is in line with the principles set out in Art. 27 (2) TRIPS, which makes it clear that such an exemption from patentability would violate the agreement. It would also be problematic from a democratic point of view, since discrepancies between legislation and major views of morality are rare and difficult to prove.[399] Founding an exclusion from patentability on moral order, even though the commercial exploitation of the invention is explicitly permitted, would indicate that the German Patent Office assumed such a discrepancy would exist. However, such discrepancies are of major significance in terms of maintaining a stable relationship between the population and the legislative power, and it is not the place of the German Patent Office to assume such a tension and resolve it independently without democratic legitimation.

e) Conclusion

In conclusion, those significant principles of constitutional ranking are under no circumstances be undermined by the German Patent Office or jurisdiction. Therefore, any discrepancies between legislation and ethical viewpoints within society may not be solved through patent administrative action.[400] The only acceptable exception, however, becomes significant where the process of adaptation by legislation is too cumbersome and does not allow for an appropriate and urgent reaction. An example would be an unintended lack of regulation within a piece of legislation which usually triggers the judiciary to employ analogous applications.[401]

Romandini states that even the tendency to regulate all areas of life will not decrease such situations and since patent law is usually the first legal area that has to assess new technologies, the significance of moral order in patent law prevails.[402]

It seems that the only thing of sufficient certainty is the consideration that the definition for moral order used in German civil law is too specific to its field of law and therefore non-transferable to patent law.[403] Other than that, the arguments and

---

[399] *Romandini*, 255; *Rogge*, GRUR 1998, 305.

[400] *Romandini*, 256.

[401] The classification of an analogous application of a certain provision and its violation by the commercial exploitation of an invention as either part of the legal or moral order is difficult; however, it seems to be more appropriate to consider it to be part of the legal order.

[402] *Romandini*, 256 with reference to the embryonic stem cell research which was almost unregulated by the time the first patent applications had to be examined by the European and the British Patent Offices.

[403] *Melullis*, in: Benkard, PatG Sect. 2 re. 50; *MGK/Moufang*, Art. 53 re. 37; *Singer/Stauder/Schatz*, Art. 53 re. 17.

considerations are often circular.[404] It seems that using both terms in a uniform manner is the only reasonable and practical approach.[405] Yet, the legal literature still attempts to distinguish between the two elements. The proposed arguments for the necessity of both aspects and the significance of their reciprocal relationship are entirely unconvincing. For the purposes of this thesis, both terms will are used as one or interchangeably.

IV. Commercial Exploitation as a Requirement of Moral Violations

The discussions about the morality of certain technologies usually focuses directly on the device itself. Most legal arguments even address the invention and its potential uses. However, the TRIPS treaty and all the respective supranational and national patent regimes actually focus on the "commercial exploitation" of the invention. An invention may not be patentable only where the commercial exploitation of the invention violates morality or ordre public. It seems that this distinction must bear at least some significance. Yet, even the official guidelines of the EPO address the invention directly without mentioning the need for commercial exploitation.[406] Therefore, the following section will analyze whether this criterion has actual relevance and why it was included at all.

1. TRIPS Considerations and the Term itself

Analyzing the underlying Art. 27 (2) TRIPS is not ultimately supportive, since it does not provide a more precise definition of the term "commercial exploitation". The general interpretation of the Article is in line with the previous interpretation; any use of the invention with the intent to earn a profit is considered commercial exploitation.[407] Hence, scientific research with or based on the invention and the gratuitous distribution of products based on the invention are not considered commercial exploitation.[408]

It is possible, however, to interpret Art. 27 (2) TRIPS in a different way: Any state that fails to prohibit any use of an invention that is excluded from patentability based

---

[404] *Melullis*, in: Benkard, PatG Sect. 2 re. 50, especially the paragraphs re. the relevant legal and moral order norms are almost identical and even the referenced jurisprudence is partly the same.

[405] With an overview: *Goebel*, Mitt. 1999, 173.

[406] EPO Guidelines for Examination – Part G patentability 4.1 "Matter contrary to 'ordre public' or morality".

[407] *Porter*, Human Embryos, Patents, and Global Trade, p. 343, 355; *Rott*, Patentrecht und Sozialpolitik unter dem TRIPS-Abkommen, 221; *Kienle*, WRP 1998, 699.

[408] *Carvalho*, The TRIPS Regime of Patent Rights, 211 et seq.; *Rott*, Patentrecht und Sozialpolitik unter dem TRIPS-Abkommen, 221.

IV. Commercial Exploitation as a Requirement of Moral Violations

on ethical considerations is in violation of the TRIPS-Agreement.[409] This interpretation can only be based on the understanding of the term "commercial" in a broad way, simply meaning "non-private". Scientific research may be a non-profit activity but still non-private and therefore – in a certain sense – commercial.

At first, this interpretation seems difficult to accept, since Art. 31 (2) lit. (b) TRIPS itself mentions "public non-commercial use". This use suggests that "commercial" cannot be reasonably differentiated from "private". Otherwise, the combination of "public non-commercial use" would be tautological. Also, Art. 31 (2) lit. (b) TRIPS describes aspects of "reasonable commercial term and conditions". The concept of "reasonable terms and conditions" that are merely "non-private", is meaningless. This is due to the fact that the concept of Art. 31 (2) lit. (b) TRIPS basically describes FRAND licensing.

It might be argued that it is not necessary for the TRIPS agreement to use the term "commercial" consistently throughout its Articles. The foregoing reasoning is therefore likely and reasonable but not definitive.

It is, however, additionally supported by the intention of Art. 31 (2) lit. (b) TRIPS. Without a universal prohibition of the commercial exploitation of inventions that are excluded from patentability, it was anticipated that developing nations would establish exclusions of patentability based on legal or moral order. The purpose of this was to enable a generic production and imitation industry within a developing nation.[410] A methodical abuse of the exclusion of patentability for the sake of protectionism or the pursuit of profit defeats the very purpose of the possibility of the exclusion based as expressed in Art. 31 (2) lit. (b) TRIPS. The formulation and identification of this intention makes it clear that the exclusion from patentability does not necessarily cover scientific research or the gratuitous distribution of products based on the inventions. Such modes of exploitation are not in danger of being abused due to the particular purposes which were intended to be prevented by Art. 31 (2) lit. (b) TRIPS. Hence, the generally accepted interpretation of "commercial" persists.[411]

However, the German Patent Act also distinguishes between "commercial" and "private" which further proves that those terms are not meant be interpreted as synonyms.[412] This generally agreed upon interpretation and the fact that this term bears little to no relevance for the major analysis of the question under consideration render any further discussion of this problem at this point unreasonable.

---

[409] *Straus*, Optionen bei der Umsetzung der Richtlinie EG 98/44, 46 and *Addor/Bühler*, 2004, 383, 390 et seq.

[410] *Rott*, GRUR Int. 2003, 103, 112.

[411] *Meiser*, Biopatentierung und Menschenwürde, 180; *Guglielmetti*, NLCC 2008, 396, 401; *Romandini*, 235.

[412] See Sect. 11 No. 1 PatG for the terms commercial (gewerblich) and private (privat).

The term "commercial exploitation" is therefore identical in its meaning in the German Patent Code, the European Patent Convention and the TRIPS Articles. As mentioned before, some authors tend to group patent applications that are likely to be affected by the exclusion provision. The first such grouping describes inventions which are not allowed to result in products or actually applied procedures, since their existence alone violates relevant prohibitive legislation.[413] Examples are reproductive cloning, methods to execute the death penalty (within the European Union) and genetic modifications of the human genome. While the first and the last are straightforward examples, since they are already subject to the EU Biotech Directive, the concept of an invention related to the death penalty makes further analysis necessary. Even though the death penalty has been abolished within Germany and the European Union in general, it does not necessarily mean that every conceivable use of the invention is automatically illegal. Unless the invention somehow specifies in its technical set-up that it can only be used as a method for performing the death penalty, no restriction exists on contraptions resulting in the death of a human.

The other group relates to inventions whose commercial exploitation violates the legal or moral order, even if scientific research with the invention or private use is still permitted. The most relevant example of this distinction is the production of psychotropic drugs which are legal to produce in a private or scientific environment. However, they are prohibited when it comes to commercial production and distribution.[414] In such cases, patentability is excluded without violating the TRIPS agreement or European law. The reverse case, where the commercial exploitation of an invention does not constitute a violation of the moral or legal order, but instead the non-commercial use does, is hardly imaginable and therefore not practically relevant for the present analysis.

2. Standard for Commercial Use

In terms of the aspect of commercial use, any form of use according to Sect. 9 PatG is included, specifically, the economic exploitation of the invention which describes the realization of the technical teaching within the patent application.[415]

Most important in identifying the restrictive scope of application of the provision is the fact that the commercial use only constitutes an exclusion from patentability according to Sect. 2 PatG if the only conceivable commercial uses are those which violate the moral or legal principles.[416] If only one of several conceivable uses violates these principles, the violation is insufficient to trigger the exclusion clause of

---

[413] *Romandini*, 242.

[414] *Romandini*, 243.

[415] *Melullis*, in: Benkard, PatG Sect. 2 re. 28.

[416] BPatG, GRUR 2007, 1049, 1051; *Schulte/Moufang*, Sect. 2 re. 31; *Melullis*, in: Benkard, PatG Sect. 2 re. 30.

Sect. 2 PatG.[417] Even in cases where the violation of moral or legal principles of one specific conceivable use is of considerable severity, the exclusion clause it not applicable.[418]

These considerations are usually summed up by the following wording: possible misuse of a legal teaching in individual cases is insufficient to deny patent protection to an inventor – in fact, the commercial use of an invention as a whole has to be completely incompatible with the moral and legal order.[419] In line with this reasoning is the principle that a possible abuse of the invention which is not intended by the patent application is irrelevant for the assessment. This line of reasoning still applies even if the abusive commercial use would clearly violate the moral or legal order.[420] The only relevance is in relation to the intended or proper use and execution of the invention.

This reasoning functions solely as a clarification, since the assessment standard is already very narrow and any consideration of individual ways of using the invention in a way which violates moral or legal order is absolutely irrelevant – intended or otherwise. Again, the only exception is a case where no non-violating use is conceivable.[421]

Taking the aspects about all conceivable uses into account, it is clear that a prohibitive provision that includes exceptions usually does not constitute a relevant piece of legislation for the assessment of the legal order, since uses that are allowed by the legal order are already included in the provision. A violation of the provision by an invention therefore automatically includes a very conceivable use that is non-violating, since it is already included in the provision.[422]

a) German Jurisprudence Regarding Commercial Use

Examples in German jurisprudence include the treatment of water[423] and a construction lift.[424] In each case a specific piece of legislation prohibited the use of the patented invention in a specific way or with a specific substance, yet, a method of using the technical teaching was deemed to exist beyond the specifically prohibited way.

---

[417] BGH, GRUR 1973, 585 – IUP, BGH GRUR 2010, 212 Rn. 24, etc; *Melullis*, in: Benkard, PatG Sect. 2 re. 30.

[418] *Breier/Straus*, Gentechnologie, S. 137; *Melullis*, in: Benkard, PatG Sect. 2 re. 30.

[419] *Melullis*, in: Benkard, PatG Sect. 2 re. 31; BGH, GRUR 1983, 729, 730 – Hydropyridizin.

[420] RGZ 149, 224, 229; *Melullis*, in: Benkard, PatG Sect. 2 re. 32; RGBl. 04, 35, 36; RGZ 149, 224, 229.

[421] EPA, GRUR Int. 1993, 240, 241; *Melullis*, in: Benkard, PatG Sect. 2 re. 32.

[422] BPatG, Mitt. 1972, 135, 137; *Melullis*, in: Benkard, PatG Sect. 2 re. 33.

[423] BpatG, Mitt. 72, 135, 137.

[424] BPatGE 5 129, 134.

While German jurisprudence still officially uses this standard,[425] the European Patent Organization seems to have developed a different approach. The EPO decided in a case regarding a process directed at producing genetically modified animals that any patent claims that are ambiguous and therefore apply to both animal and human cells have to be restricted in such a way that no patent claim may relate to humans.[426] The same reasoning was applied in a patent application where the claims covered a method for euthanizing animals; however, the specific claim was formulated in a way that also covered humans.[427] It was explicitly stated that a patent claim may only remain admissible when all potentially relevant subjects conform to requirements of the EPC.

One might think that the German FPC would agree with this method of interpretation.[428] It was decided that the same reasoning applies to patent claims that cover both biological material with an unobjectionable origin and biological material that was produced by destroying omni-potent stem cells. However, the decision was very specific and based on one of the explicit case groups of Sect. 2 PatG. The standard has to be different, because the wording is different from the general clause in Sect. 2 (1) PatG. In addition, such a standard would drastically reduce the scope of permissible claims for ordinary inventions rather than biotechnological ones. Otherwise, any invention that is intended to cause harm, especially weapons, would necessarily incorporate claims that also cover violations of ordre public.

Referring to the foregoing example of the "obviously" violating patent which includes a method of executing the death penalty, any weapon invention includes a patent claim describing its function as it might be used in the execution of the death penalty. Therefore, the standard of the decision is non-transferrable to the general clause. Otherwise, the patent claims for such inventions would be severely limited and exclude a large number of patentable inventions in practice. Transference of the standard fails to be logically satisfying and has to be rejected.

The restricted effect nature of the *Krebsmaus* decision is also supported by the different jurisprudence of the EPO regarding Art. 53 lit. (a) and (b) EPC. Art. 53 lit. (b) EPC excludes from patentability plant or animal varieties or essentially biological processes for the production of plants or animals. However, the court decision was made that a patent application is still permissible, even if patent claims are included that cover excluded plant varieties as well.[429] Otherwise, inventions with general claims that address multiple varieties would remain without patent protection.

---

[425] With an exception of BPatG, Mitt. 2007, 278. – "Neuronale Vorläuferzellen".
[426] *Romandini*, 894.
[427] T 315/03, Abl. EPA 2006, 15, Egr. Nr. 12.2.4.
[428] *Romandini*, 245.
[429] *Romandini*, 245.

b) Legal Discussion of Commercial Use

Romandini tries to distinguish between the two regulations. He describes the general clause of Art. 53 lit. (a) EPC as being intended to deter companies from investing in technological advancements whose commercial exploitations violate significant legal principles.[430] Furthermore, supposedly, this function cannot be fulfilled, if patent claims for an otherwise excluded patent application simply include admissible types of use.

This line of argument might work for the specific biotechnological field which *Romandini* examines; however, without that context, the definition and conclusion are unsustainable. As mentioned above, for ordinary, i.e. non-biotechnological inventions, this approach is nonsensical, since the types of applications are vastly more diverse than in the field of biotechnology. Applying the same strict standard would cripple patentability in almost any technological field in which a type of application exists which is potentially harmful to humans or animals.

That said, it is also the case that the basis of the argument, the description of the intention of the regulation of Art. 53 lit. (a) EPC is less definitive than *Romandini* makes it seem. While it is possible that one aspect of the exclusion of patentability is to function as a steering element for investment, this could quite easily also be achieved by simple prohibitive legislation. In addition, as mentioned in the preceding chapter analyzing the need for such provisions in general, the conclusion was mainly based on the aspect of official recognition and approval of inventions violating legal or moral order. Taking this important and significant aspect of the intention for the provision into account, *Romandini*'s conclusion becomes less convincing. The function of abstaining from officially recognizing and approving an invention which possibly violates legal or moral order can very well still be achieved, if the specific patent claims also cover types of application that do not pose the threat of being a violation of legal and moral order.

The effect of official recognition or approval is therefore significantly reduced. This development can be observed in the practice of any patent office where potentially dangerous inventions or even inventions that are explicitly and specifically harmful to human beings, such as weapons, are considered to be contributing to the general well-being of society.

Another argument made by *Romandini* targets the abstract nature of the possible results of applying the strict version of any hypothetical commercial exploitation and describing them as arbitrary.[431] He states that a patent application is permissible where the state of the art allows for a generalization of the patent claim which then include a non-violating type of application. Identifying a single non-violating application seems arbitrary to him, since a patent is excluded from patentability if such a generalization is not possible. While it might seem that the characteristic of being

---

[430] *Romandini*, 245.
[431] Id at 246.

able to generalize patent claims to include a variety of types of applications including non-violating interpretations is arbitrary, *Romandini* fails to deliver a deeper analysis of this argument.

The fact that an invention includes violating or non-violating patent claims is based on the decision to implement the patentability exclusion regulation. The cause for such a categorization lies ultimately within the aspects of the invention itself. Regarding the ability to generalize a patent claim to include non-violating types of application, it is apparent that the specific characteristic which enables generalization of a concept within a technological invention is also inherent to the invention itself.

Additionally, the claim of arbitrary categorization can further be refuted by assessing the results of each individual patent application process. A patent with no means of modification, such that it includes exclusively violating types of application, is rejected while another may be accepted. In the acceptance of the application and the granting of the patent lies the assessment that a non-violating type of application exists which is ultimately useful to society and its technological advancement. Without an exclusively violating set of patent claims, the danger of officially recognizing or approving an ethically questionable invention ceases to exist. Those aspects make it clear that the distinction between the two patent applications based on their capacity for modification to include patent claims that conform with patent law is not arbitrary or at least not more arbitrary than the distinction between violating and non-violating patent claims in the first place.

In addition, there is an argument in the legal discussion that the approach based on evaluating every patent claim of an invention in order to identify any hypothetically violating type of application burdens the examiner with an almost impossible task and unnecessarily lengthens the examination process; however, this is also countered by *Romandini* with reference to *Guglielmetti*,[432] asserting that that argument is based on the confusion of the application of the invention with the use of its results, as stated by *Guglielmetti*. The scope of protection of a patent is entirely different from the effects of the protection.

The example given addresses the particular problems with the type of application of inventions that provide for the possibility of using them in a way which violates legal or moral order. Inventing a new type of knife and trying to obtain a patent for it poses the problem that such a knife has the potential to be used in a variety of ways that violate ordre public by being used for torture or murder. It is then argued that the application of the invention, the technical solution captured in the patent claim, is merely providing the product, the knife in the example. Such a supply is legally and morally unobjectionable, while any conflict with the legal system is caused only by an improper use of the product based on the invention. Being merely a type of use of the product, such acts are inherent to the application of the invention or the technical

---

[432] *Romandini*, 246 and *Guglielmetti*, NLCC 2008, 396, 403 et seq.

solution. Granting such a patent would also not in any way promote or facilitate such improper actions.

This argument of distinction certainly seems to provide a solid solution to the inherent problem. However, it tends to fall short of offering a definite and final solution. The distinction between the application of the invention and the use thereof are, in fact, different aspects of the patent. On the other hand, the regulation of Art. 27 (2) TRIPS, Art. 53 (a) EPC and Sect. 2 (1) PatG all include the formulation of "commercial exploitation" of the invention. It is true that the sale of knives may not violate the moral and legal order. Yet, it has to be considered that distribution as a means of commercial exploitation does not refer to the provision of the product "knife" but is instead directly targeted at the distribution of the products which are based on the invention.

A distinction between the two aspects of "scope of protection" of the patent and "effects of the patent" is not razor-sharp but rather represents a gradient. In addition, the "scope of protection" – when referring to the scope of the patent claims – is evidently different from the aspect of "commercial exploitation" which clearly targets the effects of the patent. In the knife scenario, the main question regards relates to the problem of "dual use"[433] technology and how patent law can deal with it efficiently. Clearly, the solution cannot be to exclude knife technology from patentability altogether, just because some uses of knives violate legal or moral order. The term "improper" used by *Romandini* technically does not fit, since the application of the knife for torture is still a technically correct use of the knife. To determine the "proper" use of a knife by including the intention of the inventor also fails to provide the desired result, since the device is usually of neutral status and does not include a specific intention.

c) Romandini's *Case Group Solution*

Romandini seems to be aware of the shortcomings of the solution by including a different case group. This group is characterized by providing a product which must not be produced without violating the ordre public.[434] He concludes that in such cases, the patent protection has to be rejected because it would otherwise support a technology whose commercial exploitation violates fundamental legal principles. This conclusion is remarkable, since it is very similar to the regulation wording but it fails to draw a distinction for the first case example which included the "knife" scenario.

Romandini uses three examples to illustrate the second group:

---

[433] Originally referring to the use of rockets which can be used for both space travel and the transportation of military warheads. The transferal does not work in its entirety, since in the original sense, both uses were legal and in the case under discussion, only one of them is.

[434] *Romandini*, 247.

(a) In case of a procedural patent, the patent claim may be inadmissible if one realization of the procedure exists that may be in violation of the legal or moral order. The specific example is a patent that provides a procedure to euthanize mammals which is therefore also applicable to human beings.[435]

A further analysis of this example shows that it is confusing and potentially conflicts with the "knife" scenario from before. Displaying the procedure for euthanizing mammals is the "scope of protection" in this scenario, and what it is actually applied to – either humans or animals – is an aspect of the "effects of the patent" – to retain the chosen terms. According to the German legal discussion, such an invention would probably be admissible since it includes perfectly legal means of commercially exploiting the invention – the same way a knife does. It seems that the relevant distinction here is the difference in probability or the specific "threat" to human life or the overall ethically forbidding concept of human euthanasia that triggers a different response which requires a harsher and strict judgement to exclude the invention from patentability.

(b) The second example refers to a patent that describes a product and also explains the specific purpose; such a patent shall not be granted patentability where the realization of a specific purpose includes a single case which violates the legal or moral order. Specific technologies such as anti-personnel mines, torture devices and synthetic drugs are considered to be in that group.[436] Even though the production of such a product might be legal, the specific purpose allegedly violates the legal order.

Interestingly, this example group introduces a new factor into the complex equation of determining the ethical requirements to qualify for patent protection: the intention of the inventor in terms of how the invention is supposed to be used. Usually, the intent is part of a different assessment and does not constitute any element of the actual invention. Any technology might be intended for use in a certain way. Including the intention in a patent document might actually prove risky for the inventor and also might result in different assessments of patentability based solely on whether the inventor included his intended use for the invention – which might actually represent an arbitrary distinction.

(c) The third example group given by *Romandini* addresses patent claims that involve a chemical or biological substance without mentioning a specific purpose. Where it is impossible to produce any of the necessary substances without violating the legal or moral order, the scope of protection has to be restricted or patent protection in general rejected.[437] However, according to *Romandini*, it is

---

[435] *Romandini*, 247, fn. 900.

[436] *Romandini*, 247, fn. 901.

[437] Id. A possible example of such a case is the Brüstle decision of the ECJ which concerned a patent claim that relied on using a certain kind of stem cell, the production of which required the destruction of very potent embryonic stem cells.

IV. Commercial Exploitation as a Requirement of Moral Violations

irrelevant to the question of patent protection whether the combined substances can potentially be used in illicit applications, as long as admissible applications of the invention exist.[438] *Romandini* agrees further with the relevant decision that such a restriction may be achieved with a so-called ethical "disclaimer".[439] While it might be possible to design the patent application in such a way, it illustrates the importance of the intention laid out within the patent description and adds a somewhat arbitrary factor to the examination process.

It is correct to assume that such an application may not necessarily violate the legal or moral order; however, this argument seems to be contradictory to the explanations given in the context of the "knife" examples. Even though the results for both examples follow the same principle, it is unclear how *Romandini* distinguishes between the two aspects. A method of tempering a knife in a certain way might fall under the violation of legal or moral order.[440] If it does not, its methods of application are equally irrelevant. The only difference to the biological or chemical substance example seems to be the fact that it concerns a biological or chemical substance. Creating two seemingly identical examples to convey the same argument would only lead to a hendiadys, however, the following explanations made by *Romandini* show inconsistency in the application of his established principle.

Where all possible methods of application would violate legal or moral order or the substances only have a specific field of application, the invention has to be rejected in totality according to *Romandini*.[441] While it is in line with the general definition of commercial exploitation in Sec. 2 PatG and Art. 53 lit. (a) ECP it contradicts the explanations provided by *Guglielmetti*, which are adapted by *Romandini*.

The distinction between the invention and its underpinning technology and a subsequent application of the products based on the invention is falsely regarded as a clear and unambiguous line in terms of the scope of protected patent claims and irrelevant factors in the assessment of the morality of patents. Applying this principle precisely in the same way to the biological or chemical substance example, the potential applications of the invention should still be considered irrelevant.

It might be argued that the principle does not apply in a case where only illicit applications exist but *Romandini* does not propose such an exception. Furthermore, the distinction made by *Guglielmetti* is clearly based on an allegedly

---

[438] *Romandini*, 247.

[439] *Romandini* disagrees with the invention to such an extent that the existence of possible illicit methods of application of the invention is insufficient to reject the patent in general but is a basis for a restriction of the patent claims to non-violating varieties.

[440] Such as the ancient myth of quenching a steel sword by stabbing it into a human being, which supposedly would lead to a stronger blade.

[441] *Romandini*, 247.

precise interpretation of the wordings of the relevant norms, the scope of patent protection as regards patent claims and the limitations thereof. He clearly states that (abusive) applications of an invention are not part of the protected invention, the assessment of which is based on the technological process or teaching, hence it is not covered by the patent protection in general. In conclusion, the logically resulting irrelevance of the invention's application for examining the patent should remain unaffected by any form of subsequent applications of the patent invention.

Without a conclusive application of the principle or a coherent argument for exceptions, this category by *Romandini* does not provide a satisfying solution for the different aspects of violating or non-violating patent inventions.

It becomes apparent that neither the very strict approach of focusing on a single hypothetical non-violating application nor the approach of restricting any hypothetical violating types of application seems to be a reasonable and practicable approach to the difficult matter of patentability and ethics. This dilemma and the insufficiency of the solutions are mirrored in the jurisprudence where neither approach is consistently applied – ultimately contributing to the confusing and unsatisfying status quo.

3. Relevant Moment of Commercial Exploitations

Since the commercial exploitation of an invention is logically subsequent to the act of inventing the specific technological advancement, it is usually agreed upon within the legal discussion that only future acts can constitute commercial exploitations according to the relevant German and European regulations.[442] Yet, the question of how patents may be assessed, where they are unobjectionable regarding their application but violate the legal or moral order during the inventive process, is still subject to debate in the German legal field.[443]

a) Black Letter Analysis of Art. 53 EPC and Art. 27 (2) TRIPS

Based on the wording of Art. 53 EPC the EPO decided that any violations in the invention process preceding the application are irrelevant to the application process or at least that such an event is not covered by the regulation.[444] Other legal experts reject this reasoning and argue for an inclusion under the patentability restrictions of Art. 53 EPC, where the development process for the invention includes a violation of

---

[442] Schweizer Bundesrat, Botschaft zur Änderung des Patentgesetzes und zum Bundesbeschluss über die Genehmigung des Patentrechtsvertrags und der Ausführungsordnung vom November 23rd, 2005, 58.

[443] *Romandini*, 248.

[444] T 315/02, July 6th, 2004, Abl. EPA 2006, 1, Egr. Nr. 4.2.

IV. Commercial Exploitation as a Requirement of Moral Violations

the moral or legal order.[445] While the wording of the regulation is still respected, the patentability restriction is based on Art. 53 EPC via an analogous application. The need for the analogous application is seen in maintaining the uniformity of the legal system, otherwise a patent applicant might be able to obtain a patent, even if he stole the invention or obtained the necessary knowledge in another illicit way. Incentivizing such behavior via a patent would contradict the intentions not only of the patent regime, but also violate a greater principle within the legal system that seeks to prevent any reward for illicit behavior in general.

Counter arguments against this proposal of an analogous application are as follow: Art. 27 (2) TRIPS states, where a patent application is exempt from patentability based on violations of the legal or moral order, the national legislator also has to prohibit the commercial exploitation of that invention. If that is that not the case, the exclusion of the patent from patentability violates the TRIPS agreement.[446] Applying this interpretation to the situation of the present case, it is obvious that only the obtainment of the patent application was in violation but not the commercial exploitation. The commercial exploitation is not prohibited by any state legislation, which would bar the legislator from excluding the patentability in the first place.

Romandini responds to that argument by addressing the overall concept of the TRIPS agreement and distinguishing between the TRIPS agreement and the problem of obtaining an invention in an illicit manner. An illicitly obtained patent addresses the problem of competitors trying to fight the advantage of the inventor within the specific nation. While the analogous application of Art. 53 lit. (a) EPC functions as a means to provide such a mechanism, the regulations of the TRIPS agreement are intended to regulate such means in the form of exemptions from patentability.

Where the establishment of an exclusion from patentability is in line with the TRIPS regulations, the means of establishing such an exemption are irrelevant – it might be a piece of legislation or the analogous application of an existing legislative exemption. Therefore, the argument against analogous application is supposed to have no effect because it confuses two different aspects.

While this is technically a precise interpretation of the regulation within the TRIPS agreement, it fails to address all doubts about the contradictory nature of allowing the commercial exploitation of an invention on the one hand, but prohibiting the granting of a patent for the same invention on the other. The regulation itself specifically mentions in Art. 27 (2) TRIPS the invention and its exploitation. Additionally, the Article is titled "Patentable Subject Matter" and thereby clearly relates to the invention and its inherent characteristics which excludes the circumstances of its development. Therefore, the originally stated principles embedded in Art. 27 (2) TRIPS states that a legislator is prohibited from barring patentability for inventions

---

[445] *Romandini*, fn. 907 and 909.
[446] *Straus*, Optionen bei der Umsetzung der Richtlinie EG 98/44, p. 54.

whose commercial exploitation has been explicitly permitted in another piece of legislation.

By exempting an illicitly obtained invention from patentability, even though the commercial exploitation is permissible, it seems to directly contradict the TRIPS agreement. However, *Romandini* circumvents this apparent contradiction by interpreting the regulation of Art. 27 (2) TRIPS to be non-exhaustive.[447] First, he draws a comparison to Art. 21 (2) UPOV[448] which specifically includes a clarification that the reasons for annulment in Art. 21 (1) UPOV are exhaustive. Yet, it is claimed that the lack of such a clarification in Art. 27 TRIPS is a definitive indicator for a conscious decision to ensure the list of exemptions for patentability in Art. 27 TRIPS remain non-exhaustive.[449] However, this is not an entirely convincing argument, since the reason to include or refrain from including a specific regulation on the exhaustive character is not explicitly communicated by the regulation or lack thereof.

Yet, such an intent can be identified as arising during the development process of the TRIPS agreement, where supposedly the delegates of the United States tried to determine the exhaustive character of Art. 27 TRIPS but failed due to the opposition of developing countries.[450] This historic argument certainly makes a convincing case for the non-exhaustiveness of Art. 27 (2) TRIPS but it does not render the exemptions in subsection 2 as mere examples, giving total liberty to the Contracting States to arbitrarily establish other exemptions by introducing state legislation.[451] *Romandini* argues that the specific regulation of Art. 27 (2) TRIPS provides a restriction on national patent exemptions which requires a distinction to be made between exemptions which are related to patentability and exemptions which are not related to patentability.[452] The term "patentability" is, in that context, somewhat misleading since the exemptions exclude certain inventions from patentability, so technically all such exemptions ultimately relate to patentability.

What *Romandini* refers to are the positive and negative characteristics that are inherent to an invention and are required for in order for the invention to be eligible for patent protection – meaning "patentability" the characteristic of the invention rather than "patentability" the legal result of an examination.[453]

This definition results in the following application of the TRIPS agreement: an exemption of patentability that is based on a characteristic of the inventions that is

---

[447] *Romandini*, 250.

[448] The International Union for the Protection of New Varieties of Plants or UPOV (Union internationale pour la protection des obtentions végétales, UPOV).

[449] *Romandini*, 250.

[450] *Carvalho*, The TRIPS Regime of Patent Rights, 373; *Séguin*, Genomic Medicine and Developing Countries: Creating a Room of Their Own, 9 Nature Reviews Genetics 487, 493 (2008).

[451] *Romandini*, 250.

[452] Id.

[453] Id.

neither a positive requirement for patent protection nor an exception mentioned in Art. 27 TRIPS is inadmissible.[454] Other exemptions which are not based on "patentability" (in the sense of the positive and negative characteristics inherent to the invention) are supposedly not covered by Art. 27 TRIPS and hence not affected by its restrictions on national legislation. Ultimately, this would result in the admissibility of national legislation exempting patentability based on the illicit manner in which the invention was obtained, even though the TRIPS agreement itself does not include such provisions. Apart from international and supranational legislations, some authors focus on the national patent systems.

b) Black Letter Analysis of the German Patent Act

Romandini mentions Sect. 21 (1) No. 3 PatG as an example of such admissible legislation; however, Sect. 21 PatG is a mechanism of revoking a patent and therefore does not cover patentability. Even if it is argued that Sect. 21 PatG as a revocation mechanism is functioning synchronically to patentability, as is apparently indicated by Sect. 21 (1) No. 1 PatG which mentions the lack of patentability according to Sect. 1 to 5 PatG as a ground for revocation, this very fact indicates that the legislator distinguishes between patentability and the grounds for revocation. Sect. 2 PatG, which relates to the violation of moral and legal order, is independently mentioned in Sect. 21 (1) No. 1 PatG, while the illicit obtainment of a patent (in a certain manner) is captured in Sect. 21 (1) No. 3 PatG, clearly indicating that it is different from Sect. 2 PatG context- and content-wise. Thus, the conclusion can be drawn that ensuring that there has been no illicit obtainment of an invention is not part of the patentability requirements and therefore is not a violation of the legal or moral order in its interpretation of Sect. 2 PatG.

In *Romandini*'s line of argument, it seems clear that this exemption from patentability (or technically right to revocation) relates to the behavior of the inventor and not the invention – the rights of an inventor and the lack thereof are indeed not regulated by the TRIPS agreement which therefore does not affect Sect. 21 PatG. The author of this analysis agrees with *Romandini* insofar as Sect. 21 PatG does not violate the TRIPS agreement; however, it is not precise to base the exemption on an analogous application of Art. 53 EPC.

Firstly, as mentioned above, the legal mechanism of Sect. 21 PatG differs from Sect. 1 to 5 PatG. Art. 53 EPC directly and exclusively relates to the exceptions to patentability which are part of the examination process. An analogous application would therefore necessarily result in an additional exception of patentability, which Sect. 21 PatG evidently is not. It also makes practical sense to distinguish between those two aspects and their legal realization, since requiring the patent office to include the means of development in their examination process over-burdens the examiner with regard to assessing information that is not included in the patent

---

[454] *Rott*, Patentrecht und Sozialpolitik unter dem TRIPS-Abkommen, 52.

application. *Romandini* agrees with the practical reservations but refers to the practice of objecting third parties which may provide such information.[455] Still, this practice is more of an aspect of revocation courts than the patent application process which intends to assess the patent itself.

Lastly, the effect of such legal differentiation is relevant. The Swiss Federal Council, assessing the same problem in patent law, decided against the exemption from patentability, since the patent itself does not violate legal or moral order nor does its commercial exploitation. By revoking the patent, anyone, including the illicitly behaving inventor, would still be able to exploit the invention commercially; the injustice created would not be resolved.[456] *Romandini* also disagrees with these explanations by focusing on the incentivizing aspect of a patent. The injustice is incorporated in the right of the illicit inventor to exclude other competitors and thereby obtain an advantage through illicit acts. Inversely, a competitor would be at a disadvantage by complying with the national law.[457]

While it is true that the situation is more complex than the Swiss Federal Council makes it seem, it raises an interesting point. The discrepancies between *Romandini* and the explanation given by the Council are not really contradictory but rather a result of a misunderstanding. Since the court focuses specifically on the patent and any injustice embodied by it, the conclusion is correct in stating that the patent itself is unobjectionable and a revocation of the patent would result in the elimination of a perfectly admissible patent. However, it is also correct, as *Romandini* describes, to accept the injustice of the fact that the patent is owned by a market participant who does not deserve the patent as a right of exclusion because of illicit obtainment which violates the intention of patent law to incentivize admissible research and technological advancement. These two different aspects of the situation are perfectly represented by the regulatory approaches of Sect. 2 PatG and Sect. 21 PatG. While Sect. 2 PatG addresses the injustice of a patent which itself violates the legal and moral order via its commercial exploitation and Sect. 21 PatG addresses the injustice of granting a patent to an inventor who has obtained it illicitly. In the first instance, the injustice is the patent itself, while in the latter it is the fact that a certain inventor has obtained a specific patent.

Finally, *Romandini* does not explicitly address the fact that Sect. 21 (3) PatG only covers a very specific way of obtaining a patent which would render it illicit. Only in a case where the significant content of a patent was obtained without consent, from the descriptions, technical drawings, models, devices or equipment of another person or a process devised by another person, would its obtainment be considered illicit and be the basis for revocation of the patent. This is, however, implied in his further explanations, where he acknowledges the need for more consideration regarding the

---

[455] *Romandini*, 252.

[456] Schw. Bundesrat, Botschaft zum Bundesgesetz über die Forderung an überzähligen Embryonen und embryonalen Stammzellen, November 20th, 2002, p. 58.

[457] *Romandini*, 251 et seq.

origin of patents since most of the patents in Germany are developed abroad.[458] *Romandini* implies, with his demand for an assessment of the development of the invention according to the country of application, that he understands the limitations of Sect. 21 (3) PatG.

c) Interim Result

The significance of the question about whether preceding violations of morality or public order can be relevant to the patentability of an invention is negligible in the present case. The foregoing legal assessment supports the decision of the author to exclude this aspect from further empirical evaluation. In addition, the aspect of commercial exploitation has no significant impact on the discussion of morality in patent law either.

V. Conclusion

As seen in the individual explanations, a general standard for both the aspects of ordre public and morality does technically exist. However, both standards are vague and include elements which in themselves require a standard. Relying on sub-definitions results in the effect that the general definition is not actually defined in an applicable manner but rather replaced with a different more extensively worded term.

As regards ordre public, the crucial aspect of the definition relates to the level at which significance provisions or any legislation have to be in order to become relevant for the exclusion of patentability. Furthermore, even if a definition for that threshold of significance has been given, it is unclear in what way the invention or its application for commercial use has to violate the specific provision. In particular, for provisions at the very top of ordre public, such as human rights or human dignity, the nature of such a violation is usually not obvious or direct. If an indirect violation is sufficient, the field of application becomes much broader.

In the realm of morality, the uncertainties grow even further. It seems to be of general agreement that only "high principles" or "universally binding fundamentals" of morality are important and significant enough to be considered in the realm of patentability. Once again, not only is this standard almost as broad as the concept of morality itself but it does not provide a more detailed approach to the subject, and even the definitions given are impractical and contradictory. These uncertainties make it impossible to characterize the relationship between patent morality and ordre public as two independent elements.

However, some general features of the entire term "morality and ordre public" can be summarized. Both aspects require a qualified version of morality and ordre public

---

[458] *Romandini*, 252, as well as *Guglielmetti*, NLCC, 396, 404.

respectively. The characteristics of that qualification are usually described by imaging morality and public order as a construct with a pyramidal form in which only the very top is relevant to the aspects of patentability.[459] Therefore, the threshold at which a provision can be considered to be of sufficiently high rank within the structure is very high.

This structural comparison of both elements indicates that the concept of immorality and illegality in patent law is reversed compared to other areas of law. Most legal scholars and even members of the judiciary are unaware of this unique relationship. Identifying this relationship is of considerable help in addressing attempts to define morality or ordre public in patent law.

Of note is also the fact that weapon technology has never been subject to German jurisprudence and it is usually only mentioned when it comes to the introduction of circumstances where moral considerations generally do not interfere with aspects of patentability. This view of weapons as patentable devices strongly implies the general view of Sect. 2 PatG as a classic form of an exemption from the rule that patentability is generally regarded to be beneficial and not subject to moral considerations. Such a fundamental aspect of the function of patent law also implies that the legal literature interprets the German Patent Act to be based on the assumption that technological advancement is inherently good and beneficial, even in the case of weaponry. However, weapon technology is usually a subject which is highly prone to ethical discussion and prohibitive legislation. In German legislation, in particular, weapons are subject to severe and restrictive regulation. As such, patent law seems out of sync with the rest of the legal system.

---

[459] Even if some of the decisions regarding legal order include provisions of lesser structural height, those usually protect legal assets which are very high ranking such as human life and bodily integrity.

D. Patentability and Moral Concerns in U.S. Patent Law

The U.S. Constitution is one of the oldest legal documents that specifically mentions the concept of a patent.[1] Therefore, the legal culture of the U.S. patent law regime is heavily influenced by its dynamic historic development. To acquire a basic understanding of the significance of recent developments, the first part of this chapter gives an overview of the historic patent law development (I.).

In the second part, the analysis turns towards the recent changes in patentability requirements in the light of biotechnology (II.). A significant section of this part addresses the *Rifkin* case which specifically tested the moral limits of the U.S. patent system.

Subsequently, the chapter applies the human dignity-centered approach of the EU and German patent law systems to the U.S. The role played by human dignity in the U.S. and more specifically in the U.S. patent system is also analyzed (III.).

In a micro-functional comparative analysis, the following sections compare the European and German patent regimes versus the U.S. system with regard of judicial reasoning (IV.) and the relationship of state powers (V.).

The final part presents a first conclusion for the overarching question of this thesis as well as recommendations (VI.).

I. Historic Development

As the most significant difference between the German and European approach of taking legal order or moral order into account, the United States Code, Title 35 Patents (35 USC) does not include a specific provision regarding ordre public or morality.[2] The patentability requirements for inventions are limited to non-obviousness and novelty. The U.S. therefore does not make use of Art. 27 (2) of the TRIPS agreement.

---

[1] Art. I Section 8 Clause 8 of the United States Constitution grants the US Congress the enumerated power "to promote the progress of science and useful arts, by securing for limited times to authors and inventors the exclusive right to their respective writings and discoveries."

[2] *Colston/Galloway*, Modern Intellectual Property Law (3rd edition, Routledge 2010), 532; *MacQueen*, Contemporary Intellectual Property: Law and Policy (Oxford University Press 2008).

Yet, between 1817 and 1999 the common law of patentability included the "moral utility doctrine". The doctrine was used to address morality's place in patent law. *Lowell v. Lewis*[3] is usually regarded as the beginning of the patent moral utility doctrine. More recently, *Juicy Whip, Inc. v. Orange Bang, Inc.*[4] ultimately rejected the moral utility doctrine.[5]

1. Genesis of the Moral Utility Doctrine

In *Lowell v. Lewis*, Justice *Joseph Story* reasoned that – concerning a morally innocuous water pump – a newly invented water pump need not be better than existing pumps to be useful according to § 101 of the Patent Act. "All that the law requires is that the invention should not be frivolous or injurious to the well-being, good policy, or sound morals of society."[6] Remarkably, this general standard from 1817 regarding the nature of patents is identical to the patentability exemption of the German and European equivalent.

Justice *Story* continued to give negative examples which do not fulfill the utility requirement: "[A] new invention to poison people, or to promote debauchery, or to facilitate private assassination, is not a patentable invention."[7] For the purposes of this analysis it is useful to focus on the last example. The example is arguably close to weapon technology. In addition, the rejection of assassination devices is limited to the "private" sector. Such a restriction regarding the market is peculiar and demonstrates the relevance of potential consumers of the patent application in question. Justice *Story* even restated his definition in the *Bedford v. Hunt* decision[8] where he explained:

> "A useful invention (…) is (…) one as may be applied to some beneficial use in society, in contradistinction to an invention, which is injurious to the morals, the health, or the good order of society. (…) It is sufficient, that it has no obnoxious or mischievous tendency, that it may be applied to practical uses, and that so far as it is applied, it is salutary. (…) The law

---

[3] 15 F Cas. 1018, 1019 (Story, Circuit Justice, C.C.D. Mass. 1817); *Ladas*, Patents, Trademarks, and Related Rights: National and International Protection (Harvard University Press 1975).

[4] 185 F.3d 1364, 1366-67 (Fed. Cir. 1999).

[5] See: *Bagley*, Patent First, Ask Questions later: Morality and Biotechnology in Patent law, 45 Wm & Mary Law Review, 469, 476–77 (2003) who describes the shift away from the moral utility doctrine following the U.S. Patent Act of 1952; *Bently/Sherman*, Intellectual Property Law (4th edition, Oxford University Press 2014), 245; *Machin*, Prospective Utility: A New Interpretation of the Utility Requirement of Section 101 of the Patent Act, 87 California Law Review 421, 425 (1999); *Machlup*, An Economic Review of the Patent System: Study of the Subcommittee on Patents, Trademarks, and Copyrights of the Committee on the Judiciary (US Government Printing Office 1958).

[6] 15 F Cas. 1018, 1019 (Story, Circuit Justice, C.C.D. Mass. 1817).

[7] 15 F Cas. 1018, 1019 (Story, Circuit Justice, C.C.D. Mass. 1817).

[8] Bedford v. Hunt, 3 F Cas. 37, 37 (Story, Circuit Justice, C.C.D. Mass. 1817).

(...) simply requires, that it shall be capable of use, and that the use is such as sound morals and policy do not discountenance or prohibit."[9]

Not only do these explanations underline the original definition, they also allow for a clear assessment of the fundamental considerations of patent law itself. By requiring the invention to be of "some beneficial use in society", Justice *Story* referred to the main function of patent law as being to ultimately benefit society. He indicated that technological advancement is no end in itself. In the further development of the moral utility doctrine, Justice *Story* laid the framework for using this approach to specifically exclude two types of patent applications: gambling devices "injurious" to the morals of society and inventions with a "mischievous tendency" to deceive the public.

The selection of these specific devices illustrates the content of the moral utility doctrine. An analysis will indicate, how these devices are shaped by the developing and dynamic legal culture of the U.S.

2. Specific Decisions Regarding the Moral Utility Doctrine

Neither of those specific inventions directly relates to modern controversies. It can be noted, however, that the standard of gambling devices and "mischievous tendency" seems rather low, especially, when it comes to a comparison with the German or European Patent law restrictions. These previously mentioned restrictions rely significantly on human dignity or fundamental freedom of constitutional value. Yet, as has been analyzed above, even in German jurisprudence, several different examples of rejected patent applications exist as well. These decisions of patent ineligibility were based on morality or ordre public by applying a set of values that do not directly relate to fundamental freedoms or human dignity specifically.[10]

Therefore, the following section analyzes both specific technologies mentioned by Justice *Story*, in order to gain insights into the moral considerations that have shaped the moral utility doctrine.

a) Gambling Devices

Applying the fundamental remarks of Justice *Story*, the Norther District of Illinois invalidated a patent under the moral utility doctrine. In the decision *National Automatic Device Corp v. Lloyd*[11] a patent was challenged concerning a "Toy Automatic Race-Horse" for exclusive use in gambling establishments. The patent owner applied for an injunction to prevent an infringing use of the patented invention. However, the court refused to grant the injunction based on the explanation that the invention of the

---

[9] Bedford v. Hunt, 3 F Cas. 37, 37 (Story, Circuit Justice, C.C.D. Mass. 1817).
[10] Id.
[11] National Automatic Device Corp. v. Lloyd, 40 F. 89, 90 (C.C.N.D. Ill. 1889).

patent "was not a useful device, within the meaning of the patent law".[12] Furthermore, in 1897, the Court of the Northern District of California decided, in line with the moral utility doctrine, to invalidate patents for a card-playing slot machine[13] and a coin return device for slot machines.[14] A similar fate was meted out to a patent for a lottery vending machine.[15] The reasoning behind these decisions was based on each game's morality which was in turn characterized by the ratio of skill to luck necessary to beat the game. A game of skill was considered to be of moral use for society while a game of chance was immoral. Therefore, inventions of respective gambling devices were excluded from patentability. Exactly what ratio of skill to luck was necessary to distinguish one game type from another was subject to extended legal discussion. The suggested standard ranged from exclusion of patentability where succeeding at the game was a "mere matter of luck"[16] to the validation of a pinball machine because "[the skill in] operating the device was not wholly absent."[17]

aa) Legal Analysis of the Reasoning

Analyzing decisions about gambling devices makes it clear that the standard of the moral utility doctrine was much lower than the German and European equivalents. Gambling was illegal in most states in the U.S. when those decisions were made. It can be assumed that these decisions did not draw a distinction between morality and public order in the sense of the German and European legislation. The lack of a distinction might also support the hypothesis that both terms are very similar and a distinction is not necessary. Yet, the assessment of the devices by the courts was usually limited to their intended use and did not involve a further analysis of commercial exploitation as with the German and European approach. Focusing on the intention of an inventor makes it significantly easier for a court to apply moral considerations to the overall assessment of patentability.

U.S. courts even went so far as to discuss whether the intended place of use for an invention had the potential to render the invention itself immoral. Early decisions excluded gambling devices from patentability, even if they were exclusively used in gambling establishments. In addition, patentability was still denied, even if the devices in question had the potential for innocuous purposes.[18] In contrast, the Seventh Circuit Court later decided that a patent for "a bogus coin detector for coin

---

[12] Id.

[13] Reliance Novelty Co. v. Dworzek, 80 F. 902, 904 (C.C.N.D. Cal. 1897).

[14] Brewer v. Lichtenstein, 278 F. 512, 514 (7th Cir. 1922).

[15] Chicago Patent Corp v. Genco, Inc., 124 F.2d 725, 728 (7th Cir. 1941).

[16] Norther District of Illinois, Meyer v. Buckley Mfg. Co. 15 F. Supp 640, 641 (N.D. Ill. 1936) regarding a game where the objective is to pick up a toy from a case of toys.

[17] Chicago Patent Corp. v. Genco, Inc, 124 F2d 725, 728; *Volokh*, The Mechanisms of the Slippery Slope, 116 Harvard Law Review 1026, 1029 (2003).

[18] In National Automatic Device Corp. v. Lloyd, 40 F. 89, 90 (C.C.N.D. Ill. 1889), the race horse toy patent exclusion was based on its exclusive use in gambling establishments.

operated vending machines" was valid. This validation seemed inconsistent, since the invention was actually only used on gambling devices. The court explained that the invention was "[not] incapable of serving any beneficial end".[19] In 1966, even the Supreme Court of the United States weighted in and specified the standard of the moral utility doctrine. The court sharpened the definition and rebranded it the "specific beneficial utility doctrine."[20] Content-wise, Justice *Fortas* noticed the discrepancies in the previous decisions and explained that an invention was useful under patent laws so long as it had at least one specific utility that benefited the public.[21] The question of moral utility was transformed into a question of whether a "specific benefit exists in currently available form."[22]

Those explanations are of general interest when analyzing the standard of the moral utility doctrine. The flexibility of the dichotomy of "potential beneficial use" to "only actual immoral use" used by the courts eroded the certainty around patentability. However, both standards are much more practical for a court to assess than the German approach of identifying "all potential uses". German courts generally only have the power to invalidate a patent or patent application if not even a single potential use is considered to be compliant with morality or order public. Again, the U.S. approach was more court-friendly by including a much lower standard for defining when potential or actual use is relevant for the overall assessment. In particular, the standard clarified by the U.S. Supreme Court is similar but still more practically relevant. The specific benefit to society had to exist "in currently available form" whereas the standard of German jurisprudence lets a single hypothetical use suffice for the validation of patentability.

To understand the decisions of the courts in deciding that gambling was specifically opposing sound morals and policy, it is necessary to assess the moral opposition to gambling in the United States during those times.

bb) Historic Development of Morality with regard to Gambling Devices

Before the 1920s and 1930s the general acceptance of gambling was so low that it reached near prohibition status. This era marked the time when courts were also invalidating patents for gambling devices.[23] The strong rejection of gambling in society was partly due to high levels of corruption in the gambling business which led almost all states in the U.S. to ban gambling.[24]

---

[19] Fuller v. Berger, 120 F. 274, 276 (7th Circuit 1903).

[20] Benner v. Manson, 383 U.S. 519 (1965) regarding a case unrelated to gambling devices.

[21] Id at 534, 535.

[22] Id at 533, 534–535.

[23] *Muntig*, An Economic and Social History of Gambling in Britain and the USA, 28 (Manchester Univ. Press 1996), 52.

[24] *Rose*, Gambling and the Law: The Third Wave of Legal Gambling, 17 VILL. SPORTS & ENT. L.J. 361, 369–73.

After the definition of the very broad standard of the U.S. Supreme Court regarding patentability, the patent applications for gambling devices were no longer a subject of the decisions. By raising the bar higher, the U.S. Supreme Court decision marked the turning point after which gambling device patents were regularly upheld, as with the slot machine in 1977.[25] This point in time is sometimes interpreted as the moment when court doctrine was changed in the modern era to grant patents on gambling devices.[26] For matters of patentability, it is highly interesting that the courts observed these changes and decided accordingly. In *Fuller v. Berger*, Seventh Circuit Judge *Grosscup* stated that "the national conscience is seen to be outspoken against the practice [of gambling]. Nothing could be conceived more conclusively showing a general conscience, and a general conception of policy."[27]

This observation is highly relevant for the analysis. The explanation by Judge *Grossup* refers to the standard of morality and public policy in patent law. He furthermore describes a method of identifying such a standard. Identifying moral acceptance or opposition within a society is also a subject in the ongoing discussion of German and European Patent law.[28]

After the change in terms of public acceptance of gambling during the Great Depression, the legalization of casino gambling in Nevada in 1931[29] and the creation of state lotteries in 1964,[30] the courts followed suit and stopped invalidating patents for gambling devices.

b) Deceptive Devices or Devices with Mischievous Tendencies

The other major subjects of invalidating patents according to the moral utility doctrine were devices intended to deceive consumers. One of the first cases which noted this tendency was involved the Indiana Supreme Court in 1851. Even though the court lacked the jurisdiction to invalidate the federal patent in question, it cited the original case of *Lowell v. Lewis* in a footnote, stating that a patent for a rake might be invalid.[31] Said rake was advertised to be significantly more efficient than other rakes, even though that was not the case, so the jury found the rake to be a fraudulent sale.[32] In turn, the court made its suggestion that such a product might not be eligible for patent protection under the moral utility doctrine.

---

[25] Ex parte Murphy, 200 U.S.P.Q. (BNA) 801, 803 (B.P.A.I. Apr. 29, 1977).

[26] *Keay*, AIPLA Quaterly Journal, Volume 40, Number 3, 414, re. 28.

[27] 120 F. at 279–80 (Grosscup, J., dissenting).

[28] See above.

[29] *Muntig*, An Economic and Social History of Gambling in Britain and the USA, 28 (Manchester Univ. Press 1996), 52.

[30] Id at 53.

[31] Fowler v. Swift, 3 Ind. 188, 190 n. 1 (1851).

[32] Fowler v. Swift, 3 Ind. 188, 189 n. 1 (1851).

A later decision, which actually invalidated patents or patent applications, concerned a patent for a procedure to make unspotted tobacco plants appear spotted.[33] During the time of the decision, spotted tobacco plants were considered to produce qualitatively superior tobacco compared to unspotted plants. Based on this, the court did not accept the explanations of the plaintiffs that the procedure allegedly also improved the leaf quality of the plants and decided that the patented procedure was intended to deceive the public. The invention was therefore ineligible for patent protection. Another other court case focused on the patentability of so called "Oxydonor" which was a simple electric device, allegedly able to cure all diseases. The patentee claimed all illnesses and diseases were caused by electrical equilibrium disturbances in the body. Addressing the unscientific and unsubstantiated claims, the Eight Circuit Court decided that the patent application for such an ineffective medical device was intended to deceive the public. The court explained that the claims of the patent were at best "an imaginary hypothesis" and a "mere pretense".[34] However, the court also mentioned that the explanations given by the patentee were merely a means to obtain a patent for a simple electric device lacking novelty.[35] The direct application of the moral utility doctrine seemed to be intermixed with the problem of circumventing the requirements of novelty.

aa) Legal Analysis of the Reasoning

Both decisions illustrate clearly that courts originally considered consumer protection of significant value as the basis for a patent exception. With that being said, the focus seems primarily to have been on the intention of the patentee. Giving more relevance to the intention is significantly different to the prior gambling decisions and the general approach in German and European Patent law. In counterdistinction, the latter focus on values and moral standards that might be violated by the commercial exploitation of the patent. In German and European Patent law, the patent is the sole object of assessment. This focus on morality is based on the intended use of the device and the intention of the patentee. It differs from the more refined standard development of gambling jurisprudence which distinguished between the potential applications of an invention and the actual ones.[36] These two cases do not allow for a general standard to be established, especially considering that the first decision was more of an *obiter dictum* than an actual legally binding decision.

In the 1980s, federal courts made it clear that the moral utility doctrine was insignificant in cases where deceptive devices were involved. An invention – which was also the subject of jurisprudence in Germany[37] – for radar detectors made it

---

[33] Rickard v. Du Bon, 103 F. 868, 869 (2nd Cir. 1900).
[34] Mahler v. Animarium Co., 111 F. 530, 535–537 (8th Cir. 1901).
[35] Mahler v. Animarium Co., 111 F. 536 (8th Cir. 1901).
[36] Id.
[37] BGHZ 183, 235, 242.

possible to identify radar speed controls. Therefore, arguably, the device was primarily intended for the evasion of government control. However, the invention was still regarded as useful by the Northern District of Texas.[38] This decision is often cited as part of the "downfall" of the moral utility doctrine regarding deceptive devices. However, the device in question did not deceive its user or the potential buyer. The device also worked as promised. The question of whether devices that are intended to undermine government control or render it inefficient are eligible for patentability is therefore substantially different from the general idea of deception. This shift in judicial reasoning affected the moral utility doctrine in its entirety.

bb) Decline of the Moral Utility Doctrine

The explanations given by these U.S. courts also address the role of legislator and judiciary when it comes to prohibitive measures in the field of technology. The Federal Circuit Court followed these considerations. In *Juicy Whip, Inc. v. Orange Bang, Inc.*,[39] – a case regarding the patentability of a juice dispenser with a fake display reservoir on top to appeal to potential customers and a hidden juice reservoir that contained the actually dispensed juice – the patent was upheld. The court explicitly decided against the general applicability of the moral utility doctrine. It further explained that it was the responsibility of the federal and state legislator to decide on "the health, good order, peace and general welfare of the community" through patent law.[40] It is noteworthy that other cases exist and were only decided a couple of years earlier, which still upheld the doctrine.[41] A lot of scholars involved in the legal discussion identify the end of the moral utility doctrine based on the additional court notes which state that "years ago courts invalidated patents on gambling devices on the ground that they were immoral but that is no longer the law."[42] Stating the discontinuation of the moral utility doctrine explicitly and clearly is rightfully a very convincing argument. It is relevant to observe, however, that the decision made in *Juicy Whip, Inc. v. Orange Bang, Inc.* is still in line with the doctrine itself. The actual case itself offered no prompt for actually addressing the validity of the moral utility doctrine. The device was not inherently deceptive and a potentially moral application was possible. In its decision, the court further explained, that "[it found] no basis in section 101 [of the U.S. patent code] to hold that inventions can be

---

[38] Whistler Corp. v. Autotronics, Inc., 14 U.S.P.Q.2d (BNA) 1885, 1886 (N.D. Tex. July 28, 1988).

[39] 185 F.3d 1364 (Fed. Cir. 1999).

[40] 185 F.3d 1368 (Fed. Cir. 1999) – with reference to Webber v. Virginia, 103 U.S. 344, 347–48 (1880).

[41] Tol-O-Matic, Inc. v. Proma Produkt-Und Marketing Gesellschaft, 945 F.2d 1546, 1552 (Fed. Cir. 1991) (noting that the usefulness requirement "has ... been interpreted to exclude inventions deemed to be immoral"), and Am. Standard. Inc. v. Pfizer Inc. 722 F. Supp. 86, 150 (D. Del. 1989) (noting that to be useful, the patent's "purpose must not be illegal, immoral or contrary to public policy").

[42] Id at 1367.

ruled unpatentable for lack of utility simply because they have the capacity to fool some members of the public."[43] Clearly, a general standard of deception did not exist, since other decisions before used different standards to justify the invalidation of a patent. Therefore, this remark by the Federal District Court did not address the core principle of the moral utility doctrine. The explanation singled out an aspect of morality that was never the basis for an actual decision in the first place.

Additionally, in *Juicy Whip, Inc. v. Orange Bang, Inc.*, the court suggested that the Congressional intent would be a more reliable source of information than the moral utility doctrine.[44] Since the U.S. legislative body had not made any rules regarding the invalidity of gambling devices or deceptive contraptions, such inventions had to be patentable under that approach. Consequently, the moral utility doctrine was pronounced "dead".[45]

In terms of judicial acceptance of an inherent responsibility of the judiciary, that can be considered to be accurate. From a legal point of view, it might be argued that the moral utility doctrine was just modified in terms of its standard of application. In a similar way to the German or European approach, the intention of the legislator and the public acceptance of certain industries and trades are vital and significant aspects that the courts have to factor into their decisions. From a German and European civil law approach it seems that the moral utility doctrine was certainly a step towards establish judicial responsibility and corresponding power when it comes to morality and public policy in patentability. However, the doctrine was not refined enough or sufficiently well-established to be applicable in a general way. Additionally, it lacked abstract standards and certainty with regard to area and scope of application.

After *Juicy Whip, Inc. v. Orange Bang, Inc.* the moral utility doctrine was understandably considered to be dead law.

3. Recent Development and Status Quo

Without the moral utility doctrine, U.S. patent law was rendered a place without moral concerns. However, in the 2002 decision of *Geneva Pharmaceuticals, Inc. v. Glaxosmithkline PLC*, the court stated the general requirements for the utility of a patent "if it will operate to perform the functions and secure the results intended, and its use is not contrary to law, moral principles, or public policy." Either the court decided to re-apply the moral utility doctrine or it cited law that included a passage that was no longer an active requirement for patentability. Yet, the decision did not make use of moral considerations to exclude patentability. The moral character of the invention was not even addressed. Hence, it seems that this quote was simply a

---

[43] 185 F.3d 1351 (Fed. Cir. 1999).

[44] 185 F.3d at 1368.

[45] *Keay*, 418; *Walsh*, Stemming the Tide of Stem Cell Research: The Bush Compromise, 38 John Marshall Law Review 1061, 1065 (2004).

misrepresentation of the law; a potential mistake describing recently outdated patentability requirements.

In a more substantial decision, the absence of morality concerns within the U.S. patent system was supported with the *Diamond v. Chakrabarty* decision from 1980. This decision validated the patentability of a live, human-made organism capable of breaking down multiple components of crude oil.

In other cases from the late 20th century, the main reason given for rejecting the moral utility doctrine is based on the separation of state powers, especially in terms of the shift of responsibility entirely to the legislator, an argument, that is well-known from the German discussion regarding the need to include morality into the patent law system. In the U.S. common law system, the patentability approach changed from the beneficial nature of the patent to a more technical function of patent law.

Another similar argument to the German and European discourse is brought up by *Rosenberg*. He observes that "[w]hat is immoral varies from generation to generation (...) [and] cases denying the protection of the law on the ground of immorality are not of this generation." German scholars tried to solve the problem of the dynamic nature of morality shifts within society by adding a feature of qualification. *Chisum* also argues that morality still has a place in the U.S. patent system as part of a public policy doctrine. He explains that it should be required that a "patent will be withheld only if the invention cannot be used for any honest and moral purpose."

At least until late 2012 the United States Patent and Trademark Office has stated on its website that inventions "offensive to the public morality" cannot receive patent protection.[46] In the recent technological concepts of genetic engineering technology and related scientific advancements, the USPTO and the Supreme Court of the United States have indicated that moral or ethical issues still have to be taken into account when it comes to patentability.[47] The explanations in *Mayo Collaborative Servs v. Prometheus Labs*[48] also indicate that due to recent limitations of the eligible subject matter of the U.S. Patent Code, the U.S. patent law may "not yet be amoral."[49] Numerous authors in the legal debate also argue that morality has a definite place within the assessment of patentability.[50] Other authors oppose such views and state

---

[46] Patents, USPTO, http://www.uspto.gov/inventors/patents/jsp#heading-3; *Keay*, AIPLA Quarterly Journal, Volume 40, Number 3, p. 410, re. 3.

[47] *Keay*, 410.

[48] 132 S. Ct. 1289 (2012).

[49] *Keay*, 411; *Walter*, Beyond the Harvard Mouse: Current Patent Practice and the Necessity of Clear Guidelines in Biotechnology Patent Law, 73 Indiana Law Journal 1025, 1031 (1997); *Warren-Jones*, Vital Parameters for Patent Morality – A Question of Form, 2 Journal of Intellectual Property Law & Practice 832, 841 (2007); *Whitehill*, Patenting Human Embryonic Stem Cells: What is so Immoral? 34 Brooklyn Journal of International Law 1045, 1053 (2008).

[50] *Philips*, Half-Human Creatures, Plants & Indigenous Peoples: Musings on Ramifications of Western Notions of Intellectual Property and the Newman-Rifkin Attempt to Patent a Theoretical Half-Human Creature, 21 Santa Clara Computer & High Tech Law Journal, 383

that according to the "American view" "morality should (...) have nothing to do with patents".[51]

In 2021, the United States Patent and Trademark Office's Manual of Patent Examining Procedure does not include any reference to morality or public policy in its requirements for patentability – unlike the German and European equivalents. Sect. 706 of the Manual even goes so far as to cite *Juicy Whip, Inc. v. Orange Bang, Inc.* and explains: "A rejection under 35 U.S.C. 101 for lack of utility should not be based on grounds that the invention is frivolous, fraudulent or against public policy. See Juicy Whip Inc. v. Orange Bang Inc., 185 F.3d 1364, 1367-68, 51 USPQ2d 1700, 1702-03 (Fed. Cir. 1999)."[52]

Apart from these general and theoretical explanations, the practical application without any concern for morality was significantly challenged with the rise of biotechnology.

II. Rise of Biotechnology and Genetic Engineering

The era of genetic engineering marked a spike in legal and general discussion about morality in patent law, especially in Germany and the European Union. A very similar development took place in the U.S., where the patent law just recently abandoned its regard for morality and ordre public. Genetic research in the U.S. was on the rise with the famous General Electric biologist *Ananda Chakrabarty* producing genetically engineered life forms.[53] Public and scientific acceptance of genetic engineering was high in the U.S., even though in the early beginnings, the focus on medical advancements was addressed by concerns about availability to the public which the concept of patentability generally opposes. This concern about availability

---

(2005); *Dresser*, Ethical and Legal Issues in Patenting New Animal Life, 28 Jurimetrics Journal 399, 410–424 (1988) with a specific focus on moral and ethical challenges in animal patenting; *Fendrick/Zuhn*, Patentability of Stem Cells in the United States, 5:a020958 Cold Spring harb Perspect Med 1 (2015); *Lindvall*, Stem Cell Therapy for Human Neurodegenerative Disorders – How to Make it Work, 10 Nature Medicine 42, 45 (2004); *Mandra/Russo*, Stem Cells and Patenting and Related Regulatory Issues: A United States Perspective, 7 Bio-Science Law Review 143, 150 (2004).

[51] *Enerson*, The Risk of Reviving the Moral Utility Doctrine, 89 Cornell L. Rev. 685 (2004), 12.

[52] Sect. 706.03(a) Rejections Under 35 U.S.C. 101 [R-07.2015], 9th Edition of the Manual of Patent Examining Procedure.

[53] *Chang*, Patent Scope, Antitrust Policy, and Cumulative Innovation, 26 The RAND Journal of Economics 34 (1995), 40; *Kevles*, Ananda Chakrabarty Wins a Patent: Biotechnology, Law, and Society, 25 Hist. Stud. Physical & Biological Scl. 111, 114–116 with one of his most famous creations, a bacterium capable of consuming parts of crude oil; also relevant in that context: *Chapman*, Virgin Birth in a Hammerhead Shark, 3 Biology Letters 425 (2007); *Marshall*, Ethicists back Stem Cell Research, White House Treads Cautiously, 285 Science 502, 510 (1999).

is not linked to general morality considerations, however. Most opposing parties cited the patent approach of several scientists from the University of Toronto. These scientists patented a medically significant process of producing insulin with the sole intention "to prevent the taking out of a patent by other persons", so that "no one could secure a profitable monopoly" from the invention.[54] Over time, these concerns grew stronger, as the U.S. government encouraged cooperation between universities and commercial entities. The intention was to enable universities to profit commercially from their academic research.[55] Universities were further incentivized by the Bayh-Dole Act which motivated them to patent and commercialize results from federally funded research.[56] Such an increase in intertwining of scientific research and commercial exploitation was fueling already existing opposition. However, the opposition was not based on moral considerations of the subject matter. The concerns focused on endangering free scientific research which was regarded as under threat from the abundance of patents in the field of biotechnology.[57]

It can be observed that the concerns about patenting biotechnology in the U.S. differed greatly in comparison to the situation in the European Union and Germany. The scientific community in the U.S. even called for increased regulation, monitoring of industrial ties and research studies. Even other solutions, such as anti-tempering solutions, were proposed to secure the freedom of scientific research, unhindered by an over-thickened patent landscape.[58] After the famous decision of *Diamond v. Chakrabarty*,[59] the United States Patent and Trademark Office even started to grant patents and accepted patent applications related to non-human animal life such as a genetically modified oyster and a transgenic mouse.[60]

---

[54] *Chapman*, The Ethics of Patenting Human Embryonic Stem Cells, 19 Kennedy Institute of Ethics Journal 261 (2009) 266; *Kevles*, Principles, Property Rights, and Profits: Historical Reflections on University/Industry Tensions, 8 Accountability Res. 293, 294 (2001); *Johnson*, Human ES Cells and a Blastocyst from One Embryo: Exciting Science but Conflicting Ethics? 2 Cell Stem Cell 103, 105 (2008).

[55] Most notably the 1980 Tax Reform Act which gave tax benefits to corporations funding academic and scientific research.

[56] *Kevles*, Principles, Property Rights, and Profits: Historical Reflections on University/Industry Tensions, 8 Accountability Res. 301 (2001); *Davis*, Patented Embryonic Stem Cells: The Quintessential "Essential Facility"?, 94 Georgetown Law Journal 205 (2005), 211; *Miller*, The Effect of Federal Funding Restrictions for Embryonic Stem Cell Research on Colleges and Universities: The Need for Caution when Ethical Objections to Research are Raised, 41 Journal of College and University Law 147, 157 (2015).

[57] *Heller/Eisenberg*, Can Patents Deter Innovation? The Anticommons in Biomedical Research, 280 SCIENCE 698, 698 (1998); *Muscati*, "Some More Human than Others": Assessing the Scope of Patentability Related to Human Embryonic Stem Cell Research, Jurimetrics 201, 240 (2004).

[58] *Keay*, 423 with further references.

[59] 447 U.S. 303 (1980) (No. 79–136).

[60] *Kevles*, The Advent of Animal Patents: Innovation and Controversy in the Engineering and Ownership of Life, in Intellectual Property Rights in Animal Breeding and Genetics 17,

1. Jeremy Rifkin as the "Most Hated Man in Science"

The situation began to shift with the movement started by *Jeremy Rifkin*. He headed the opposition against genetic engineering research and transgenic patents. The movement directly addressed moral concerns regarding bio-genetic research and agitated against researchers and research institutions. Books and articles written by him raised moral arguments against biotechnology in general.[61] In the context of the *Chakrabarty* decision, *Rifkin* advised the court to invalidate the patent since it could lead to "significant moral and ethical issues"[62] and ultimately to "the end of human life as we and all other humans know it."[63] Being the most prominent figure to oppose biotechnological engineering made *Rifkin* highly unpopular within the scientific community.[64] Chief Justice *Burger* of the U.S. Supreme Court discredited *Rifkin's* warnings and predictions as "a gruesome parade of horribles".[65] Justice *Burger* explained further that the warnings were irrelevant to the weighting against the potential beneficial outcomes of genetic engineering. He once more emphasized that the proper forum for the weighting process for this complex issue was the legislator and not the judiciary.[66]

These general arguments are, by now, very well known, but mention of the "weighting" process is an interesting area for comparison with German and European law. In these jurisdictions, especially regarding the same subject matter of stem cells, human dignity played the most significant role. Human dignity is also allegedly above the weighting process due to its absolute nature as an absolute value. Com-

---

21–22 (Max Rothschild & Scott Newman eds., 2002); *Mills*, Biotechnological Inventions: Moral Restraints and Patent Law (Revised Edition) (Ashgate Publishing Limited 2010).

[61] *Rifkin*, This is the Age of Biology, Guardian, July 28th, 2001, at 20; Jeremy Rifkin, The Sociology of the Gene, 79 Phi Delta Kappan 648 (1998). In counterdistinction to the German and European discussion, Rifkin used the method of painting grim and dystopian predictions of the future influenced by genetic modifications and the cloning of human beings.

[62] *George*, The Stem Cell Debate: The Legal, Political and Ethical Issues Surrounding Federal Funding of Scientific Research on Human Embryos, 12 Albany Law Journal of Science & Technology 747 (2001), 750; Brief for Peoples Business Commission as Amicus Curiae Supporting Petitioner at 5, Diamond v. Chakrabarty, 447 U.S. 303 (1980) (No. 79–136) at 25; *Gerecht-Nir/Itskovitz-Eldor*, Cell Therapy Using Human Embryonic Stem Cells, 12 Transplant Immunology 203 (2004), 205; *Mireles*, States as Innovation System Laboratories: California, Patents, and Stem Cell Technology, 28 Cardozo Law Review 1133, 1149 (2006).

[63] Brief for Peoples Business Commission as Amicus Curiae Supporting Petitioner at 5, Diamond v. Chakrabarty, 447 U.S. 303 (1980) (No. 79–136) at 31.

[64] Dubbed by the 1987 TIME Magazine "The Most hated Man In Science" and as stated by microbiologist *Newell-McGloughlin:* "Having the endorsement of Jeremy Rifkin means nothing." (Erik Stokstad, A Kinder, Gentler Jeremy Rijkin Endorses Biotech, or Does He?, 312 Science 1586, 1587 (2006).

[65] Chakrabarty, 449 U.S. at 316.

[66] Chakrabarty, 449 U.S. at 317.

paring the two discussions supports the hypothesis that the question of morality in patent law is actually subject to the result of the weighting process.

Most of the genetic engineering patents were considered to be beneficial to human life and society.[67] Consequently, *Rifkin*'s arguments were considered be in opposition to public interest and his crusade against biotechnology titled "romanticism, in its most dangerous anti-intellectual form, [without] respect for knowledge and its humane employment."[68] However, bringing ethical and moral considerations into the patent law system had significant impact regarding human-animal chimeras and Myriad Genetics' BRCA breast cancer gene patents.

2. Re-Introducing Morality Concerns into U.S. Patent Law

Trying to bring moral considerations back into the discussion about patentability, *Rifkin* himself tried to file a patent with human-animal chimera as the subject matter. This patent challenged the subject matter doctrine which was defined in *Chakrabarty* as very broad. According to the *Chakrabarty* decision, patentability was to "include anything under the sun that is made by man."[69] The subject matter doctrine was later reiterated in *Bilski v. Kappos* and further explained that "Congress plainly contemplated that the patent laws would be given wide scope."[70] Only discoveries of natural phenomena are considered to be subject to implicit exception of patentability and therefore not patentable.[71]

In the attempt to reignite debate about morality in patent law, *Rifkin* – with the support of biology professor *Stuart Newman* – filed a patent application for human-animal chimeras that could be up to fifty percent human. Additionally, they intended to exercise their own pure understanding of scientific advancement by using the patent to prevent others from commercially exploiting human-animal chimeras.[72] To

---

[67] Brief for Peoples Business Commission as Amicus Curiae Supporting Petitioner at 5, Diamond v. Chakrabarty, 447 U.S. 303 (1980) (No. 79–136).

[68] *Gould*, On the Origin of Specious Critics, Discover, Jan. 1985, at 34.

[69] Chakrabarty, 447 U.S. at 309.

[70] Bilski v. Kappos, 130 S. Ct. 3218, 3225 (quoting Chakrabarty, 447 U.S. at 308) (referring to business methods and their patentability).

[71] Prometheus, 132 S. Ct. at 1293 (2012) (citing Diamond v. Diehr, 450 U.S. 175, 185 (1981); Bilski, 130 S. Ct. at 3233-34; Chakrabarty, 447 U.S. at 309; O'Reilly v. Morse, 15 How. 62, 112-20 (1854); Le Roy v. Tatham, 14 How. 156, 175 (1853); *Gerecht-Nir/Itskovitz-Eldor*, The Promise of Human Embryonic Stem Cells, 18 Best Practice & Research Clinical Obstetrics & Gynaecology 843 (2004), 850; *McCoy*, Biotechnology and Embryonic Stem Cells: A Comparative Analysis of the Laws and Politics of the United States and Other Nations, 8 Loyola Law and Technology Annual 63, 86 (2008); *Menell*, Forty Years of Wandering in the Wilderness and No Closer to the Promised Land: Bilski's Superficial Textualism and the Missed Opportunity to Return Patent Law to Its Technology Mooring, 63 Stanford Law Review 1289 (2011).

[72] *Dickson*, Legal Fight Looms over Patent Bid on Human/Animal Chimaeras, 392 Nature 423 (1998).

create a more emotional impact and significant effect, *Rifkin* and *Newman* addressed the fear of human-animal chimera research in the sense that such a patent would come dangerously close to granting property rights over human beings, similar to slavery.[73] The approach was highly effective, triggering scientific articles regarding the application and even a statement by a media advisory of the United States Patent and Trademark Office. The media advisory explained that the intended application regarding human-animal chimeras might not be eligible for patentability. Surprisingly, the restriction was based on the "public policy and morality aspects of the utility requirement"[74] directly quoting *Lowell v. Lewis* and the moral utility doctrine – a legal argument from almost two centuries ago that was supposedly no longer good law.[75] A more media-effective statement was issued by the United States Patent and Trademark Commissioner *Bruce Lehman* who said that "there [would] be no patents on monsters."[76]

Consequently, the patent application of *Rifkin* and *Newman* was rejected by the USPTO. The decision was not based on moral utility in any form, though. Instead, the USPTO noted that the broad scope of patentable subject matter laid down in *Chakrabarty* included three limits – laws of nature, physical phenomena and abstract ideas. It further acknowledged that the patent application of a human-animal chimera did not fit directly into any of the three exceptions for patentability. However, the USPTO decided it was part of another category of subject matter which was not intended to be profiting from patent protection according to the legislator.[77] Further attempts by *Rifkin* to obtain the patent remained unsuccessful.[78]

Ultimately, the United States Trademark and Patent Office circumvented the reintroduction of the moral utility doctrine by interpreting the patentable subject matter doctrine in a different way. The interpretation relied on the intention of the federal legislator, even though no remark on the matter was actually ever made by the legislator itself. Arguing that such subject matter was considered to be ineligible for patentability based on the legislative intent is strikingly similar to the German and European approach of legal order or ordre public, which in itself also represents one

---

[73] *Magnani*, The Patentability of Human-Animal Chimeras, 14 Berkeley Tech. L.J. 443, 444 (1999).

[74] Media Advisory 98–6: Facts on Patenting Life Forms Having a Relationship to Humans, USPTO (Apr. 1, 1998), https://www.uspto.gov/about-us/news-updates/facts-patenting-life-forms-having-relationship-humans.

[75] Id.

[76] "Morality" Aspect of Utility Requirement Can Bar Patent for Part-Human Inventions, 55 Patent, Trademark and Copyright Journal, (BNA) 555, 556 (Apr. 9, 1998).

[77] Patent Application is Disallowed as "Embracing" Human Being, 58 Patent; Trademark and Copyright Journal, (BNA) 203, 203 (June 17, 1999).

[78] U.S. Patent Application No. 8,993,564 (Final Office Action Aug. 11, 2004) and U.S. Patent Application No. 8,993,564 (Notice of Abandonment Mar. 2, 2005), *Warnock*, Report of the Committee of Inquiry into Human Fertilization and Embryology (HM Stationary Office 1984).

facet of moral considerations. The solution by the USPTO was criticized for being legally imprecise. However, there were several interests that had to be considered. The USPTO wanted to reject the application. It did not want to re-introduce the morality utility doctrine to uphold the consistency of jurisprudence. Finally, it intended to explain that moral considerations are entirely up to the patent legislator. Achieving all these goals was impossible without bending the existing legal standards.

Even though Rifkin did not succeed with his patent application, he would have another shot at challenging the U.S. patent system.

3. Myriad Breast Cancer Genes Patent Case

In the mid-90s, the company Myriad Genetics applied for numerous patents involving BRCA1 and BRCA2 DNA which were genetic markers indicating hereditary breast cancer. Those patents were granted by the United States Patent and Trademark Office[79] and used by Myriad Genetics in patent litigation against diagnostic laboratories and universities.[80] This behavior led to Myriad Genetics having monopoly status for providing the genetic breast cancer test and this monopoly made it impossible for patients to get a second medical opinion from other laboratories.[81]

Once the development had come to *Rifkin*'s attention, he again decided to campaign against the patent applications by arguing that the patent would obstruct medical research and prevent women from being able to obtain adequate and affordable testing.[82] This time, his objections did not directly relate to the subject matter of the patent but rather the effects of patenting. The German and European patentability restrictions also assess the commercial exploitation of a patent and its potential violation of ordre public. Similarly, *Rifkin*'s arguments focused on the consequences for the specific market that the patents would affect.

---

[79] Ass'n for Molecular Pathology v. USPTO, 653 F.3d 1329, 1339 (Fed. Cir. 2011).

[80] Myriad Genetics v. Oncomed, Nos. 2:97-cv-922, 2:98-cv-35 (D. Utah 1998) and Myriad Genetics v. Univ. of Pa., No. 2:98-cv-829 (D. Utah 1998); *Hoffman*, Modest Proposal: Toward Improved Access to Biotechnology Research Tools by Implementing a Broad Experimental Use Exception, 89 Cornell Law Review 993 (2003).

[81] *Pins*, Impeding Access to Quality Patient Care and Patient Rights: How Myriad Genetics' Gene Patents Are Unknowingly Killing Cancer Patients and How to Calm the Ripple Effect, 17 Journal for Intellectual Property. 377, 379–380 (2010); *Hoxha*, Stemming the Tide: Stem Cell Innovation in the Myriad-Mayo-Roslin Era, 30 Berkeley Technology Law Journal 567, 588 (2015); *Landry/Zucker*, Embryonic Death and the Creation of Human Embryonic Stem Cells, 114 Journal of Clinical Investigation 1184, 1199 (2004); *Mitalipova*, Human Embryonic Stem Cell Lines Derived from Discarded Embryos, 21 Stem Cells 521 (2003).

[82] *Radick*, Discovering and Patenting Human Genes, in Body Lore and Laws 63, 74 (Andrew Bainham et al. eds, 2002); *Abeleen*, 7 William & Mary Business Law Review 855 (2016); *Lemley*, Life After Bilski, 63 Stanford Law Review 1315, 1320 (2011); *Murray*, The Stem-cell Market – Patents and the Pursuit of Scientific Progress, 356 New England Journal of Medicine 2341, 2350 (2007).

Gathering a group of women's rights advocates, healthcare professionals and affected women, *Rifkin* filed a law suit against Myriad Genetics, co-owners of the patent from the University of Utah Research Foundation and the United States Patent and Trademark Office.[83] The law suit was mainly based on the argument that the patent impeded breast cancer research.[84] It went further by explaining that it felt like a moral obligation to provide women with access to testing and results, therefore a patent which would establish a monopoly was obstructing healthcare professionals from acting according to a moral obligation.[85] In the German and European context, numerous methods exist to protect research and development environments as well as privileges for the healthcare sector.[86] Another balance to significant processes and technologies can be found in the FRAND licensing scheme which forces patent holders to grant licenses given a specific set of substantial requirements.[87]

Overall, the reasoning of the plaintiff group explained that the gene patents were slowing down the discovery, development, and dissemination of knowledge for patients seeking preventive breast cancer care.[88] As it turned out, those arguments convinced the district court, and all of Myriad's patents for the specific DNA and the diagnostic and research methods were invalidated. Legally, the decision was based on the patent subject matter doctrine and it was found that those specific patent claims did not meet the requirements of said doctrine laid out in 35 U.S.C. § 101.[89] The court even acknowledged the moral implications for the healthcare sector and society overall by explaining that the questions on how to "best harness [...] [this genetic information] for greater goods presents difficult questions touching upon innovation policy, social policy, medical ethics, economic policy, and the ownership of what some view as our common heritage."[90] Deciding such policy implications, however, was considered to be too complex for a single judgment and it was stated that "the resolution of these disputes of fact and policy are not possible within the context of these motions".[91]

---

[83] Complaint at 3-13, Ass'n for Molecular Pathology v. USPTO, 669 F. Supp. 2d 365 (S.D.N.Y. 2009) (No. 09 Civ. 4515).

[84] Brought forth by the Association for Molecular Pathology.

[85] 10 Complaint at 3-13, Ass'n for Molecular Pathology v. USPTO, 669 F. Supp. 2d 365 (S.D.N.Y. 2009) (No. 09 Civ. 4515), 28–29.

[86] Sect. 11 No. 2 PatG which allows research and testing of an invention.

[87] A license with fair, reasonable, and non-discriminatory terms (FRAND).

[88] Complaint at 3-13, Ass'n for Molecular Pathology v. USPTO, 669 F. Supp. 2d 365 (S.D.N.Y. 2009) (No. 09 Civ. 4515), 3–4; *Riley/Merrill*, Regulating Reproductive Genetics: A Review of American Bioethics Commissions and Comparison to the British Human Fertilisation and Embryology Authority, 6 Columbia Science & Technology Law Review 1, 17 (2005).

[89] Ass'n for Molecular Pathology, 702 F. Supp. 2d at 238.

[90] Id at 193.

[91] Id at 211.

This explanation is directly in line with the well-known argument of the separation of state powers and the responsibilities of regulation, but it is still noteworthy that the court decided in favor of the plaintiffs organized by *Rifkin*.[92]

In 2011, the Court of Appeals for the Federal Circuit affirmed most of the decision by the district court. The focus on the patentable subject matter doctrine became more apparent, since the circuit court stated that the claims made by Myriad Genetics were abstract. The mental steps involved in the invention did not constitute eligible subject matter for patent protection.[93] Only the patents on the isolated DNA molecules were upheld, since "the molecules as claimed do not exist in nature".[94] By addressing the status of naturally occurring vs. artificial, the circuit court focused more narrowly on the aspects of patent subject matter doctrine. The court was careful to avoid considerations regarding morality or public policy. Judge *Moore* mentioned those aspects briefly by pointing out that the patents "raise substantial moral and ethical issues related to awarding a property right to isolated portions of human DNA – the very thing that makes U.S. human, and not chimpanzees."[95] She also addressed the effect of the patent on the healthcare and research environment. Based on this effect, she noted that voiding the patents would be likely to be more harmful to the advancement of science than upholding the patents.[96] Ultimately, she also expressed the notion that the dispute was a matter of legislation and not relevant to the judiciary.[97]

In contrast, Judge *Bryson* stated his concerns about the morally questionable consequences in a dissenting opinion: "In my view, [the] claims are not directed to patentable subject matter, and if sustained the court's decision will likely have broad consequences, such as preempting methods for whole-genome sequencing, even though Myriad's contribution to the field is not remotely consonant with such effects."[98] Still, the moral aspects of the patent claims did not form the main focus of his opinion. He instead followed the *Chakrabarty* decision and the particular exception from patentability for products of nature.

Yet, the decision was not final and was referred to the United States Supreme Court, which granted *certiorari* and made additional statements expanding the natural law exception to patent subject matter doctrine. The Supreme Court referenced *Mayo Collaborative Servs. v. Prometheus Labs* and explained that expansions

---

[92] *Oppenheimer*, Patents 101: Patentable Subject Matter and Separation of Powers, 15 Vanderbilt Journal of Entertainment & Technology Law 1, 14 (2012).

[93] Ass'n for Molecular Pathology v. USPTO, 653 F.3d 1329, 1334 (Fed. Cir. 2011), vacated sub nom. Ass'n for Molecular Pathology v. Myriad Genetics, 132 S. Ct. 1794 (2012).

[94] Id.

[95] Ass'n for Molecular Pathology v. USPTO, 653 F.3d 1329, 1334 (Fed. Cir. 2011), 1371.

[96] Id. ("Unsettling the expectations of the biotechnology industry now, based on nothing more than unsupported supposition, strikes me as far more likely to impede the progress of science and useful arts than advance it.")

[97] Id at 1373.

[98] Id at 1373 (Bryson, J., concurring in part and dissenting in part).

of the natural law exception to patent subject matter doctrine have to be undertaken by means of public policy.[99] It was stated that inventions which have the effect, impermissibly, of inhibiting research of natural laws should not be patented. Interestingly, Justice *Breyer* applied this exception to a process that was technically non-natural and therefore not covered by the proper meaning of the doctrine. He explained that the court could not "uphold (...) patents that claim processes that too broadly preempt the use of a natural law."[100] Furthermore, this principle includes patent applications that "disproportionately [tie] up the use of the underlying natural laws, inhibiting their use in the making of further discoveries".[101]

The given explanations and adjustments of the patent subject matter doctrine do not expressly include moral considerations or expressly mention public policy. Yet, they include aspects of policy in a requirement of patentability that, originally, was only intended as a technical requirement to determine the differences between discoveries and inventions. The inclusion of such aspects indicates – albeit only to the slightest degree – that the patent system of the United States is considered by the jurisprudence to lack a specific characteristic in the legislation to address certain considerations of public policy. Such an element seems to be necessary to ensure that an invention is at least potentially beneficial to society.

In its decision on remand, the Federal Circuit court came to the same legal conclusions and even repeated the statements regarding moral and ethical issues.[102] In addition, the need to acknowledge the separate powers and responsibilities of the legislative and judicial branch were restated, as well as the dissenting opinion by Justice *Bryson*.[103]

The most significant result of the whole set of decisions in the *Myriad Breast Cancer Gene* case is the establishment of the expansion of the law of nature doctrine. Accordingly, isolated genes that are not found in nature would still likely be ineligible for patent protection under the product of nature exception as per Sect. 101 because the patents "impermissibly tie up research on fundamental genetic information". The importance of this specific exception is the fact that impeding research on fundamental genetic information is considered to be an unintended effect of the patent

---

[99] Ass'n for Molecular Pathology v. Myriad Genetics, 132 S. Ct. 1794 (2012) (mem.), vacating 653 F.3d 1329 (Fed. Cir. 2011).

[100] Mayo Collaborative Servs. v. Prometheus Labs., 132 S. Ct. 1289 (2012) (citing O'Reilly v. Morse, 15 How. 62, 112-20 (1854); Gottschalk v. Benson, 409 U.S. 63, 71-72 (1972)).

[101] Mayo Collaborative Servs. v. Prometheus Labs., 132 S. Ct. 1294 (2012).

[102] Ass'n for Molecular Pathology v. Myriad Genetics, No. 2010-1406 (Fed. Cir. Aug. 16, 2012) with Justice Moore concurring in part at 81; *Burk/Lemley*, Biotechnology's Uncertainty Principle, 54 Case Western Reserve Law Review 691 (2003), 699; *Levine*, Federal Funding and the Regulation of Embryonic Stem Cell Research: The Pontius Pilate Maneuver, 9 Yale Journal of Health Policy, Law, and Ethics 552, 555 (2009).

[103] Ass'n for Molecular Pathology v. Myriad Genetics, No. 2010-1406 (Fed. Cir. Aug. 16, 2012) with Justice Moore concurring in part at 81 and Justice Bryson concurring in part and dissenting in part at 87.

legislation. It means that the court decided the outcome based on considerations of the benefit of genetic research for society as a whole.

4. Ultimate Place of Morality within the Patent Subject Matter Doctrine?

It can be determined that the U.S. has not explicitly incorporated morality concerns into the requirements for patentability. However, it is sometimes argued that the incorporation of public policy aspects into patent subject matter doctrine represents a similar approach to that in the European or German models of patentability exclusions.[104] Technically, that is incorrect, since the European and German models include independent and separate sections relating to morality and ordre public considerations. It is true that a patent application violating that requirement is ineligible for patent protection and therefore not included in the patent subject matter. However, the European and German patent legislation also includes separate sections specifically about the subject matter and refers to the same natural occurrences vs. artificial inventions dispute.[105]

Secondly, the European and German sections on patentability exceptions based on moral or legal order are not applicable to the patent subject directly, but require a violation of the commercial exploitation of the patent.[106] This requirement is sometimes overlooked in the legal discussion, but it is still necessary to account for the commercial value and relevance of the patent itself. The approach of U.S. patent

---

[104] *Dondorp/Wert*, Embryonic Stem Cells Without Moral Pain (Health Council of the Netherlands 2005) 12; *Keay*, 438; with further and more philosophical concerns: *Burns*, Happiness and Utility: Jeremy Bentham's Equation, 17 Utilitas 46 (2005), 50 et seq.; *Merges*, Intellectual Property in the New Technological Age (Wolters Kluwer Law & Business 2007); *Mueller*, Patenting Human Embryonic Stem Cells in the United States: The Legal and Ethical Debate, 14 CASRIP Newsletter 1 (2007).

[105] Sect. 2 (2) PatG; *Crowne*, The Utilitarian Fruits Approach to Justifying Patentable Subject Matter, 10 John Marshall Review of Intellectual Property Law 753 (2011), 756; *Olson*, Taking the Utilitarian Basis for Patent Law Seriously: The Case for Restricting Patentable Subject Matter, 82 Temple Law Review 1 (2009).

[106] Sect. 2 (2) PatG, except for the Sect. (3), et seq. where it is simply the subject matter; *David*, The Role of Intellectual Property Rights in Biotechnology Innovation (Edward Elgar 2009); with more general considerations: Caulfield, Biotechnology Patents, Public Trust and Patent Pools: the Need for Governance? in: The Role of Intellectual Property Rights in Biotechnology Innovation (David Castle ed., Edward Elgar 2009); *Devolder/Ward*, Rescuing Human Embryonic Stem Cell Research: the Possibility of Embryo Reconstitution After Stem Cell Derivation, 38 Metaphilosophy 245 (2007), 250; in general: *Knoppers*, Commercialization of Genetic Research and Public Policy, 286 Science 2277, 2287 (1999); *Schlechter*, Promoting Human Embryonic Stem Cell Research: A Comparison of Policies in the United States and the United Kingdom and Factors Encouraging Advancement, 45 Texas International Law Journal 603, 642 (2009); *Snead*, The Pedagogical Significance of the Bush Stem Cell Policy: A Window into Bioethical Regulation in the United States, 5 Yale Journal of Health Policy, Law, and Ethics 491, 501 (2005); *Snow*, Stem Cell Research: New Frontiers in Science and Ethics (University of Notre Dame Press 2003).

jurisprudence to include policy consideration into the natural law doctrine has a very narrow scope of application and has only been somewhat effective in the field of biotechnology.

This argument of public policy is not the result of a precise and straightforward legal argument, since the application of the "product of nature exception" to non-natural processes is incongruent. Additionally, it is arguably not intended for inclusion in the exception, since the exception functions as a barrier to address the issue of discovery vs. invention. An immoral invention is still an invention, and attempts to address the moral consideration with the natural vs. non-natural approach are ill-advised. Modifying the scope of application requires a legal stretch in reasoning which could even go too far for other immoral inventions that have no connection to natural phenomena whatsoever.

The base-line aim of the Federal Circuit Court was to prevent the "impermissibl[e] tie-up [on] research on fundamental genetic information". Patents primarily have an exclusionary effect on research or the commercial exploitation thereof. Thinking in line with that argument would mean that other patents might also impermissibly tie up relevant research with benefits for society and the product of nature exception might not be applicable. Apart from that, other inventions also involve morality concerns but cannot be discussed under the specific product of nature exception.

The decision of the Federal Circuit Court was so significant that it even affected the jurisprudence of the Canadian Supreme Court.

5. Influence on Canadian Jurisprudence

In 2002, the Supreme Court of Canada followed the U.S. approach not in terms of legal method but in material content. It was decided that the Canadian patent law system exempts patents for higher life forms such as mice from patent protection.[107] Even though the group of plaintiffs in the case were morally motivated and warned about ethical threats, the court stated: "The sole question in this appeal is whether the words 'manufacture' and 'composition of matter', within the context of the Patent Act, are sufficiently broad to include higher life forms."[108] Direct concerns about moral considerations or public policy were not the focus of the decision, but rather, it was based on the interpretation of the sections of the Patent Act relating to patentable subject matter.

The court expressly stated that "it is irrelevant whether this Court believes that higher life forms such as the onco-mouse ought to be patentable."[109] In line with the U.S. approach, the Canadian court sought the intention of the legislator and explained that "it is possible that Parliament did not intend to include higher life forms

---

[107] Harvard Coll. v. Canada, [2002] 4 S.C.R. 45, 53 (Can.).
[108] Id.
[109] Id.

in the definition of 'invention'".[110] Once again, a judicial branch rejected responsibility and referred to the legislator.[111] Furthermore, the court addressed its own lack of competence to decide fundamentally complex issues in an abstract fashion;[112] it explained: "Neither the Commissioner of Patents nor the courts have the authority to declare a moratorium on 'higher' life patents until Parliament chooses to act."[113] Highly interesting to the present analysis is the understanding of the court regarding the issue at hand, revealing that patent protection is considered a balance of "competing social interests" and therefore not an absolute.[114]

Additionally, the court interprets the Canadian Patent Act in such a way that the fundamental intention of promoting ingenuity can at times be "balanced against other considerations."[115] Apart from the general considerations and intentions of the Canadian Patent Act, the court focused on the wording of the legislation. It tried to find a "line" which separates life forms eligible for patent protection and others that are ineligible for patent protection. The difficulty of this and possibly arbitrary approach was directly addressed by the court which stated that "if the line between lower and higher life forms is indefensible and arbitrary, so too is the line between human beings and other higher life forms."

This distinction points to the deeper issue of valuing human and animal life and its moral and ethical implications. By addressing the "common sense differences" between lower and higher life forms, the court explained that it is easier "to analogize a micro-organism to a chemical compound or another inanimate object than it is to analogize an animal to an inanimate object."[116] Even the dissenting opinions still agreed on the limited competence and authority of the court, with Judge *Binnie J.*

---

[110] Harvard Coll. v. Canada, [2002] 4 S.C.R. 45, 53 (Can.).

[111] Id. "While some policy concerns, such as the environmental and animal welfare implications of biotechnology, are more appropriately dealt with outside the patent system, other concerns are more directly related to patentability and to the Scheme of the [Canadian Patent] Act." and E. "The balance between other [the objective of the Canadian Patent Act to encourage human inventiveness] competing policy considerations is for Parliament to strike."

[112] Id. "It is not an appropriate judicial function of the courts to create an exception from patentability for human life given that such an exception requires one to consider both what is human and which aspects of human life should be excluded. (...) This Court does not possess the institutional competence to deal with issues of this complexity, which presumably will require Parliament to engage in public debate, a balancing of competing social interests and intricate legislative drafting."

[113] Harvard Coll. v. Canada, [2002] 4 S.C.R. 45, 53 (Can.) F. The Court's Moratorium.

[114] Id. and in general regarding the issue: *Dutfield*, Intellectual Property Rights and the Life Science Industries: Past, Present and Future (World Scientific 2nd ed. 2009), 15.

[115] Harvard Coll. v. Canada, [2002] 4 S.C.R. 45, 53 (Can.). B. 3, The Object of the Act.

[116] Harvard Coll. v. Canada, [2002] 4 S.C.R. 45, 53 (Can.). C. (with McLachlin C.J. and Major, Binnie and Arbour JJ. (dissenting): The oncomouse is patentable subject matter. The extraordinary scientific achievement of altering every single cell in the body of an animal which does not in this altered form exist in nature, by human modification of the genetic material of which it is composed, is an inventive "composition of matter" within the meaning of S. 2 of the [Canadian] Patent Act).

II. Rise of Biotechnology and Genetic Engineering 169

explaining: "The legal issue is a narrow one and does not provide a proper platform on which to engage in a debate over animal rights, or religion, or the arrogance of the human race."[117] The list of potential moral implications and issues revolving around the field of biotechnology are very similar to the considerations in the German and European discussion of the *Brüstle* case.[118]

In the dissenting opinion of *Binnie J.* it is expressed that the actual question of the interpretation of the statute is whether the past legislator intended to protect such inventions that were not anticipated at the time of the enactment of the original patent legislation or at any time before the specific invention was brought forth.[119] He supports the interpretation of the Canadian Patent Act and points out that the Commissioner of Patents was given no discretion to refuse a patent on the grounds of morality, public interest, public order or any other ground if the statutory criteria are met.[120] However, it seems that Judge *Binnie J.* is not entirely convinced that the court should not ideally have some sort of competence or authority in that regard. The issue of whether a granted patent represents government approval of the invention, as has been discussed already, is addressed in the dissenting opinion as well and directly rejected: "In 1993, it [the Canadian Parliament] repealed the prohibition (…) against patenting an 'invention that has an illicit object in view.' It thereby made it clear that granting a patent is not an expression of approval or disapproval. (…) Parliament thereby signalled *(sic)*, however passively, that these important aspects of public policy would continue to be dealt with by regulatory regimes out the [Canadian] Patent Act."[121]

Overall, the Canadian Supreme Court and the dissenting opinions addressed the central issues of morality in patent law. Some of the findings are supportive of the solution presented solution for the overall question of inclusion of morality into patent law, especially the distinction between regulation and patentability.[122] Hence, the Canadian approach is very similar to U.S. patent jurisprudence. The other side of the coin is also stated in the dissenting opinion: "This [commercial value of biotechnology in a global perspective] is not to suggest that because something is beneficial it is necessarily patentable."[123] However, the decision simultaneously emphasizes the importance of incentivizing biotechnological research via patent

---

[117] Harvard Coll. v. Canada, [2002] 4 S.C.R. 45, 53 (Can.) dissenting 1.

[118] Id.

[119] Id at 10. Dissenting.

[120] Id at 11. Dissenting.

[121] Id at 14. Dissenting.

[122] Id at 15 Dissenting. (Discussing Bill C-13 which prohibits the cloning of human beings, modifying the gene line identity of human beings and the use of human embryos for industrial or commercial purposes: "At the same time, Bill C-13 would not prevent inventions in that regard being patented in Canada. This illustrates, again, the fundamental distinction made by Parliament between patentability of an invention and regulation of activity associated with an invention.").

[123] Harvard Coll. v. Canada, [2002] 4 S.C.R. 45, 53 (Can.) 18. Dissenting.

protection as pointed out by Professor *Gold* of McGill University.[124] Otherwise, the very beneficial results for society are not incentivized through investment and research.[125]

In conclusion, the legal reasoning of the Canadian court focused mainly on the distinction of discovery vs. invention or natural vs. artificial matter compositions. Legally speaking, the decision is based on the court's understanding of patentability based on statute interpretation and therefore somewhat similar to the approach of U.S. patent law jurisprudence. Content-wise, it goes much further than the U.S. decisions, especially *Ex Parte Allen*, which found a patent of a transgenic animal to be eligible for patent protection.[126]

In addition, the United States Patent and Trademark Office approved the patent application concerning the Harvard OncoMouse.[127]

III. The Role of Human Dignity in the U.S. Patent System

The previous analysis of German and European jurisprudence indicated the significant influence of human dignity in assessing morality. In particular, the German legal system has a very unique and specific understanding of human dignity. Most notably it is considered to be an absolute value that cannot, under any circumstances, be infringed upon. Since the U.S. in its current form is a much older legal system than that in Germany or any European community, it is interesting to see how its development has been influenced by the introduction of human dignity as a legal concept.

1. Historical Development within the U.S. Legal System

In national constitutions the term "dignity" was first included in the 1930s and after World War II.[128] Italy was the first country to substantiate the term "dignity" in

---

[124] *Gold*, Biomedical Patents and Ethics: A Canadian Solution (2000), 45 McGill L.J. 413, at p. 423.

[125] "It is necessary to feed the goose if it is to continue to lay golden eggs." Harvard Coll. v. Canada, [2002] 4 S.C.R. 45, 53 (Can.) 25. Dissenting; similarly: *Moses*, Understanding Legal Responses to Technological Change: The Example of In Vitro Fertilization, 6 Minnesota Journal of Law Science & Technology 505 (2004); *Moufang*, Patenting of Human Genes, Cells and Parts of the Body? – The Ethical Dimensions of Patent Law, 25 International Review of Industrial Property and Copyright law 487, 499 (1994).

[126] See Ex Parte Allen, 2 U.S.P.Q.2d (BNA) 1425, 1426-27 (B.P.A.I. April 3, 1987).

[127] U.S. Patent No. 4,736,866 (filed June 22, 1984); *Papastefanou*, GRUR Junge Wissenschaft 2018, 120.

[128] 1937 in Art. 6 Nr. 3 of the Portuguese Constitution and in the preamble of the Irish Constitution in 1937.

the Italian Constitution by setting it as a limitation of commercial initiative in 1947.[129] Germany followed suit by not only including human dignity in its constitution but also giving it a central role in restricting state power. The term was also symbolically positioned at the very beginning of the Constitution and the following fundamental rights catalogue.[130] In a second wave, after 1975, human dignity also became a central part of other European constitutions. These constitutions either included the term as the basis of the political order[131] or in a similar way to the German constitutional structure – positioned human dignity prestigiously at the beginning of a fundamental rights catalogue.[132]

International treaties and declarations first included the term dignity in the 1945 Charter of the United Nations. The Charter mentioned the term in the preamble in of the phrase "the dignity and worth of the human person".[133] The term is also repeated in the Universal Declaration of Human Rights, both in the preamble and further established in Art. 1 which states that "All human beings are born free and equal in dignity and rights." Art. 22 of the Declaration relates "the organization and resources of each State, of the economic, social and cultural rights" to the existence of dignity for each person. The statute of UNESCO and the international treaties of 1966[134] also grant a relevant role to the dignity of human persons.

Finally, as mentioned above, the most important and most relevant convention with regard to human dignity in the European scope is the European Convention on Human Rights from 1950.[135]

a) Historical Background of the Introduction of Human Dignity

Centering the German Constitution around the concept of human dignity and its restrictive effect on state power came about as a result of the horrific experiences of the national socialist dictatorship.[136] Some of the constitutions of German federal states even included the concept of human dignity after the end of World War II.[137] Bavaria's Constitution from 1946 was the first to include the function of human dignity as a restriction for state actions and state power.[138]

---

[129] *Appel*, 107.

[130] Art. 1 Sect. 1 GG – German Constitution.

[131] Sweden, Cap. 1 § 2 Sub. 1, Portugal, Art. 1, Spain, Art. 10 I.

[132] Greece, Art. 2; Switzerland, Art. 8.

[133] UN Charter preamble.

[134] BGBl. 1973 II 1534, 1570.

[135] Even though it technically mentions human dignity only once in the preamble to the Protocol No. 13 to the Convention, it is still highly relevant to decisions focusing on human dignity.

[136] *Appel*, 108.

[137] See *Appel* 108, fn. 66.

[138] Art. 100 of the Bavarian Constitution from 1946.

In the jurisprudence of the Federal Constitutional Court of Germany, human dignity has been recognized as the highest value protected by the constitution.[139] Since the following fundamental rights are considered to be derived from the value catalogue of human dignity, the value of human dignity itself is usually not the subject of court decisions but rather the specific fundamental right. Yet, given that human dignity may not be subject to state interference or restrictions, it functions as the most powerful and last resort of protection against state intervention and is therefore also called "the constitutional emergency brake" for protecting legal interests.[140] Simultaneously, human dignity is not easily and readily applied to situations that appear to have extensive emotional implications, such as the abuse of technology.[141]

The consideration of human dignity is entirely different in the U.S. legal system. While it is recognized as an aspect of the value of human life, it is generally categorized as legally indescribable. The U.S. Constitution does not specifically include the term human dignity, even though the Bill of Rights is similar to the constitutional fundamental freedoms of European constitutions. Whether some of the personal liberties granted in the U.S. Constitution and its Amendments are also facets of human dignity will be the subject of the following analysis.

b) Legal Assessment of Human Dignity within the U.S.

The President's Council on Bioethics tried to identify consensus around the term human dignity in 2008 but ultimately failed.[142] It was stated in the Letter of Transmittal by the Council's Chairman that "…there is no universal agreement on the meaning of the term, human dignity".[143] It seems that human dignity has no independent role in the U.S. legal system, even though the U.S. also acknowledged and voted in favor of the Universal Declaration of Human Rights. Legal research in the U.S. claims that human dignity as a basis for international law is a natural law approach, which depends upon exercises of faith.[144] Furthermore, the research states: "The abiding difficulty with the natural law approach is that its assumptions, intellectual procedures, and modalities of justification can be employed equally by the proponents of human dignity and the proponents of human indignity in support of diametrically opposed empirical specifications of rights, and neither set of propo-

---

[139] Further references given by *von Vitzhum*, JZ 1985, 201, 203.

[140] *von Vitzhum*, JZ 1985, 201, 202.

[141] Specifically, the technology of extracorporeal fertilization, *Appel*, 109 with further references.

[142] *Macklin*, Dignity is a useless concept, 2003; *Pinker*, The Stupidity of Dignity, The New Republic 2008, 1 et seq.; *Beyleveld*, Human Dignity in Bioethics and Biolaw, 2001, 12 et seq.; *Pellegrino/Merrill/Schulman*, 2009, 145 et seq.

[143] Bioethics.gov. Presidential Commission for the Study of Bioethical Issues.

[144] *McDougal/Lasswell/Chen*, Human Rights and World Public Order: The Basic Policies of an International Law of Human Dignity (New Haven: Yale UP, 1980).

nents has at its disposal any means of confirming the one claim or disconfirming the other."[145]

It can be observed, on the other hand, that in several decisions, the United States Supreme Court has explicitly used the term human dignity and grants its value a prominent role. In *Lawrence v. Texas*, the Supreme Court stated that "[t]he State cannot demean their [homosexuals] existence or control their destiny by making their private sexual conduct a crime"[146] and "These matters, involving the most intimate and personal choices central to personal dignity and autonomy, are central to the liberty protected by the Fourteenth Amendment."[147] It further explained that a person's dignity is central to allowing a person's choices regarding intimate relationships: "It suffices for U.S. to acknowledge that adults may choose to enter upon this relationship in the confines of their homes and their own private lives and still retain their dignity as free persons."[148]

In *Atkins v. Virginia*, the United States Supreme Court analyzed the scope of the Eighth Amendment's prohibition against cruel and unusual punishment and whether executing a defendant suffering from mental illnesses might be in violation of said Amendment.[149] By applying the decision and explanations of Chief Justice *Warren* in *Trop v. Dulles*[150] the Supreme Court stated that "[t]he basic concept underlying the Eighth Amendment is nothing less than the dignity of man (...). The Amendment must draw its meaning from the evolving standards of decency that mark the progress of a maturing society."[151] Having interwoven the concept of human dignity with the term "standard of decency", the Supreme Court confirmed its approach by deciding that the execution of juveniles was unconstitutional.[152] Those executions had to be analyzed in light of the evolving standards of decency.[153] Other decisions regarding the Eighth Amendment's prohibition against cruel and unusual punishment also regularly refer to a person's dignity.[154] The Supreme Court also referred to a "constitutional guarantee" of human dignity.[155]

---

[145] *McDougal* et al., p. 286.
[146] Lawrence, 539 U.S. at 575.
[147] Id at 578.
[148] Id at 567.
[149] 536 U.S. 304 (2002).
[150] 365 U.S. 86 (1958).
[151] Atkins, 536 U.S. at 311 (quoting Trop, 356 U.S. at 100-01).
[152] Roper v. Simmons, 125 S. Ct. 1183 (2005).
[153] Id at 1194.
[154] Hope v. Pelzer, 53 U.S. 730 (2002).
[155] N. Y. Times v. Sullivan, 376 U.S. 254, 256 (1964) ("the right to live in human dignity as guaranteed by the U.S. Constitution and the Bill of Rights"; Screws v. United States, 325 U.S: 91, 135 (1945) (a citizen "was entitled to all the respect and fair treatment that befits the dignity of a man, a dignity that is recognized and guaranteed by the Constitution")).

c) Comparing U.S., German and European Approaches to Human Dignity

An immensely significant difference in the European and more specifically the German constitutional understanding of human dignity becomes clear in the explanations given by the U.S. Supreme Court in *Gregg v. Georgia*.[156] This relevant decision upheld the death penalty in general as not violating the Eighth Amendment, as the punishment was not meted out arbitrarily. The court additionally stated that the societal purposes of the statute, retribution and general and specific deterrence outweighed the competing human dignity concerns.[157] The reasoning explained that the Eighth Amendment "demands more than that a challenged punishment be acceptable to contemporary society. The Court must also ask whether it comports with the basic concept of human dignity at the core of the Amendment."[158] Setting those principles allows for the term human dignity to be subject to a weighting process which is theoretically excluded in European and German legal matters involving human dignity.[159] Given the structural differences in the constitutional concept of human dignity, scholars argue that the U.S. Supreme Court has not adequately recognized human dignity as a constitutional value.[160] The concept of human dignity is described as being oriented towards values of liberty, and especially liberty against the state in American constitutional understanding.[161] Accordingly, human dignity lacks meaning as an independent constitutional value[162] and is ultimately "quite alien to the American tradition".[163] Ultimately, the role of human dignity in U.S. constitutional jurisprudence is described as "episodic and underdeveloped".[164]

Having established that, it can be observed that the U.S. Supreme Court still explicitly recognizes human dignity as a value underlying several constitutional amendments. This recognition might indicate that human dignity supports or gives meaning to existing rights provided by the U.S. Constitution.[165] From the mid-1940s

---

[156] 428 U. S. 153 (1976).

[157] 428 U. S. 182.

[158] Id at 182.

[159] See. Above and Art. 1 (1) GG.

[160] *Rabkin*, Law and Human Dignity: What We Can Learn About Human Dignity from International law, 27 Harvard Journal of Law & Pub Pol'y 145, 146 ("The Founders embraced this more limited conception of international law because they understood that human dignity was not something that could be assured by government, let alone by international understanding.").

[161] *Whitman*, The Two Western Cultures of Privacy: Dignity Versus Liberty, 113 Yale Journal of Law 1151, 1161 (2004).

[162] Id at 1214 ("There is language about respect in Lawrence, but there is little that can be said to count in any certain way as law.").

[163] Id at 1221.

[164] *Jackson*, Constitutional Dialogue and Human Dignity: States and Transnational Discourse, 65 Montana Law Review, 15, 17 (2004).

[165] *Goodman*, Human Dignity in Supreme Court Constitutional Jurisprudence, p. 743. More detailed with regard to the comparison see *Eberle*, Human Dignity, Privacy, and Per-

III. The Role of Human Dignity in the U.S. Patent System

to the present, the United States Supreme Court has recognized human dignity in its decisions. In some cases, the court has based the interpretation of a constitutional guarantee on the underlying concept of dignity. In other cases, however, the Supreme Court has acknowledged human dignity concerns within a certain issue but considered competing interests to be of more significant value.[166]

The question of whether human dignity can ultimately be considered to be a true constitutional value within the U.S. legal system is difficult to answer. Most likely, any answer is not simple or straightforward. In light of the comparative analysis, it is more important to focus on the specific differences with the German and European understanding of human dignity. In an attempt to simplify the issue for the sake of practicability, the following key elements can be identified: (a) the U.S. Constitution does not expressly mention human dignity as an independent value or at all and (b) concerns of human dignity may be outweighed by other interests. In addition, (c) no absolute standard of such interests exist which prevents human dignity from being elevated to an ultimate value that cannot be outweighed by other concerns or societal interest.

Those results can now be transferred into an analysis of the relevance of human dignity in patent law and all of the consequences that such an application might result in.

2. Relevance of Human Dignity for the Patent Law System

The standard for patentability in German patent law is definitely heavily influenced by the concept of human dignity and its philosophical, ethical and metaphysical implications. Especially in the broad and in-depth discussion of human genetic bio-engineering and respective patentability, it is considered to be the most relevant factor. The previous analysis of U.S. Supreme Court cases clearly demonstrates how several morality concerns are linked to the core value of human dignity. Yet, the analysis also indicates that human dignity does not possess any standard constitutional function as an ultimate and exclusive core value. Rather, the observation was made that the more substantial and thought-out considerations were the result of a weighting process which – even if it did not mention human dignity expressly – directly addressed major facets of the human dignity concept.

A true and precise application of human dignity as an absolute value would also lead to remarkable results. Either, the debated issue raises human dignity concerns and since those cannot be outweighed by other interests, the result must, undoubtedly, be in favor of human dignity or other interests prevail and human dignity concerns are considered to be non-applicable in the debated issue. The crucial issue is therefore

---

sonality in German and American Constitutional Law, 1997, UTAH L. Rev. 963, 968–72 (1997).

[166] Very detailed review by Id. Part III.

shifted from the actual opposing interests and their weight in argument to the question of whether the issue is protected by human dignity.

The argumentation and reasoning may be similar in both cases, however, the question of how to decide on the more convincing argument in light of opposing interests cannot always be seamlessly transformed into a question of application.

Approaching such an issue in the U.S. patent system is therefore not a question of application but rather an argument – albeit a strong one – within the overall analysis of the legal issue. It is not of the same absolute character as in German [and European] constitutional law.

In biogenetic engineering, in particular, the aspect of human dignity is highly relevant, as it laid out in the reasoning above.[167] Not only has the term itself been very prominent in the discussion but so too has image of man and the discussion which follows about the point at which human dignity must be protected.[168] Otherwise, it would not have been possible to adequately assess the applicability of human dignity. It is sometimes argued that not only is the embryonic development status of a human cell worthy of protection but also the very beginning of cell development to prevent the disparagement of the fertilized ovum to "undignified biomass".[169]

a) Discussing the Legal Reasoning

Such a line of reasoning is circular, since the core argument is that without the protection of the concept of human dignity the cell would lack protection which it needs because it is supposed to be protected. This argument makes it necessary to apply the concept of absolute validity of human dignity to every aspect of the human embryonic cell which makes the consideration of other interests such as medical research technically impossible.

However, as with other aspects of law, the protection of embryonic cells is not entirely non-negotiable and is subject to certain weighting processes with different interests.[170] This is illustrated by the discussion revolving around the level of protection for embryonic cells and possible exemptions for high-tier research.[171] It has been argued that high-tier research with the aim to save human life or treatment of human suffering might be morally permissible.[172] This supposed exception has been

---

[167] See *Pinker*, 2; *Macklin* et al., Human Dignity and Bioethics, University of Notre Dame Press 2009, 17.

[168] *Eser*, Fortpflanzungsmedizin und Humangenetik – Strafrechtliche Schranken?, p. 263, 284 et seq.

[169] *Appel*, 115; *Nagl*, Gentechnologie und Grenzen der Biologie, 142.

[170] For example, the provisions on abortion in the German Criminal Code, Sect. 218.

[171] *Appel*, 116.

[172] *Appel*, 116, re, 121. Ziff. 3.1. of the BÄK-RL, Research is permissible, where it is "directly or indirectly clinically useful in the sense of prophylactic, diagnostic or therapeutic advancements".

rejected by other authors for two reasons. First, in German constitutional law, the concept of human dignity forbids the (involuntary) sacrifice of one life to save another human life.[173] Otherwise, it is argued, the dignity of a human person would become limited and quantifiable.[174] German legislation regarding stem cell research including embryonic cells is therefore regarded as insufficient, even though the originally proposed high-tier research exception was not included.[175] In the ethical discussion, a comparison to the U.S. research landscape has been drawn which allowed the process of cloning of human embryos by genetically producing identical twins.[176]

Interestingly enough, the huge collection of legal discussion concerning the concept of human dignity and its role in patentability generally fail to focus on the actual definition of dignity and its application to embryonic research. The most common approach is the extension of human dignity to embryonic cell development and the resulting equality to fully developed human beings. Accepting the legal equality of human embryos and human persons, the exclusion from patentability should then simply be an obvious step and not the result of a legal debate or weighing of different and opposing interests.

The grand debate regarding human and embryonic stem cell research is therefore mostly irrelevant for the analysis of other morally challenging technology and its potential exclusion from patentability based on morality and ordre public

b) Human Dignity in the Context of Biotechnology as a Precedent

For one, the debate around biotechnology does not focus on establishing a basic standard on how to interpret legal and moral order in the framework of patent law. It needs a refined definition in order to be applicable to other ethically challenging issues. In addition, the reasoning is very fast in ignoring the duality of the European and German legislation which includes "ordre public" and "morality". This combination of the two terms further supports the previous analysis indicating that both terms are actually identical in the context of patent law. It might be possible that "ordre public" is slightly more fathomable, since it requires some sort of legislative or administrative form and effort. Apart from that, the discussion surrounding human genetic engineering provides no further insights regarding the pair of terms "ordre public" and "morality".

Furthermore, most of the argument and line of reasoning has focused on the difficult question of applying human dignity to the developmental stages of embryonic development. Even if the analysis of certain stages has been considered, the

---

[173] *Pap*, MedR 1986, 299 et seq., 235; BVerfGE 115, 118, 120.
[174] BVerfGE 115, 118, 121.
[175] Germany Embryo Protection Act.
[176] *Elmer-Dewitt/Cloning*, Where Do We Draw the Line?, Time, No. 142 (1993), 62 et seq.

courts have taken the easy way out by simply deciding for the absolute beginning. This has left circumventive approaches for legislators with regard to abortion law and scientific research. Finally, the German and European legal debate very quickly focused solely on human dignity and its absolute value without using different approaches to morality or ordre public. Such an approach makes it difficult to transfer legal findings to another issue that is not directly related to human genetic research or other biotechnology. It barely leaves any opportunity for extracting an abstract standard or general consideration of patentability.

Having no general standard only leaves the conclusion that human dignity in a biotechnology discussion is of very limited use in the analysis of a basic standard for patentability. It might prove somewhat useful when it comes to the more specific analysis of modern weapon technology, since weapon technology is somewhat interwoven with the concept of human dignity. Human genetic research decisions and legal contributions make it undeniably clear that human dignity is a value that – theoretically – trumps all other interests. The U.S. consideration of human dignity is less absolute and might therefore be a "smarter" or at least more practical approach. The previous more in-depth analysis of similar decisions and legal approaches in the U.S. has proved this assumption to a certain extent. However, the human dignity concept in the U.S. is on the opposite end of the spectrum. The term has no definitive meaning in U.S. legal discourse and U.S. jurisprudence has not identified a consistent value and quality of human dignity. Therefore, its application in patent law might be easier than in the European or German context. Yet, it does not provide a qualitative argument. This lack of argumentative depth makes its application arguably equally meaningless in the context of patentability.

3. Summary

It can be easily observed that the U.S. has not incorporated morality concerns into the requirements for patentability. It is still possible to argue that the incorporation of potential human dignity aspects and morality into the patent subject matter doctrine results in a similar approach to European patentability exclusions.[177] However, the legal realization might be entirely different. Ultimately, though, the relevant content-related similarities outweigh the formal differences. As a result, the differences in the legal discussion and the direction of the material arguments allow for an overview of the concept and functionality of state powers within each legal system. Subsequently, those findings can be incorporated into the overall comparative analysis of the advantages and disadvantages of each approach, which ultimately form the basis for a set of suggestions to improve both legal approaches. The ideal is that those recommendations can lead to the adaptation of the positive aspects of one jurisdiction and legal system into the other one to address certain problems.

---

[177] *Keay*, AIPLA Quarterly Journal, 438.

IV. Differences in Judicial Arguments

It is correct to assume, that a patent application violating morality is ineligible for patent protection and therefore not included in the patent subject matter. However, European patent legislation also involves a separate piece of legislation specifically about the subject matter and refers to the same natural occurrences vs. artificial inventions dispute.[178] Secondly, the European sections on patentability exceptions based on morality are not applicable to the patent subject directly. Instead, they require a violation of the commercial exploitation of the patent.[179] It is still necessary to account for the commercial value and relevance of the patent itself. The approach of U.S. patent jurisprudence to include policy consideration within natural law doctrine is not the result of a legislative approach. Fundamentally, it arose as a result of the need for the USPTO to satisfy very different legal and political interests.

Legally speaking, the argument is not the result of a precise and straightforward legal argument, since the application of the "product of nature exception" to non-natural processes is incongruent. Additionally, it is, arguably, not intended by the legislator for inclusion in the exception, since the exception functions as a barrier to addressing the issue of discovery vs. invention. An immoral invention is still an invention, and trying to address the moral consideration with the natural/non-natural approach is legally imprecise. It requires a legal stretch in reasoning which may even be a step too far for other immoral inventions that have no connection to natural phenomena whatsoever. The base-line argument of the U.S. Federal Circuit Court in *Rifkin*'s human chimera case was to prevent the "impermissibl[e] tie-up [on] research on fundamental genetic information."[180] Patents primarily have an exclusive effect on research or the commercial exploitation thereof. An approach in line with that argument would mean that other patents might also impermissibly tie up relevant research which could be of benefit to society and where the product of nature exception might not be applicable.

The conclusions reached by both the U.S. and Canadian courts describe the problem as simply a question of patentable subject matter while either ignoring or dismissing the moral considerations based on a judicial lack of authority, responsibility or competence. European and German decisions have to face the moral challenges of novel and innovative inventions, since the legislation expressly grants responsibility and authority for them to do so.

In any event, the foregoing analysis demonstrates that the interpretation whereby the moral utility doctrine is labeled as "dead" is not necessarily correct. It appears, rather, to have undergone a shift and moved into the assessment of patentable subject

---

[178] Art. 52 (2) EPC.

[179] Sect. 2 (2) PatG, except for the Sect. (3), et seq. where the exclusion is based on the subject matter.

[180] Ass'n for Molecular Pathology v. USPTO, 653 F.3d 1329, 1334 (Fed. Cir. 2011).

matter.[181] Both the original cases regarding gambling devices and deceptive devices to defraud the public and the more modern cases of human-animal chimera patents arguably address the moral order and public policy. The modern cases even go further than public policy and make it easier to identify moral standards than the gambling device cases. By considering more emotionally-based moral and ethical considerations, more aspects have been addressed that were not the subject of the original moral utility doctrine. In particular, the morally questionable aspects of owning human life or building a monopoly based on processes for developing human life made these legal adjustments necessary. Most significantly, the object of moral and ethical assessment shifted from the potential use or commercial application of the patented invention (as was the case with the gambling devices) towards a direct assessment of the invention itself when it became part of patentable subject matter doctrine. In the German and European approaches, the general section for including legal or moral order is limited in that regard, since it requires a violation not of the invention itself but rather of its commercial exploitation. Therefore, the new-found home for considering morality concerns in U.S. patentable subject matter doctrine is both significantly narrower but simultaneously broader than its European and German counterparts.

In conclusion, both patent law regimes share a surprising variety of similarities now and during their historical development, specifically the judiciary assumed responsibilities for incorporating morality and public policy into the patentability assessment procedure. In the more recent development, the U.S. courts have increasingly dismissed the need to assess the morality of an invention based on the lack of judicial authority. These explanations and findings make it easier to understand the relevance of the different approaches in terms of the European and U.S. separation of state powers and their corresponding responsibilities.

V. Morality and Patentability in Relation to State Powers

In the U.S., the development from moral utility doctrine to subject matter doctrine consistently questioned the competence of the judicial branch. The question of judicial acceptance of an independent responsibility with regard to morality in patent law arose frequently.[182]

From a legal point of view, it might be argued that moral utility doctrine was simply modified in its application standard by being incorporated into the subject matter doctrine. From a specific European patent law point of view, it seems that the

---

[181] *Keay*, 439; *Daniel*, The Case For and Against Patenting of Biotechnological Inventions, in: Biotechnology, Patents and Morality (Sigrid Sterckx ed., Ashgate Publishing 2000); *Moren*, Will A Trump Administration Let Sleeping Cells Lie? 35 Nature Biotechnology 20, 24 (2017).

[182] *Oppenheimer*, Patents 101: Patentable Subject Matter and Separation of Powers, 15 Vanderbilt Journal of Entertainment & Technology Law 1, 12 (2012).

V. Morality and Patentability in Relation to State Powers

moral utility doctrine was certainly a step towards establishing a judicial responsibility and corresponding power when it comes to morality and public policy in patentability. However, as mentioned before, the doctrine was not refined enough or sufficiently well-established to be generally applicable. In addition, it lacked abstract standards and certainty with regard to the area and scope of application.

Instead of refining those standards, the main reason given for rejecting the moral utility doctrine was based on the separation of state powers – shifting the responsibility entirely to the legislator. This argument is also acknowledged in the European discussion regarding the need to include morality and legal order into the patent law system. In the U.S. law system, the question changed from the beneficial nature of the patent to the more general function and role of patent law. In the *Chakrabarty* decision, it was once more emphasized that the proper forum for weighing any complex issue was the legislator and not the judiciary.[183] The same argument was made by Judge *Moore* in the BRCA gene case where she expressed the notion that ethical dispute is a matter of legislation and not relevant to the judiciary.[184] Even Canadian courts accepted the explanations given by their U.S. counterparts and explained: "The legal issue [of patenting complex living organisms] is a narrow one and does not provide a proper platform on which to engage in a debate over animal rights, or religion, or the arrogance of the human race."[185]

In the context of the European discourse the argument by Professor *Peter Rosenberg* is equally relevant. He observes that "[w]hat is immoral varies from generation to generation (…) [and] cases denying the protection of the law on the ground of immorality are not of this generation." German authors have tried to solve the problem of the dynamic nature of morality shifts within society by adding a feature of qualification. As described in the previous sections, *Chisum* also argued that morality needs to have a place in the U.S. patent system. One possible solution might be the creation of "public policy doctrine". Such doctrine would meet his supposed patentability requirement that a "patent will be withheld only if the invention cannot be used for any honest and moral purpose."

Since the discussion in Europe is based on the EPC and its national predecessors or equivalents, the U.S. concerns about state powers are well-known in the EU legal landscape. However, they have been identified as being only a small factor in the overall discussion around justifying the judicial power of including moral considerations into patentability assessment. One of the first arguments in favor of such a mechanism is that a patent office should not be forced to participate in the preparation of inventions which violate public or moral principles.[186] This approach has been

---

[183] Chakrabarty, 449 U.S. at 317.
[184] Ass'n for Molecular Pathology v. USPTO, 653 F.3d 1329, 1373 (Fed. Cir. 2011).
[185] Harvard Coll. v. Canada, [2002] 4 S.C.R. 45, 53 (Can.) dissenting 1.
[186] *Melullis*, in: Benkard § 2 PatG re. 31.

famously apparent in the German Federal Supreme Court.[187] It is also necessary to consider the reasoning behind the fact that the granting of a patent, to some extent, indicates official recognition and appreciation, since the official participation of a state institution is, by necessity, required.[188] Even the EPO has accepted this interpretation by explaining: "Art. 53 lit. (a) [EPC] is merely intended to prevent an invention, the publication or exploitation of which would infringe the fundamental principles of 'ordre public' or morality being given an appearance of approval through a patent issued by an international authority."[189]

Additionally, aspects of legal and moral order are common in European legislation and usually function as an ultimate corrective to uphold the uniform principle of the national legal system. The general limits of every piece of legislation set by legal and moral order should also apply to patent law.[190]

Therefore, patent law can only function properly if it includes a mechanism which prohibits the incentivization of technological advancements which might negatively affect social well-being. A norm excluding inventions the exploitation of which would violate legal or moral order leads to the prevention of investment in such inventions. It also incentivizes research to develop a product which does not violate said principles but still manages to fulfill the market requirements in order to satisfy a potential demand of the market for such a product.[191]

VI. Conclusion and Recommendations

The analysis identifies the following aspects relevant to both the U.S. patent system and the European approach to patentability. Several aspects leave significant room for improvement and allow for the following recommendations:

1. Both jurisdictions acknowledge that patent law functions by incentivizing socially beneficial inventions, since technological advancement is not an end in itself. The differences in jurisprudence come about as a result of different legal cultures. In particular, the extent of judicial control and scope for moral considerations is subject to the differences in civil law and case law.

2. The European approach of including morality in the patenting process and thereby using the competence and responsibility of the executive branch is deemed necessary, since it goes beyond the effect of prohibitive legislation.

---

[187] BGH GRUR 73, 585, 586 – IUP, the terms of "social disorientation" and "levelling effect on moral principles" are often used.

[188] *Paver*, Patent World, March 1992, 12; *Beyleveld/Brownsword*, Mice, Morality and Patents, 44.

[189] T 0866/01 dated 11 May 2005, Egr. 9.7 – "Euthanasia Compositions/Michigan State University".

[190] *Teschemacher*, GRUR 1992, 134; *Pedrazzini/Blum*, GRUR Int. 1960, 151.

[191] *Romandini*, Patentierbarkeit menschlicher Zellen, 228 et seq.

VI. Conclusion and Recommendations

3. U.S. courts and the USPTO are aware of the need for administrative and judicial control in patentability matters with regard to morality. It is therefore reasonable to incorporate such responsibilities and competences in patent legislation or by establishing "public policy doctrine".
4. Human dignity in its current form as an absolute value prohibits the development of a practical and universal standard for assessing morality within the European patent system. The U.S. approach is more useful and honest in its legal and dogmatic application. However, the concept of human dignity in the U.S. is too underdeveloped to be practically applicable in a consistent manner.
5. Both patent systems might require a more refined catalogue of moral considerations to ensure legal certainty in the patentability process. Such a catalogue can only be practically established with the support of the judiciary and administrative branch.
6. The U.S., European and German patent law regimes are similar in the sense that morality in the patent law context is inherently different from morality in any other legal context. Therefore, the usual approach to ethics and morality is ultimately futile. It is necessary to be aware of this unique feature of patent law.

Naturally, adapting legal concepts and adopting ideas from a foreign legal system results in new challenges. Such transfer might be hindered by the different legal settings and structure of legislation. However, the conceptual differences are not ultimate and absolute.

E. Morality and Patentability in Chinese Patent Law

Given the relevance[1] of Asian law patent jurisdictions and the seemingly considerable differences in cultures and societal customs, it is of great interest to analyze how those patent regimes address the research questions. Those research results are promising in terms of offering insight into how cultural and societal particularities shape the understanding and function of patent law. In addition, the origin and practical relevance of intellectual property and patent law are very different in the context of Chinese legal culture.

Patent law has been the subject of lengthy and in-depth legal and political discussion in the Western world. In Chinese society, intellectual property and patent is a new phenomenon. In a first section of this chapter, China's particular interpretation of patent law will be analyzed (I.).

In order to understand the reasons for the diverging perception, it is helpful to understand the historic and political development of patent law in China (II.).

The following section then addresses the issues of legal culture and morality in a micro-functional analysis with the results from the previous chapters (III.) This analysis reveals that public perception is significantly different to the status quo in Western patent systems.

The main results with regard to Chinese legal culture are then presented in a conclusion (IV.).

I. Chinese Legal Culture and Patent Law

Compared to the very heated debates in Europe and the United Sates, patentability issues like advanced biotechnology inventions have seemingly never sparked such a fierce discussion in China.[2]

---

[1] *Normile*, 21.

[2] *Zhao*, Yuanguo, Zhongguo Zhuanlifa de Yunyu Yu Dansheng [The Drafting History of the Patent Law of China] (Zhishi Chanquan Chubanshe [Intellectual Property Publishing House] 2003) 142. Peng, 58; *Zhou*, Qi, Zhongguo ji Zhongguo Kexueyuan Ganxibao yu Zaisheng Yixue Yanjiu Gaishu [An Overview of Stem Cell and Regenerative Medicine in China and at Chinese Academy of Sciences], 28 Chinese Bulletin of Life Sciences 833 (2016); *Zhou*, Yan, Woguo Ganxibao Yanjiu Zhong de Lunli Weiji yu Falü Kunhuo jiqi Guojia Guanli de Yanjiu [Research on Ethical Crisis and Legal Issues Related to Stem Cell Research and National Regulatory Framework in China], Di San Junyi Daxue [Third Military Medical University of Chinese PLA] 12 (2009).

One of the main reason for this difference is the public perception concerning patents and inventions. Chinese patent law also includes a general morality clause almost identical to the German and European approach.[3] China utilized the option provided by Art. 27 TRIPS.

Public perception naturally influences the role of patents within the legal and moral culture. A perceived importance or lack thereof can significantly influence patent protection in relation to certain items. Perceived importance is especially relevant in cases where morally controversial inventions are concerned. To understand the current role of patent law in China, it is necessary to briefly analyze the significance of patent throughout the country's legal and historical development.

Secondly, patenting inventions in controversial areas is closely related to the views surrounding several moral and legal issues in Chinese culture. Dissecting the legal culture is useful, since it sheds light on the question of how values influence morality in Chinese patent law. The role of values is especially interesting, because it allows the potential human dignity concerns to be analyzed as a criterion for interpreting Chinese patent law.

II. Development of Patentability Concerns in China

As stated in the beginning of this section, China utilized Art. 27 TRIPS and incorporated a general morality clause into its patent law regime. In its guidelines, the Chinese State Intellectual Property Office (SIPO)[4] defines morality as "ethical or moral norms and rules regarded as justifiable and accepted by the public."[5] The first remarkable aspect of this definition is the reference to public opinion. It suggests public opinion should be the ultimate factor in deciding what is excluded from patentability.[6]

Historically, Chinese law consisted mainly of penal codes rather than a civil code. Customs and commercial traditions were used to address civil issues.[7] Using customs

---

[3] Sect. 4. Patent Law of the People's Republic of China.

[4] 国家知识产权局, Pinyin Guójiā Zhīshìchǎnquán Jú.

[5] Part II, Chapter 1 Section 3.1.2. of the SIPO Guidelines.

[6] *Cao*, Trends and Prospects of Stem Cell Research in China, 31 Chinese Medical Journal 116 (2016), 120; *Peng*, 59; compared with the public perception in the US: Caulfield, Trust, Patents and Public Perceptions: The Governance of Controversial Biotechnology Research, 24 Nature Biotechnology 1352 (2006), 1355; *Chan*, A Patent Perspective on US Stem Cell Research, 32 Nature Biotechnology 633 (2014), 634; *Murray/Spar*, Bit Player or Powerhouse? China and Stem-cell Research, 355 New England Journal of Medicine 1191, 1201 (2006).

[7] *Feng*, Intellectual Property Law in China (2nd edition, Sweet & Maxwell Asia 2003), 125; *Chen*, Chinese Law: Towards an Understanding of Chinese Law, Its Nature and Developments (Klumer Law International 1999); *Peng*, 59; *William*, To Steal A Book is An Elegant Offense: Intellectual Property Law in Chinese Civilization (Standford University Press 1995), 12 et seq.; *Braga*, The Developing Country Case For and Against Intellectual

and traditions left the civil law system rather incomplete. Intellectual property and especially patent law are relatively new advancements and consequently there was no legal background to be developed.[8] During the 19th century, after China was forced to connect with the Western world, attempts were made to include a patent system but ultimately failed.[9] After the end of the Qing dynasty, in the first half of the 20th century, the Ministry of Commerce and Industry of the Republic of China introduced the first Chinese patent law, the Temporary Statue on Technology Reward.[10] This approach offered no real protection to foreign patent holders and was rarely enforced.[11] Consequently, patent law only grew in importance following the newly issued patent law system after World War II. This piece of legislation is regarded as the first real patent law in China.[12] However, with the establishment of the Communist government in 1949, patent law became largely insignificant again.[13] Following the Cultural Revolution at the end of the 1970s, China still had not developed a modern and substantial patent system.[14]

Only in the 1980s and after an intense and lengthy debate, was a modern patent law introduced to enable China to engage with the global community on an economic and technological level.[15]

Property Protection (Wolfgang E. Siedbeck ed., The World Bank 1990), 120; *Ganea/Pattloch*, Intellectual Property Law in China (Christopher Health ed., Kluwer Law International 2005); *Tong*, Zhongguo Minfa Xue MinFa Zongze [Chinese Civil Law Science: General Principles of Civil law] (Zhongguo Gong'an Daxue Chubanshe [Peoples Public Security University of China's Press] 2003).

[8] *Peng*, 59; *Cui*, Zhuanli Fa Yuali Yu Anli [Patent Law: Cases and Materials] (Beiing Daxue Chubanshe [Peking University Press] 2012), 287.

[9] *Liu*, Deming, Now the Wolf Has Indeed Come! Perspective on the Patent Protection of Biotechnology Inventions in China, 53 The American Journal of Comparative Law 207, 210 (2005), footnote 8; *Fyre/Schlich*, Patenting Stem Cell Technologies Following Guidelines issued by the EPO, USPTO, JPO an SIPO, 4 Pharmaceutical Patent Analyst 431 (2015); *Kim*, Methods for Derivation of Human Embryonic Stem Cells, 23 Stem Cells 1228, 1230 (2005); *Kintisch*, Groups Challenge Key Stem Cell Patents, 313 Science 281 (2006).

[10] *Liu*, Deming, Reflections on Lack of a Patent System throughout China's Long History, 12 The Journal of World Intellectual Property 122, 130 (2009).

[11] *Chengsi/Zheng/Pendleton*, 9; *Peng*, 59.

[12] *Yu*, Peter, From Pirates to Partners: Protecting Intellectual Property in China in the Twenty-first Century, 50 American University Law 131, 140 (2000).

[13] *Liu*, 6; *Peng* 60, 13.

[14] During the time, the communist government introduced a "double-track" system of patents and certifications of authorship, which were modeled after the Soviet system. However, this was more of a political tool: *William*, To Steal a Book is an Elegant Offense; 58, 1995.

[15] *Yu*, Peter, Building the Ladder: Three Decades of Development of the Chinese Patent System, Drake University Law School Research Paper (2012); *Li*, Yahong, Imitation to Innovation in China: the Role of Patents in Biotechnology and Pharmaceutical Industries (Edward Elgar 2010).

In the context of patent legislation in the U.S. and European or German legal systems, this development can be described as very recent. In addition, the main takeaway is that the development was initiated due to an interest in competing and engaging internationally, instead of an inherent interest of national Chinese legal culture. Neglecting national implementation and understanding have led to the effect that the concept of patents is still a somewhat foreign notion in Chinese legal culture which better explains the perceptions around patents in general.[16]

III. Morality and Chinese Legal Culture

Even though the Chinese government has invested a lot of resources in promoting the new patent system, only a very rudimentary idea of patents exits among the Chinese populace. Most Chinese people lack a basic understanding of patent law.[17] Even among better educated populations, a significant proportion of people in China think that patents either assure a certain quality of a product[18] or directly relate to advanced technologies.[19] In addition, research has indicated that college students were unable to understand the different concepts of intellectual property or point out the differences between them.[20] The former SIPO commissioner identified the lack of understanding of intellectual property as a "fundamental shortcoming" of intellectual property research and significance in China.[21] Therefore, additional efforts by the

---

[16] *Peng*, 61.

[17] According to two studies, most people have heard of patents but especially people in rural regions acknowledge that they do not understand them well: *Hua Liu*, 103, 105, (2006) and *Wang*, Nian, Guangxi Shehui Gongzhong Zhishichanquan Renzhidu Diaocha yu Fenxi ji Silu Tantao [The Survey, Analysis, and Discussion on Public Perceptions of IP in GuangXi], 3 Xiandai Shangye [Modern Business] 175 (2016).

[18] *Meng/Meng*, 144, 146; *Liu/Ying*, Woguo Shehui Gongzhong Thishichanquan Yishi Xianzhuang Diaocha Fengxi ji Duice Yanjiu [Survey of Chinese Public's IP Protection Awareness and Some Recommendations], 10 Zhongguo Ruankexue [China Soft Science] 103, 110 (2006).

[19] *Tan*, Nongcun gongzhong dui Zhishichanquan de Renzhidu ji Guanzhudu Yanjiu [Researach on Plural Public's Awareness of and Attention to Intellectual Property Rights], 17 Journal of Northwest A&F University (Social Science Edition) 144, 149 (2017); *Tännsjö*, Why No Compromise is Possible, 38 Metaphilosophy 330, 338 (2007).

[20] *He*, Daxuesheng Zhishichanquan Jiaoyu Tanxi – Yi Shandongsheng Daxuesheng zhishichanquan Yishi Diaocho wei Jichu [Analysis on the Education of Intellectual Property for College Students], 27 Journal of Shandong Youth University of Political Science 42 (2011); *Peng*, 62.

[21] *Muquian/Zhsi*, 121; *Peng*, 62, 30; *Fu*, Regenerative Medicine Research in China: From Basic Research to Clinical Practice, 57 Science China Life Sciences 155 (2014), 156; *Liu/Fan*, Hepatitis B in China, 369 The Lancet 1582, 1590 (2007); *Meng/Meng*, Zhishi Jingji Shidai de Daxuesheng Zhishichanquan Yishi he Renzhi Zhuangkuang Yanjiu [A study on University Students' Awareness and Cognition of Intellectual Property in an Era of Knowledge-based Economy], 24 Journal of Nanjing University of Science and Technology 96 (2011).

Chinese government to further the acceptance and understanding of patents among the Chinese have been made

1. Governmental Influence on the Legal Culture in China

These efforts specifically shaped the legal culture in patent law very differently compared to the U.S. and European patent law. For example, a policy was created that allows students to gain extra advantages in entrance examinations for universities where they have successfully filed for a patent.[22] In addition, successful patent applications can be used by administrative officials facing disciplinary measures to reduce demerit punishments or eliminate disadvantageous records related to disciplinary proceedings.[23] Furthermore, even prisoners can benefit from being creative and innovative. A prison sentence can be reduced significantly if a prisoner successfully obtains a patent.[24]

Thus, it is obvious that the functions of patents in China are significantly more far-reaching than in other jurisdictions. They extend beyond the economic value of the exclusionary right and have value in other areas as well. These additional values shape the perception of patents accordingly. It might even be argued that the understanding of a patent among the Chinese public is further distorted by these measures, because it leads to the perception that a patent right is inherently positive. In the eyes of the public, only an achievement of a high standard would lead to these significant benefits granted by the state government. A patent is perceived as a guarantee of quality from the central government.[25] Consequently, this perception of approval influences the question of whether a patent is truly neutral due to its exclusionary nature. It is without reasonable doubt that the vigorous effort to promote patents by the Chinese government transform the granting of a patent into a government reward in the form of technical authority or advanced technology. Ulti-

---

[22] *Peng*, 62, 30; *Zhang*, *Xiado*, Zhanli Shizi Tiaojian [Substantial Requirements for Patent] (Chengsi Zheng ed., Law Press 2002); *Zheng*, Gongxu Liangsu Yuanze zai Zhongguo Jindai Minfa Zhuanxing zhong de Jiazhi [The Value of the Principle of Public Order and Good Morals in the Transformation of the Civil Law of Modern China], 11 Faxue [Law Science] 87, 98 (2017).

[23] *Peng*, 62; *Wu*, Zhongguo Zhuanli Fa de Fazhan Daolu: Xiandaihua, Guojiahua yu Zhanlüenhua – Zai Zhongguo Zhuanli Fa Banbu 30 Zhounian Zuotanhui Shang de Fayan] The Development Paths of the Chinese Patent Law: Modernizing, Internationalizing, Strategizing – An Address in Colloquia "the Issuing of the Chinese Patent Law" 30th Anniversary], 3 Zhishi Chanquan [Intellectual Property Journal] 10, 15 (2014).

[24] Article 78(1) of the Criminal Law of the PRC and Article 29(3) of Prison Law of the PRC., *Allison/Kirk*, 16 BMC Medical Ethics 85 (2015), 15 et seq.; *Tian*, Shengming Xingshi Zhishi Chanquan ji Guojia Zhengce [Intellectual Property Right of Life Form and National Policies] (Zhongguo Nongye Chubanshe [China Agriculture Press] 2003).

[25] *Meng/Meng*, 82; also: *Peng*, 63.

mately, a patent is understood as a government endorsement of a high-tech product.[26] Combining all these factors – the exotic nature of patent law in China, its very recent development and the endorsement effect – makes it possible to understand why, for the Chinese public, a patent is a "thing with a sense of mystery (...) even a sense of the sacred."[27]

2. Moral Considerations in Chinese Culture

In some Western countries, the prejudice persists that China is a country lacking in moral standards.[28] The prejudice is based on recent and ongoing gene editing research, especially CRISPR on human embryos.[29] Chinese scientists and the public, however, are of the opinion that this is a misrepresentation of Chinese moral culture.[30]

Similar to the debates in the European Union and the U.S., the fiercest discussion revolves around the value and scope of what is "human". The moment in time from which an embryo can be considered "fully" human and worthy of protection is highly debated and touches fundamental issues such as morals and other cultural and religious values. Therefore, most insight about the moral culture regarding technology and inventions can be obtained by analyzing the same debate in the Chinese context.

The ethical and cultural framework of morality in China rests upon three pillars – the teachings of Confucianism, Taoism and Buddhism.[31] Among those three, Confucianism is the most dominant and specifically influences social conventions in China.[32] However, in recent decades, Western culture has been influencing Chinese values, a phenomenon which has been accelerated by China's recent establishment of a market economy.[33] Although the fundamental concepts of Confucianism are dif-

---

[26] *Yin*, Zhongguo Zhuanlifa Xiangjie [Introduction to the Patent Law of China] (Zhishi Chanquan Chubanshe [Intellectual Property Press] 2011); *Peng*, 63.

[27] *Peng*, 63.

[28] *Dikötter*, Sex, Culture and Modernity in China: Her Tumultuous Life's Journey to the West (Vol. 1) (Hong Kong University Press 1995); *Hesketh*, The Effect of China's One-child Family Policy After 25 Years, 353 New England Journal of Medicine 1171 (2005); *Svendsen/ Allison*, Encyclopedia of Stem Cell Research (Vol. 1 & 2) (SAGE Publications 2008).

[29] *Puping* et al.; *Sun*, Fuqi Jian Lengdong Peitai Chuli Nanti de Falü Jiejue [Legal Countermeasures of Issues in Frozen Embryo Disposition between the Couple], 23 Goujia Jiancha Guan Xueyuan Xuebao [Journal of National Prosecutors College] 110, 121 (2015).

[30] *Peng*, 66, 48; *Furth*, A Flourishing Yin: Gender in China's Medical History (University of California Press 1999), 154; *Suss-Toby*, Derivation of a Diploid Human Embryonic Stem Cell Line from A Mononuclear Zygote, 19 Human Reproduction 670, 677 (2004).

[31] *Kirkland*, 26, 27; *Jing-Bao Nie/Renzong Qiu*, 51; *Weber*, The Religion of China: Confucianism and Taoism (Collier Macmillan 1964).

[32] *Peng*, 66.

[33] Renzong Qiu. *Piao*, Daojia de Shengming Lunli he Ganxibao Yanju de Wenti [Ethical View of Life in Taoism and Stem Cell Research], 9 Wuhan Keji Daxue Xuebao (Shehui Kexue Ban) [Journal of Wuhan University of Science and Technology (Social Science Edition)] 109, 115 (2007).

ferent from Western and especially European values, the questions raised by advanced biotechnology remain the same.

The most significant difference in the moral cultures is the concept of "humanness".[34] Chinese moral culture includes an additional "social dimension" that must be fulfilled in order for a being to qualify as a human person.[35] A human person is required to live in a society and interact with other persons. Under the teachings of Confucianism, a person is a psycho-somatic social unity with a variety of social features that are specified according to different hierarchical or semi-hierarchical relationships.[36] This idea differs from Western humanist approaches that focus on individualism.[37] However, it is not entirely foreign since European philosophers have also expressed similar ideas, such as that the essence of a person is the ensemble of social relations.[38]

Therefore, in terms of Chinese moral culture as it applies to questions of advanced biotechnology, a fetus or an early human embryo is not considered to be a human person.[39] This distinction between "person" and "embryo" influences the answer to a variety of questions regarding human stem cell research, since the alteration or destruction of toti-potent cells is not connected to a human person from a Chinese perspective.[40] However, Chinese moral culture still acknowledges biological prenatal life, even human pre-natal life. It is just not sufficient to be considered a human person.[41] This distinction is different in Western moral culture where the difference between human life and personhood is of lesser relevance for the scope of patent protection.[42] The protection of and respect for human life is deeply rooted in the Confucian moral principle and Taoism.[43] In Taoist writings, in particular, the scope of human life is extended before birth and imbued with a spiritual facet.[44] According to other Taoist teachings, the "spirit" is received from "Heaven"[45] which is somewhat similar to some Western understandings of human dignity, being something "di-

---

[34] As opposed to the term "humanity" which focuses either on humans as a collective species or on humane behavior.

[35] *Wing-Tsit*, A Source Book in Chinese Philosophy (Princeton University Press 1973).

[36] *Cheng*, Q., Daojiao Shengsi Guan Yanjiu [Research on Taoist View of Life and Death], Sichaun Daxue [Sichuan University] (2007); *Xunzi*, 123; *Peng*, 23.

[37] *Agassi*, The British Journal of Sociology, 1960, 454.

[38] *Marx*, Vol. 5, 4.

[39] *Qiu*, Reshaping the Concept of Personhood, 135, 142.

[40] Naturally, there are a huge variety of different beliefs and shapes of those beliefs within China that might disagree with that statement.

[41] *Peng*, 69.

[42] In comparison to constitutional decisions: BVerfGE, 109, 279, 311 (2004).

[43] *Peng*, 70.

[44] Both Lord Lao's One Hundred Eighty Precepts and Talking About the One Hundred Diseases mention and forbid the destruction of unborn life.

[45] *Huaninanz*, 158; *Peng*, 70.

vine".⁴⁶ Both traditional teachings include justifications for the destruction of human life, indicating that even those core values are not absolute in nature.⁴⁷

In contemporary China, these traditional teachings still influence the public viewpoint but have changed considerably in recent times.⁴⁸ Many Chinese support stem cell research or only oppose abortion on the grounds that it might endanger women's physical and mental health.⁴⁹ However, the majority of medical professionals believe that human life begins at an early stage before birth and has to be protected.⁵⁰ Especially in ethical debates which revolve around medical treatment and do not involve the destruction of embryos, an overwhelming majority supports such treatments, like therapeutic human cloning.⁵¹

In conclusion, it can be observed that in Chinese moral culture, some aspects of research and technology can be considered fundamentally morally wrong. However, the possibility for a justification always remains in the moral culture.⁵² Additionally, the Chinese moral system has a more distinct view of human life and personhood which allows for a more dynamic moral approach. This system is unlike the European patentability approach which theoretically uses human dignity as an absolute value. It shares a certain similarity with the U.S. approach regarding the possibility of dynamic and relative application of values and interests.

3. Morality in the Context of Legal Culture

Given the moral considerations of humanness and personhood, a fetus has no legal capacity under Chinese civil law. It is argued that not only is this in accordance with the moral views of the general public but that it also supports the acceptance of the one-child policy in China in recent decades.⁵³ From a theoretical approach to this

---

⁴⁶ BVerfGE, 109, 279, 311 (2004).

⁴⁷ *Peng*, 72.

⁴⁸ *Peng*, 73; *Kirkland*, "Enhancing Life?" Perspectives from Traditional Chinese Value-Systems, 36 The Journal of Law, Medicine & Ethics 26, 29 (2008); *Liu*, Chuntian, Intellectual Property Law (4ᵗʰ edition, Zhongguo Renmin Daxue Chubanshe [China Renmin University Publishing] 2009); *Moore*, The Developing Human: Clinically Oriented Embryology (9th edition, Elsevier Sauders 2013).

⁴⁹ *Karen Hardee*, 68, 76; and *Xiangxing Qui*, 176; *Peng*, 91; *Luk*, Abortion in Chinese Law, 25 The American Journal of Comparative Law 372 (1977); *Wang*, Luozhong, Woguo Zhuanxingqi Gonggong Zhengce Guochengzhong de Gongmin Canyu Yanjiu – Yizhong Liyi Fenxi de Shijiao [Study on the Participation of Citizens in Public Policy Making During China's Transition: From the Interest Analysis Perspective], 8 Zhongguo Xingzheng Guanli [Chinese Public Administration] 86, 93 (2005).

⁵⁰ *Yan Zhou*, 88–100.

⁵¹ At 90%, *Yan Zhou*, 100.

⁵² *Peng*, 74; *Moon*, Generation, Culture, and Differentiation of Human Embryonic Stem Cells for Therapeutic Applications, 13 Molecular Therapy 5, 11 (2006).

⁵³ *Jianfu Chen*, 228–229; *Harmon*, Organ Transplantation in China und Beyond: Addressing the "Access Gap", 10 Medical Law International 191, 206 (2010); *Takahashi*, In-

issue it can be observed that Chinese law is still used in certain areas as a tool of political power.[54] Without universal access to legal abortion in China, the implementation of the national population policy would have been much more difficult.[55] In the landmark case of *Yixing Frozen Human Embryo*, the courts agreed that a human embryo was neither a person nor just a simple object or property.[56] Rather, a "special respect theory" was developed.[57]

The concept of human dignity can be found within all three jurisdictions addressed within this thesis. It plays a central role in Europe but also in the U.S., even though to a far lesser extent. China, much like the U.S., has signed up to multiple international human rights instruments that include human dignity.[58] It has also ratified a variety of international treatments which relate to human dignity.[59] Following the atrocities of World War II, the concept of human dignity emerged in Europe and spread from there to the U.S. and ultimately to China.[60] By incorporating

---

duction of Pluripotent Stem Cells from Adult Human Fibroblasts by Defined Factors, 131 Cell 861, 863 (2007); *Yu*, Junying, Induced Pluripotent Stem Cell Lines Derived from Human Somatic Cells, 318 Science 1917, 1920 (2007).

[54] *Nie*, The Problem of Coerced Abortion in China and Related Ethical Issues, 8 Cambridge Quarterly of Healthcare Ethics 463 (1999); *Yuan*, Stem Cell Science On the Rise in China, 10 Cell Stem Cell 12, 18 (2012).

[55] *Nie*, 469; *Hardee*, Family Planning and Women's Lives in Rural China, 30 International Family Planning Perspectives 68 (2004); *Jackson*, Regulating Reproduction: Law Technology and Autonomy (Hart Publishing 2001); *Lanzendorf*, Use of Human Gametes Obtained from Anonymous Donors for the Production of Human Embryonic Stem Cell Lines, 76 Fertility and Sterility 132, 136 (2001); *Nie*, Behind the Silence: Chinese Voices on Abortion (Rowman & Littlefield Publishers 2005).

[56] *Peng*, 77, 115; *Zhou*, Qi, Mianxiang Weilai de Xin Yilun Yiliao Jishu Geming – Ganxibao yu Zaisheng Yixue Yanjiu Zhanluexing Xiandao Keji Zhuanxiang Jinzhan [Confronting the Coming Medical Renovation: Progress on Stem Cell and Regenerative Medicine Research], 30 Zhongguo Kexueyuan Yuan Kan [China Academic Journal Electronic Publishing House] 262, 271 (2015).

[57] *Peng*, 121; *Han*, 78; Lengdong Peitai de Lunli Wenti Yanjiu [An Analysis on the Ethical Problem of Frozen Embryos], 15 Kunming Ligong Daxue Xuebao [Journal of Kunming University of Science and Technology 15 (2015), 18; *Zaninovic*, Derivation of Human Embryonic Stem Cells (hESC), in: Human Fertility: Methods and Protocols (Zev Rosenwaks & Paul M. Wassarman eds, Springer 2014); *Zhao*, Zhuanli Xingfa de Sikao [Preliminary Study on the Morality Exclusion in Patent Examination: Thinking from Two Gelatin Patents], 3 Zhongguo Faming yu Zhuanli [China Invention & Patent] 92 (2013); *Zhou*, Chenlin, Comprehensive Profiling Reveals Mechanisms of SOX2-mediated Cell Fate Specification in Human ESCs and NPCs, 26 Cell Research 171, 187 (2016); *Zhou*, Di, Establishment and Maintenance of Three Chinese Human Embryonic Stem Cell Lines, 46 In Vitro Cellular & Development Biology-Animal 192, 201 (2010).

[58] *Peng*, 83, 150,

[59] UN Charter, etc.

[60] Though mostly in the form of international treaties, such as the Universal Declaration of Human Rights, the International Covenant on Economic, Social and Cultural Rights and The Vienna Declaration on Human Rights.

III. Morality and Chinese Legal Culture 193

the legal concept of human dignity into its law, it seems that China officially recognizes human dignity.[61]

In the foregoing chapters, it has been observed that the U.S. does not recognize human dignity in its constitution, simply because the U.S. Constitution is much older than the modern European counterparts which were prominently established after World War II. Therefore, it might be expected that the Chinese Constitution would follow a similar approach, given the fact that it is the most recent – having been established in 1982. Yet, it does not expressly mention human dignity at all, only the "personal dignity of citizens" in Article 38.[62] The background for this provision is not World War II but rather the Cultural Revolution, which saw massive violations of citizens' rights.[63] The wording, however, was modeled partly on the European constitutions. The use of European constitutions as a model can be observed in the wording "the personal dignity of citizens of the PRC is inviolable". A right that is inviolable in legal theory is equal to the absolute value of human dignity in the European and especially German context.

In practice, Chinese scholars have usually interpreted the meaning of "personal dignity" as a collective term for personal civil rights, such as name rights, portrait rights, reputation rights, etc.[64] These rights are only inviolable in general but many justifications and exceptions exist. Only recently, has a modern approach emerged demonstrating that the Chinese Constitution also protects and respects human dignity without expressly mentioning it.[65] Even these approaches are limited in a way by

---

[61] *Luo/Peng/Yuhong*, Ren de Zunyan de Falü Shuxing Bianxi [An Analysis of the Legal Attributes of Human Dignity], 5 Zhongguo Shehui Kexue [Social Science in China] 101 (2016).

[62] *Quanguo*, Renda Changweihui Bangongting Yanjiushi Zhengzhizu, Zhongguo Xianfa Jingshi [Explanation for China's Constitution] (Zhongguo Minzhu Fazhi Chubanshe [Press of Chinese Legal System] 1996).

[63] *Xu*, Chongde, Zhonghua Renmin Gongheguo Xianfa Shi [History of the Constitution of the People's Republic of China], (Fujian Renmin Chubanshe [Fujian People Press] 2003) 769; *Zhang*, Qianfan, Xianfa Xue Daolun [Introduction to Constitutional Jurisprudence] (Falü Chubanshe [Law Press, China] 2004).

[64] *Peng*, 161; *Langfang/Peng*, The Law Itself is not Above Human Beings: Comments on China's First Case on Frozen Embryos, 29 International Journal of Law, Policy and the Family 260, 263 (2015); *Li*, Haiping, Lun Ren de Zunyan zai Woguo Xianfa Shang de Xingzhi Diwei [On the Qualitative Orientation of Human Dignity in Chinese Constitution], 12 Shehui Kexue [Social Science] 101 (2012); *Liu/Sheng*, 3D Dayin Renti Qiguan Ke Zhuanlixing Yanjiu [The Patentability of 3D Printed Human Organs], 6 Keji yu Falu [Journal of Science, Technology and Law] 1098 (2015); *Qiu*, Renzong, Reshaping the Concept of Personhood: A Chinese Perspective, in: The Moral Status of Persons: Perspective on Bioethics (Gerhold K. Becker ed., Rodopi 2000); *Salter*, China and the Global Stem Cell Bioeconomy: An Emerging Political Strategy?, 1 Regenerative Medicine 671, 688 (2006).

[65] *Peng*, 162; *Laifan Lin*, 47–55, referring to the "inviolable" and its similarity to the German constitution, therefore concluding the similarity of the legal concept as a fundamental or absolute value. *Qianfan Zhang*, 507–509, similar, also *Haiping Li*, 101–110, as a supreme principle; *Zhang*, Qingkui, Yiyao ji Shengwu Jishu Lingyu Zhishi Chanquan Zhanlü Shiwu

stating that a Chinese supreme principle would be different from the European model simply because China has its own rules and regulations.[66]

The Chinese cultural distinction between the terms "person" and "life" heavily influences this debate. Usually, the interpretation focuses on the word "personal" in "personal dignity", meaning that it refers to a person and not human life in general.[67] The significance is also considerably lower than in Europe or even the U.S., since legislation or administrative acts barely mention human dignity at all or only in speeches[68] or reports.[69] These small and non-binding remarks are considered to be a "positive response" by the Chinese government to the international pressure to protect human dignity.[70] Legislative measures sometimes include the phrase dignity but only in describing legislative intent and the formulation of goals.[71] Compared with its very prominent role in Europe and its legal significance there, it becomes apparent that the role of human dignity is very different in China. Even in the U.S. where human dignity has a more flexible role, it is at least substantially used in jurisprudence to a certain extent.[72]

The concept of "human dignity" in China has been shaped by two major factors. First, it is partly an import from the Western legal culture and is attributed to a

---

[Strategy and Practice of Intellectual Property in the Fields of Medicine and Biotechnology] (Zhishi Chanquan Chubanshe [Intellectual Property Press] 2008).

[66] *Haiping Li*, 104, *Peng*, 85; *Harn*, Keeping the Gates Open for Human Embryonic Stem Cell Research, 13 Cardozo Public Law, Policy and Ethics Journal 525 (2015), 530; *Li/Cai*, The Scope of Patent Protection for Gene Technology in China, 32 Nature Biotechnology 1001, 1007 (2014); *Zhang*, Xin, Derivation of Human Embryonic Stem Cells from Developing and Arrested Embryos, 24 Stem Cells 2669, 2674 (2006).

[67] *Peng*, 85, who points out how this mainly influenced the discussion around biotechnology; *Lin*, Ren de Zunyan yu Ren'ge Zunyan – Jianlun Zhongguo Xianfa Di 38 Tiao de Jieshi Fangan [Personal Dignity and Personality Dignity: on the Interpretation of Article 38 of the Chinese Constitution], 3 Zhejiang Shehui Kexue [Zhejiang Social Sciences] 47, 50 (2008).

[68] President Hu Jintao at the Yale University in 2006: "the Chinese civilization always gives prominence to the principle of putting the people first and respects the dignity and value of the human being"; President Xi Jinping, 273 – The Governance of China.

[69] Prime Minister Wen Jiabao in the Report on the Work of the Government at the Third Session of the 11th National People's Congress in 2010: "all the things we do aim at improving people's welfare, letting them have more dignity and making society fairer and more harmonious"; *Qiu*, Renzong, Renlei Peitai Ganxibao Yanjiu de Lunli Wenti [Ethical Issues of Human Embryonic Stem Cell Research], 7 Qun Yan [Popular Tribune] 18 (2002).

[70] *Peng*, 86; *Yuhong Hu*, 101; UNDP China and Development Research Center of the State Council of China, China National Human Development Report 2016: Social Innovation for Inclusive Human Development (China Translation & Publishing House 2016); *Qiu*, Renzong, Cong Zhongguo "Ganxibao Zhilia" Re Lun Ganxibao Linchuang Zhuanhua Zhong de Lunli he Guanli Wenti [Behind the Vogue for "Stem Cell Therapy": Ethical and Regulatory Issue in Clinical Translation of Stem Cells in China], 3 Kexue yu Shehui [Science & Society] 8 (2013).

[71] *Peng*, 86, 167, 168.

[72] *Xu*, Haiyan, Lun Tiwai Zaoqi Renlei Peitai de Falü Diwei ji Chufen Quan [The Legal Status of Early Embryos and the Right of the Disposition of Frozen Embryos], 29 Faxue Luntan [Legal Forum] 146 (2014).

"person" instead of a "human being". It can be concluded, that this strips the idea of human dignity of its very fundamental and absolute function in European legal culture. With a lack of significance and no absolute nature, human dignity becomes much easier to handle. In that regard, the approach might be similar to the U.S. system which also employs a much more flexible approach. However, the Chinese system barely uses the term within legal reasoning or legislation at all. On a scale of significance, the Chinese system is even further from the European approach in terms of the concept of human dignity.

Combining this aspect with the fact that patent law itself is a foreign element and therefore often misunderstood within Chinese legal culture, it can be safely assumed that the role of human dignity in Chinese patent law is insignificant. To further the research and identify the Chinese use of its patentability clause, it is necessary to identify other possible values and legal concepts that influence morality in the context of patentability.

The most influential decades in recent Chinese history have been characterized by military conflict.[73] During these conflicts, the Chinese military would often suffer defeat due to technological inferiority.[74] Being defeated by superior technology left the Chinese with the impression that advancement in the areas of science and technological were absolutely necessary to make "the country wealthy and the military powerful."[75] Not only is it believed that an investment in science and technology can strengthen the military but also that it can "figure out all problems faced by China."[76] This concept and the perceived value of technological advancement have led to the rise of scientism in China.[77] It is also one of the reasons why patent law – as the major intellectual property law to incentivize technological advancement – was introduced into the Chinese legal system. It was further supported by *Deng Xiaoping* in 1988, when he stated that "science and technology is the first productive force."[78] Developing this philosophy within the Chinese education system has led to a huge prioritization of the importance of scientific fields. Increasing the focus on science has further increased the Chinese perception that advancement in science and technological stand for the growth of the economy, the progress of so-

---

[73] Starting with the Opium War in 1840 and throughout the 20th century to World War II and the Cultural Revolution.

[74] *Yuhong Hu*, 101; UNDP China and Development Research Center of the State Council of China, China National Human Development Report 2016: Social Innovation for Inclusive Human Development (China Translation & Publishing House 2016); *Peng*, 87.

[75] *Peng*, 87.

[76] *Qiu*, 51, 55.

[77] *Peng*, 87; *Quan*, Pige Mingjiao Zhuanli de Lunli Wenti, Zenme Jiejue [How to Solve the Problem concerning Patents upon the Methods of Using Leather Waste to Make Edible Gelatin]; *Xinjing Bao*, The Beijing News, A03 (May 3, 2012); *Xu/ Yu*, Prevalence and Control of Diabetes in Chinese Adults, 310 Jama 948 (2013).

[78] *Peng*, 87.

ciety and ultimately the prosperity of China itself.[79] With this mentality that science and technology represent a scared ideal, that not only provides economic growth but also the foundation for national pride, China has been very reluctant to restrict patentability based on moral considerations.[80] The broad scope patentability also explains why patent protection has such a different perception among the Chinese public. The close connection between scientism and patents as tools for technological advancement is supported by China's desire to "catch up" to Western countries and develop a scientific environment and technological advancement by investing in very modern and experimental technologies in particular, such as advanced biotechnology.[81]

By importing and adapting to a scientific research focus, China has not been uninfluenced by the international research community. Therefore, China has been, at the very least, a recipient of international research norms,[82] which include Western concerns about patentability as well. However, the influence is limited to the scientific community and barely affects the general public. An example of this kind of specific concern would be aspects of advanced biotechnology and even here, the impacts on the Chinese moral landscape have been considerably small.[83]

---

[79] *Xi Jinping*, Tan Zhiguo Lizheng [Xi Jinping: the Governance of China] (Waiwen Chubanshe [Foreign Languages Press] 2014); *Wu/Yu*, Jinping Xi: Chuangxin Ganwei Tianxia Xian [Xi Jinping: Innovation, Dare to be the First in the World], Renmin Ribao [People's Daily] 2, 11 (2017); *Peng*, 88.

[80] *Peng*, 88; also *Zhang*, Joy, The Cosmopolitanization of Science: Stem cell Governance in China (Palgrave Macmillan 2012).

[81] *Peng*, 88; *Qiu*, Xiangxing, Renlai Peitai Ganxibao Yanjiu Lunli Wenti de Diacho he Taolun [A Survey and Discussion on Ethical Issues of Human Embryonic Stem Cell Research], 25 Yixue yu Thexue [Medicine and Philosophy] 8 (2004); *Wu*, Zhishi Chanquan Zhanlüe Shishi de Guoji Huanjing yu Zhongguo Changjing [The International Environment of Implementing Intellectual Property Strategy and China's Situation], 2 Faxue [Law Science] 3 (2012); *Zhao*, Xu, Renlei Peitai Ganxibao Yanjiu de Lunli Guan Fenxi [A Study on Ethical Values of Human Embryonic Stem Cell Research], 1 Lunli Xue Yanjiu [Studies in Ethics] 82, 99 (2012).

[82] *Peng*, 88; *Yue/Yue*, 6; *Sleeboom-Faulkner*, National Risk Signatures and Human Embryonic Stem Cell Research in Mainland China, 12 Health, Risk & Society 491, 496 (2010); *Zhang*, Ping, Shengwu Yixue Lingyu zhong de Zhishi Chanquan Baohu [Intellectual Property Protection in the BioMedicine Field], 39 Journal of Peking University (Health Sciences) 101, 108 (2007).

[83] *Chen*, Hong, The Derivation of Two Additional Human Embryonic Stem Cell Lines from Day 3 Embryos with Low Morphological Scores, 20 Human Reproduction 2201 (2005); *Chen*, O., Patent biotechnology invention in China, 32 European Intellectual Property Review 9 (2010), 12; *Jiang*, Regulating Human Embryonic Stem Cell in China: A Comparative Study on Human Embryionic Stem Cell's Patentability and Morality in US and EU (Springer 2016); *Peng*, 89, *Xu Zhao*, 82, 88; *Liu*, Yinliang, Shengwu Jishu de Falü Wenti Yanjiu [Studies on Legal Issues for Biotechnology] (Kexue Chubanshe [Science Publishing House] 2007; *Pera*, Human Embryonic Stem Cell Technology in China, 113 Journal of Cell Science 5, 18 (2000).

IV. Conclusion

The conclusion on how legal culture in China shaped patent law can be based on the following observations.

1. Patent law was very recently imported to China and the concept is still not very well established among the public generally.
2. Chinese legal culture is substantially influenced by a focus on technological advancement and thereby connects patent law to other areas of law, which is highly unusual in other countries.
3. The Chinese value system does not recognize human dignity as a fundamental and absolute value and its legal significance is very low compared to its significance in other legal systems, especially Germany and Europe.

That does not mean, however, that the Chinese legal culture is totally devoid of moral standards.[84] On the contrary, this very approach to patent law makes it more dependent on legal culture than the other legal systems which have been analyzed. Since the Chinese public has established and accepted a connection of patentability and state endorsement, it is difficult from an administrative perspective to grant a patent to a morally concerning invention. This is especially difficult where the public disagrees with the specific technology. However, concerns about a certain field of research such as advanced biotechnology are not influenced by this concept since the importation of morality is very limited while the importation of law is very practical.[85]

In conclusion, the importation of patent law into China, especially a general moral restrictions clause is heavily dependent on Chinese legal culture. However, given the unique nature of patent law and its general reversal of illegality and immorality, the incorporation of such a general moral restrictions clause is very likely to be difficult

---

[84] *Cheng*, L., Ethics: China Already Has Clear Stem-cell Guidelines, 440 Nature 992 (2006), 998; *Deng/Luo*, Lun Zeren Lunli Shijioa Xia Lengdong Peitai Baohu Guize de Sifa Xuzao – Cong Woguo Shouli Lengdong Peitai de Jicheng Jiufen'an Qieru [Judicial Enforcement of Frozen Embryo Protection Rules from the Perspective of Ethics of Responsibility: The First Succession Dispute Case Concerning Frozen Embryos in China], Quanguo Fayuan Di 26 Jie Xueshu Taolunhui Lunwenji [the 26th Symposium of Courts in China] 1262 (2015), 1271; *Farrand*, Human Embryonic Stem Cells and Patent Law in the EU and China: Convergence in Standards Through Divergence in Institutions, 3 Intellectual Property Quarterly 260 (2016), 262; *Qiu*, Jane, Stem-cell Research and Regenerative Medicine in China, 3 National Science Review 257, 264 (2016).

[85] Consequently, for advanced biotechnology and stem cell research, the Chinese public has no strong moral resentments against stem cell research in general but there is certain understanding that inventions that use human embryonic stem cell show a certain level of respect for the underlying moral issues, which is a far lower hurdle than in the Western patent systems; *Chen*, H., Stem Cell Governance in China: from Bench to Bedside? 28 New Genetics and Society 267 (2009); *Qiu*, Jane, China Goes Back to Basics on Research Funding, 507 Nature 148, 161 (2014); *Salter*, Patenting, Morality and Human Embryonic Stem Cell Science: Bioethics and Cultural Politics in Europe, 2 Regenerative Medicine 301, 306 (2007).

and subject to misunderstandings. The fact that patent law itself is a foreign concept in Chinese law further exacerbates the difficulty of applying a general provision. In addition, in the Chinese system of morality and patent law, the necessary observation of the reversal of illegality and immorality has not yet been made in the legal discourse. This arguably incomplete understanding leads to a lack of decision-making on the subject as most administrative officials have no guidelines to work with and are reluctant to exclude any patent based on morality.[86]

---

[86] A similar situation is apparent in Taiwan and Japan: *Sumikura*, The Issues Surrounding Patent Protection for Human-Embryonic Stem Cells and Therapeutic Cloning in Japan, in: Patentschutz und Stammzellenforschung: Internationale und rechtsvergleichende Aspekte (Josef Drexl et al., eds, Springer 2009).

F. Summary and Comprehensive Assessment

The multitude of legislation, national and supranational patent regimes and the vague and infinite content of the concept of morality are easily considered an overburden for any analysis. However, addressing the research question and the subquestions in a comprehensive manner makes it easier to categorize the results.

Ultimately, the previous observations and analyses can be summarized and result in the following statements:

1. *How is morality shaped in the context of patent law?*

   Identifying moral concerns in patent law can be the subject of heated social debates. These debates can raise a variety of moral concerns, from different political, philosophical, religious or metaphysical viewpoints. However, moral concerns can also be subject to a careful analysis of international treaties and national pieces of legislation. Therefore, morality in the context of patent law is shaped inconsistently. Some technologies raise a substantial variety of concerns while others are never even considered to raise moral concerns at all. This effect is increased by the unequal use of patents. Not all technologies are subject to patent applications, therefore not all technologies are subject to a patentability assessment.

   Finally, morality concerns in patent law are affected by a misunderstanding of the use of a patent right. In particular, interest groups outside of the legal discussion are prone to consider a patent as a right of use.

2. *What role does legal culture play within the foundation of patentability?*

   The question of how morality in patent law is addressed, is directly linked to the very question of what purpose patent law has. Strong opinions within the legal debate, most notably in the U.S., argue that patent law incentivizes innovation as an end in itself. Consequently, such an approach argues for the elimination of moral requirements in patent law. However, it has been demonstrated that all relevant patent law jurisdictions still feel the need to impose some moral restrictions on patentability. How these moral restrictions are incorporated into patent law is dependent on the legal culture of each jurisdiction. Especially in China, where the legal culture is fundamentally different from the U.S. or Europe, it can be observed that patent law is treated as a foreign object within the legal system. As a first step to assessing the function of the concept of morality within any patent law jurisdiction, it is absolutely necessary to understand the legal culture behind it.

3. *Is there a timeframe for adopting morality within a patent system?*

The analysis of the Chinese patent law system strikingly demonstrates that a quick and practical adoption of the moral restrictions clause within a patent system is not possible. Rather, the concept of morality within patent law requires a clear understanding of the function of patent law. Moreover, for a meaningful understanding of patent law, it is necessary to clearly decide what purpose patent law has within a society. Both of those issues are conceptually lacking in the Chinese patent system. In addition, decisions on patentability regarding moral concerns are rare and always linked to a specific technology. Those factors make it almost impossible to create a general standard of morality within patent law. Furthermore, even in systems with a lengthy history of patent decisions, such as the U.S. or Germany, a clear definition of morality within patent law has still not been identified. It can be concluded that addressing the problem of general moral considerations within patent law is not simply a question of time.

4. *How can basic ideas of statehood influence the understanding of patentability?*

During the analysis, it became clear that the issue of morality in patent law is linked to the understanding of the separation of state powers. Where an invention could be deemed to be immoral and therefore not eligible for patent protection, the question arises as to who specifically has the responsibility and capability to decide. In Germany and Europe, it is both the legislator for specific inventions but also the administrative branch when it comes to the general moral restrictions clause. The latter decision can then be subject to judicial control. In the U.S., on the other hand, it was originally just the judicial branch directly, since they developed the moral utility doctrine. However, with a changing legal culture came a shift in power from the judicial branch to the legislator. Especially where there are morality concerns, the argument that such decisions should only be made by the legislator is dominant. This concept of dividing state power between the legislator, the executive and the judiciary influences how patent law is set up. And this is another aspect which is influenced by legal culture. China serves as a good example, because its legal culture includes a focus on strong central government which naturally gives ample power and responsibility to the patent offices. In Germany and the EU, where a more equal distribution of powers is intended, patent officials are hesitant to decide upon issues of morality.

5. *What makes the application of morality in patent law more difficult than in other areas of law? What is the respective relationship between immorality and illegality in this specific context?*

Several issues arise that increase the difficulty of addressing morality in patent law. First and foremost, the identified reversal of the relationship of immorality and illegality is a unique and foreign concept within the legal landscape. Secondly, the assessment of the commercial exploitation of an invention includes a certain element of prognosis. Elements of prognosis lead to uncertainty and in-

F. Summary and Comprehensive Assessment

volve a difficulty in pinpointing the actual effect an invention will have on society. Furthermore, any debates are linked to a specific technology which makes it nearly impossible to identify a general standard of morality. Ultimately, all these difficulties lead to sparse jurisprudence and legal research on this important topic. And, in countries like China, where patent law itself is a new concept that has yet to be fully embraced and understood by the general public, those difficulties increase significantly.

Additionally, morality has a distinct and unique meaning in patent law. This unique meaning stems from the feature of patent law that dictates that an invention may not be excluded from patent law just because it is illegal. In other words, an invention might be considered illegal but not immoral in the framework of patent law. This dependence is a reversal of the general concept of illegality and immorality in all other areas of law. In addition, since Art. 27 (2) TRIPS expressly states this relationship between patentability and illegality, all relevant patent law jurisdictions share this unique feature. However, most jurisdictions lack awareness of this reversal which makes its application and determination even more difficult. Effectively, for an invention in patent law to be considered immoral it has to be illegal and this requires an additional qualifying element. What exactly this "qualifying element" is, is not understood in a meaningful way in any of the analyzed jurisdictions. Several explanations attempting to explain the issue in the German and European jurisdictions exist but they do not provide practical or definitive answers. Ultimately, this unique role of morality in patent law is either misunderstood or only dealt with marginally, which ensures that it remains ill-defined.

Ultimately, the assessment of a patent application may not develop into a citizens' referendum.[1] A referendum would drastically change the reliability of patent decisions. In addition, technical details of medical or biotechnological inventions are likely to overextend the assessment capabilities of an average citizen. Therefore, a purely empirical approach seems inherently unsuitable. Ultimately, the question of how to determine the principles of morality while still maintaining the need for professionalism in a patent office is still unanswered.

A referendum would also be largely influenced by emotional considerations, besides being absolutely impractical regarding the sheer amount of patent applications.[2] A more practical approach would seem to be the establishment of an institutional body, such as an ethics committee, which assesses patents in a more legal and patent-specific light. Such a body could be integrated within the patent office itself and separate the technological aspects from the ethical considerations, solving the problem of technological focus which has the potential to outshine anything else.[3]

---

[1] *Baier*, Values and Morals, 234; *Murray*, Social Science & Medicine, 1987, 646.
[2] For example: total patent applications in the U.S. in 2018: 597, 141.
[3] See the criticism re. the weapon technology by *Vorwerk* and *Horn*.

F. Summary and Comprehensive Assessment

6. How can the current situation of applying morality in patent law be improved?

To give a definite and comprehensive definition of the moral standard within patent law is – even theoretically – impossible. However, it is necessary to be aware of the unique set-up and properties of morality within patent law. In particular, the reversal of immorality and illegality has to be addressed explicitly. In a second step, it is necessary to determine the fundamental function of a given national patent law. In addition, it has to be accepted that the fundamental function includes a moral restriction on inventions – at least to some degree. From this point on, it is possible to directly address the question of what exactly the qualifying element that leads from illegality to immorality in the meaning of patent law is. By using this approach, the relationship between morality, patent law and legal culture can be explored and provides valuable insights for answering specific questions about the morality of a specific invention. With regard to the value system, the indirect and exclusionary nature of a patent right makes it difficult to apply human dignity as an absolute value in a practical and reasonable way. Therefore, the application of human dignity should be used with particular caution within patent law. Only in this way is it possible to achieve a meaningful and applicable result. In summary, to improve the current situation, an attempt to provide a definitive and general standard is futile. Yet, the answers could be more accessible in the future, if the necessary awareness is raised to enable the right questions to be asked.

In order to address the last question and the relationship of legal culture in patent law, it is necessary to use the previous results in a respective analysis.

Given the responses to the individual research questions, an overall conclusion to the overarching question can be drawn.

How does legal culture affect the perception of morality in patent law regimes and can a better understanding improve the imprecise relationship of the two?

I. It is of crucial importance to raise awareness about how interpreting the fundamental function of patent law influences the role of morality. Additionally, even if the argument that an invention has to have some sort of social benefit is rejected, it is necessary to be aware that moral issues still arise. A truly neutral patent law is highly unlikely to exist.

II. It is also important to know that technological advancement can be much more dynamic than legislation. Patent law is potentially confronted early on in technological development. This creates a need for dynamic reaction. Even if a parliamentary decision of morality is preferred, it is practically impossible to leave decisions about morality entirely up to the legislator. It is helpful to understand that decisions regarding a patent application are very specific because they only apply to a certain technology.

III. Additionally, the role of governmental approval in granting a patent has to be considered. There are always going to be technologies and devices that will be

F. Summary and Comprehensive Assessment 203

deemed so immoral by a majority within society that even the grant of a patent is considered government approval – albeit legally incorrect. A patent law regime at least has to be aware of the difficulty of being purely technology-focused.

IV. The unique relationship of immorality and illegality in patent law creates a paradox. In patent law, the common relationship between immorality and illegality is reversed. However, the understanding of morality in patent law is still rooted in morality in a general sense. It is difficult if not impossible to solve this paradox. However, understanding this role reversal is necessary in order to formulate more precise legal arguments.

V. A standard of morality in patent law cannot be universally accepted across different patent systems. It has to be approached by a better incorporation and understanding of legal culture. Cultural aspects of interpreting patent law have to be included as well.

VI. Developing a satisfying and consistent standard of morality requires patience. Given the rarity of immoral technologies, decisions and discussions of morality in patent law are likely to remain sparse. Moreover, once they occur, they tend to over-emphasize considerations that are only applicable to a certain technology.

VII. Ultimately, aspects of legal culture and societal interests can be balanced in a proportionality approach. Given the nature of a patent as an exclusionary right makes its factual influence less significant than a right of use. However, this is only meaningful, if no interests are categorically excluded from this approach. Therefore, using human dignity as an absolute value makes the assessment of morality in patent law much more difficult, if not impossible.

Bibliography

Abeelen, Derek Van den: Harnessing Human Potential: Induced Pluripotent Stem Cell Patentability Under the Lens of Myriad, 7 William & Mary Business Law Review 855, 2016.

Ahrens, Claus: Genpatente – Rechte am Leben? – Dogmatische Aspekte der Patentierbarkeit von Erbgut, GRUR 2003, 89.

Alexander, Daniel: The Case For and Against Patenting of Biotechnological Inventions, in: Sigrid Sterck (ed.), Biotechnology, Patents and Morality, Ashgate Publishing 2000.

Alford, William P.: To Steal A Book is An Elegant Offense: Intellectual Property Law in Chinese Civilization, Stanford University Press 1995.

Allison, Kirk C. et al.: Historical Development and Current Status of Organ Procurement from Death-row Prisoners in China, 16 BMC Medical Ethics 85, 2015.

Amit, Michal/*Itskovitz-Eldor*, Joseph: Derivation and Spontaneous Differentiation of Human Embryonic Stem Cells, 200 Journal of Anatomy 225, 2002.

An, Jian: Zhonghua Renmin Gongheguo Zhuanli Fa Siyi [The Interpretation of Patent Law of the People's Republic of China], Qunguo Renmin Daibio Dahui Changwu Weiyuanhui Fazhi Gongzuo Weiyuanhui [The Commission of Legislative Affairs of the Standing Committee of the National People's Congress] (ed.), Zhongguo Falü Chubanshe [Law Press, China] 2009.

Bagley, Margo A.: A Global Controversy: The Role of Morality in Biotechnology Patent Law, in: Peter K. Yu (ed.), Intellectual Property and Information Wealth: Issues and Practices in the Digital Age Vol. 2, Praeger 2006.

Bagley, Margo A.: Patent First, Ask Questions Later: Morality and Biotechnology in Patent Law, 45 William and Mary Law Review 469, 2003.

Bagley, Margo A.: Stem Cells, Cloning and Patents: What's Morality Got to Do with it? 39 New England Law Review 501, 2004.

Bahadur, Geeh/*Morrison*, Michael: Patenting Human Pluripotent Cells: Balancing Commercial, Academic and Ethical Interests, 25 Human Reproduction 14, 2010.

Baharvand, Hossein et al.: Generation of New Human Embryonic Stem Cell Lines with Diploid and Triploid Karyotypes, 48 Development, Growth & Differentiation 117, 2006.

Baier, Kurt: Moral Reasons and Reasons to be Moral, 231–256, in: Values and Morals, 13, Springer Science and Business Media, 1978.

Bak, Rasmus O./*Gomez-Ospina*, Natalia/*Porteus*, Matthew H.: Gene Editing on Center Stage, Trends in Genetics 2018, 34 (8): 600–611.

Barad, Lili et al.: Human Embryonic Stem Cells vs Human Induced Pluripotent Stem Cells for Cardiac Repair, 30 Canadian Journal of Cardiology 1279, 2014.

Barfield, Claude/*Calfee*, John E.: Biotechnology and the Patent System: Balancing Innovation and Property Rights, The AEI Press 2007.

Barrangou, Rodolphe/*Doudna*, Jennifer A.: Applications of CRISPR technologies in research and beyond, Nature Biotechnology 2016, 34 (9): 933–941.

Batista, Pedro Henrique D.: Zur Patentierung menschlicher embryonaler Stammzellen – Kritische Würdigung der Entscheidung des EuGH im Fall Brüstle, GRUR Int. 2013, 514–518.

Baumbach/Rasch: Kann man das menschliche Genom und damit den Menschen patentieren? Mitt. 1992, 209–217.

Bayer, Hans: Patent und Ethik im Spiegel technischer Evolution, GRUR 1994, 541–559.

Benkard, Georg: Patentgesetz, Gebrauchsmustergesetz, Patentkostengesetz, 11th edition, Munich 2015. referenced as: *Editor*, in: Benkard, PatG Sect.

Bently, Lionel/*Sherman*, Brad: Intellectual Property Law, 4th edition, Oxford University Press 2014.

Bergman, Karl/*Graff*, Gregory D.: The Global Stem Cell Patent Landscape: Implications of Efficient Technology Transfer and Commercial Development, 25 Nature Biotechnology 419, 2007.

Beyleveld, Deryck: Human Dignity in Bioethics and Biolaw, Oxford University Press 2001.

Blackburn, Simon: The Oxford Dictionary of Philosophy, 2nd edition, Oxford University Press 2005.

Bouvet, Philippe: Patentability of Inventions Involving Human Stem Cells in Europe, 9 Journal of commercial biotechnology 40, 2002.

Braga, C. Primo: The Developing Country Case For and Against Intellectual Property Protection, in: Wolfgang E. Siedbeck (ed.), The World Bank, 1990.

Bregman-Eschet, Yael et al.: The Ripple Effect of Intellectual Property Policy: Empirical Evidence from Stem Cell Research and Development, 19 Journal of Technology Law & Policy 227, 2014.

Breith, Hans-Jürgen: Sind die gesetzlichen Regelungen über die Geheimhaltung von Patenten und Gebrauchsmuster noch zeitgemäß?, GRUR 2003, 587–592.

Brevini, Tal/*Gandolfi*, Fran: Parthenotes as a Source of Embryonic Stem Cells, 41 Cell Proliferation 20, 2008.

Brokowski, Carolyn: Do CRISPR Germline Ethics Statements Cut It?, The CRISPR Journal, 2018, 1 (2): 115–125.

Brownsword, Roger et al.: Human Genetics and the Law: Regulation a Revolution, 61 The Modern Law Review 593, 1998.

Bunke, Christoph: 40 Jahre Rote Taube – Die Entwicklung des Erfindungsbegriffs, Mitt. 2009, 169–175.

Burdach, Stefan: Patentrecht: Eine neue Dimension in der medizinischen Ethik?, Mitt. 2001, 9–16.

Burk, Dan L./*Lemley*, Mark A.: Biotechnology's Uncertainty Principle, 54 Case Western Reserve Law Review 691, 2003.

Burk, Dan L./*Lemley*, Mark A.: Policy Levers in Patent Law, 89 Virginia Law Review 2003, 1575–1696.

Burns, James H.: Happiness and Utility: Jeremy Bentham's Equation, 17 Utilitas 46 (2005.

Busche, Jan: Die Patentierung biologischer Erfindungen nach Patentgesetz und EPÜ, GRUR Int. 1999, 299–304.

Busche, Jan: Patentrecht zwischen Innovation und ethischer Verantwortung, Mitt. 2001, 4–10.

Byrnes, Malcolm W.: The Flawed Scientific Basis of the Altered Nuclear Transfer-oocyte Assisted Reprogramming (ANT-OAR) Proposal, 3 Stem Cell Reviews 60, 2007.

Calame, Thierry: Öffentliche Ordnung und gute Sitten als Schranken der Patentierbarkeit gentechnologischer Erfindungen: Eine Untersuchung des Europäischen Patentübereinkommens und des schweizerischen Patentgesetzes unter Berücksichtigung des internationalen Rechtsumfelds, Basel 2001.

Callaway, Ewen: UK scientists gain licence to edit genes in human embryos, Nature 530 (758), 2016.

Cameron, Nigel M. de S.: Pandora's Progeny: Ethical Issues in Assisted Human Reproduction, 39 Family law quarterly 745, 2005.

Cao, Jingwen et al.: Trends and Prospects of Stem Cell Research in China, 31 Chinese Medical Journal 116, 2016.

Castle, David: The Role of Intellectual Property Rights in Biotechnology Innovation, Edward Elgar 2009.

Caulfield, Timothy: Biotechnology Patents, Public Trust and Patent Pools: the Need for Governance? in: David Castle (ed.), The Role of Intellectual Property Rights in Biotechnology Innovation, Edward Elgar 2009.

Caulfield, Timothy et al.: Trust, Patents and Public Perceptions: The Governance of Controversial Biotechnology Research, 24 Nature Biotechnology 1352, 2006.

Chalmers, Damian et al.: European Union Law: Cases and Materials, Cambridge University Press 2010.

Chan, Albert: A Patent Perspective on U.S. Stem Cell Research, 32 Nature Biotechnology 633, 2014.

Chang, Howard F.: Patent Scope, Antitrust Policy, and Cumulative Innovation, 26 The RAND Journal of Economics 34, 1995.

Chapman, Audrey R.: The Ethics of Patenting Human Embryonic Stem Cells, 19 Kennedy Institute of Ethics Journal 261, 2009.

Chapman, Demian D. et al.: Virgin Birth in a Hammerhead Shark, 3 Biology Letters 425, 2007.

Chen, Haidan: Stem Cell Governance in China: from Bench to Bedside? 28 New Genetics and Society 267, 2009.

Chen, Hong et al.: The Derivation of Two Additional Human Embryonic Stem Cell Lines from Day 3 Embryos with Low Morphological Scores, 20 Human Reproduction 2201, 2005.

Chen, Jianfu: Chinese Law: Towards an Understanding of Chinese Law, Its Nature and Developments, Klumer Law International 1999.

Chen, Qiongdi: Patent biotechnology invention in China, 32 European Intellectual Property Review 9, 2010.

Cheng, Linzhao et al.: Ethics: China Already Has Clear Stem-cell Guidelines, 440 Nature 992, 2006.

Cheng, Qun: Daojiao Shengsi Guan Yanjiu [Research on Taoist View of Life and Death], Sichaun Daxue [Sichuan University], 2007.

Chung, Young et al.: Human Embryonic Stem Cell Lines Generated Without Embryo Destruction, 2 Cell Stem Cell 113, 2008.

Cohen, Jon: CRISPR, the revolutionary genetic "scissors," honored by Chemistry Nobel, Science 2020, 489.

Cohen, Stanley N.: Construction of Biogically Functional Bacterial Plasmids In Vitro, 70 Proceedings of the National Academy of Sciences 3240, 1973.

Colston, Catherine/*Galloway*, Jonathan: Modern Intellectual Property Law, 3rd edition, Routledge 2010.

Condic, M. L.: Alternative Sources of Pluripotent Stem Cells: Altered Nuclear Transfer, 41 Cell Proliferation 7, 2008.

Condic, Maureen L./*Condic*, Samuel B.: The Appropriate Limits of Science in the Formation of Public Policy, 17 Notre Dame Journal of Law, Ethics and Public Policy 157, 2003.

Cora, Diamond: Consequentialism in Modern Moral Philosophy and in "Modern Moral Philosophy", Human Lives – Critical Essays on Consequentialist Bioethics, 1997, 13–38.

Crespi, Stephen R.: Biotechnology patents and morality, Trends in Biotechnology 1997, 123–129.

Crowne, Emir: The Utilitarian Fruits Approach to Justifying Patentable Subject Matter, 10 John Marshall Review of Intellectual Property Law 753, 2011.

Cui, Guobin: Zhuanli Fa Yuali Yu Anli [Patent Law: Cases and Materials] Beiing Daxue Chubanshe [Peking University Press], 2012.

Curley, Duncan/*Sharples*, A.: Patenting Biotechnology in Europe: The Ethical Debate Moves on, 24 European Intellectual Property Review 565, 2002.

Cyranoski, David: China's embrace of embryo selection raises thorny questions, Nature 548 (7667): 272, 2017.

Cyranoski, David/*Reardon*, Sara: Chinese scientists genetically modify human embryos. Nature 1028, 2015, 124–130.

Daughtry, Brittany/*Mitalipov*, Shoukrat: Concise Review: Parthenote Stem Cells for Regenerative Medicine: Genetic, Epigenic, and Developmental Features, 3 Stem Cells Translational Medicine 290, 2014.

Davis, Amy Rachel: Patented Embryonic Stem Cells: The Quintessential "Essential Facility"?, 94 Georgetown Law Journal 205, 2005.

Dederer, Georg: Stammzellpatente: Causa finita?, GRUR 2013, 352–357.

Dederer, Georg: Human-embryonale Stammzellforschung vor dem Aus? – Anmerkung zum Urteil des EuGH vom 18. Oktober 2011, Rs C-34/10, Europarecht, 2012, 336–341.

Dederer, Georg: Zum Patentierungsausschluss von embryonalen Stammzellen und Stammzellenderivaten, GRUR 2007, 1054–1059.

Demaine, L. T./*Fellmeth*, A.: Reinventing the Double Helix: A Novel and Nonobvious Reconceptualization of the Biotechnology Patent, 55 Stanford Law Review 303, 2002.

Deng, Zhiwei/*Luo*, Lishi: Lun Zeren Lunli Shijioa Xia Lengdong Peitai Baohu Guize de Sifa Xuzao – Cong Woguo Shouli Lengdong Peitai de Jicheng Jiufen'an Qieru [Judicial Enforcement of Frozen Embryo Protection Rules from the Perspective of Ethics of Responsibility: The First Succession Dispute Case Concerning Frozen Embryos in China], Quanguo Fayuan Di 26 Jie Xueshu Taolunhui Lunwenji [the 26th Symposium of Courts in China] 1262, 2015.

Devolder, Katrien/*Ward*, Christopher M.: Rescuing Human Embryonic Stem Cell Research: The Possibility of Embryo Reconstitution After Stem Cell Derivation, 38 Metaphilosophy 245, 2007.

Dickson, David: Legal Fight Looms over Patent Bid on Human/Animal Chimaeras, 392 Nature 423, 1998.

Dikötter, Frank: Sex, Culture and Modernity in China: Her Tumultuous Life's Journey to the West, Vol. 1, Hong Kong University Press 1995.

Dolder, Fritz: Patente auf der Grundlage biologischen Ressourcen aus Entwicklungsländern, Mitt. 2003, 349–354.

Dondorp, Wybo/*Wert*, Guido de: Embryonic Stem Cells Without Moral Pain, Health Council of the Netherlands 2005.

Dörries, Ulrich H.: Patentansprüche auf DNA-Sequenzen: Ein Hindernis für die medizinische Forschung?, Mitt. 2001, 15–21.

Drahos, Peter: Biotechnology Patents, Markets and Morality, European Intellectual Property Review 1999, 1–12.

Drahos, Peter: Biotechnology Patents, Markets and Morality, 21 European Intellectual Property Review 441, 1999.

Dutfield, Graham: Intellectual Property Rights and the Life Science Industries: Past, Present and Future, 2nd edition, World Scientific 2009.

Eberle, Herbert: Human Dignity, Privacy, and Personality in German and American Constitutional Law, 1997, UTAH L. Rev. 963, 968–72, 1997.

Enzthaler/Zech: Stoffschutz bei gentechnischen Patenten – Rechtslage nach Erlass des Biopatentgesetzes und Auswirkung auf Chemiepatente, GRUR 2006, 529–534.

Erramouspe, Matthew: Staking Patent Claims on the Human Blueprint: Rewards and Rent-Dissipating Races, 43 UCLA Law Review 961, 1995.

Eyre, David E./*Schlich*, George W.: Patenting Stem Cell Technologies Following Guidelines issued by the EPO, USPTO, JPO an SIPO, 4 Pharmaceutical Patent Analyst 431, 2015.

Falvey, Rod et al.: Intellectual Property Rights and Economic Growth, 10 Review of Development Economics 700, 2006.

Farrand, Benjamin: Human Embryonic Stem Cells and Patent Law in the EU and China: Convergence in Standards Through Divergence in Institutions, 3 Intellectual Property Quarterly 260, 2016.

Fendrick, Sarah E./*Zuhn*, Donald L.: Patentability of Stem Cells in the United States, 5:a020958 Cold Spring harb. Perspect Med 1, 2015.

Feng, Peter: Intellectual Property Law in China, 2nd edition, Sweet & Maxwell Asia 2003.

Ferrer, Marcela et al.: The Scientific Muscle of Brazil's Health Biotechnology, 22 Nature Biotechnology DC8, 2004.

Feuerlein, Andreas: Patentrechtliche Probleme der Biotechnologie, GRUR 2001, 561–565.

Fiechter, Armin: Preface, in: Armin Fiechter (ed.), History of Modern Biotechnology II, Springer 2000.

Fitt, Robert: New Guidance on the Patentability of Embryonic Stem Cell Patents in Europe, 27 Nature Biotechnology 338, 2009.

Ford, Ralph: The morality of biotech patents: Different legal obligations in Europe?, European Intellectual Property Review 1997, 315–318.

Fu, XiaoBing: Regenerative Medicine Research in China: From Basic Research to Clinical Practice, 57 Science China Life Sciences 155, 2014.

Fuchs, Andreas: Patentrecht und Humangenetik, Mitt. 2000, 1–9.

Furth, Charlotte: A Flourishing Yin: Gender in China's Medical History, University of California Press 1999.

Galasso, Alberto/*Schankerman*, Mark: Patents and Cumulative Innovation: Casual Evidence from the Courts, 130 The Quarterly Journal of Economics 317, 2015.

Ganea, Peter/*Pattloch*, Thomas: Intellectual Property Law in China, Christopher Heath (ed.), Kluwer Law International 2005.

George, Erin P.: The Stem Cell Debate: The Legal, Political and Ethical Issues Surrounding Federal Funding of Scientific Research on Human Embryos, 12 Albany Law Journal of Science & Technology 747, 2001.

Gerecht-Nir, Sharon/*Itskovitz-Eldor*, Joseph: Cell Therapy Using Human Embryonic Stem Cells, 12 Transplant Immunology 203, 2004.

Gerecht-Nir, Sharon/*Itskovitz-Eldor*, Joseph: The Promise of Human Embryonic Stem Cells, 18 Best Practice & Research Clinical Obstetrics & Gynaecology 843, 2004.

Gervais, Danie: The TRIPS Agreement: Drafting History and Analysis, 3rd edition, Sweet & Maxwell 2008.

Goebel, Frank P.: Ist der Mensch patentierbar? Zur Frage der Patentfähigkeit von Humangenen, Mitt. 1995, 153–160.

Goebel, Frank P.: Bio-/Gentechnik und Patentrecht. Anmerkungen zur Rechtsprechung, Mitt. 1999, 173–179.

Golan-Mashiach, Michal et al.: Design Principle of Gene Expression Used by Human Stem Cells: Implication for Pluripotency, 19 The FASEB Journal 147, 2005.

Gold, E. Richard/*Gallochat*, Alain: The European Biotech Directive: Past as Prologue, 7 European Law Journal 331, 2001.

Gould, Stephan J.: On the Origin of Specious Critics, Discover, Jan. 1985, 28.

Gramm, Werner: Die gewerbliche Anwendbarkeit, GRUR 1984, 761–769.

Green, Ronald M.: Stem Cell Research: A Target Article Collection Part III – Determining Moral Status, 2 The American Journal of Bioethics 20, 2002.

Grund, Martin: Patentierbarkeit von transgenen Pflanzen, Tieren und ESTs nach der Transformation der Eu-Biotechnologierichtlinie und der EPA-Entscheidung G 1/98, Mitt. 2000, 328–335.

Grund, Martin/*Burda*, Martin R.: Zum BGH Vorlagebeschluss an den EuGH zur Auslegung der Biopatentrichtlinie – Neurale Vorläuferzellen, Mitt. 2010, 214–221.

Grund, Martin/*Keller*, Christian: Patentierbarkeit embryonaler Stammzellen, Mitt. 2004, 49–55.

Grundmann, Helge E.: The Economic Arguments for Patents and Their Validity for Developing Countries, 19 Indian Economic Journal 193, 1970.

Gudel, Diether: Zum Problem der gesetzwidrigen Erfindungen, GRUR 1966, 235–236.

Haase, Alexandra et al.: Generation of Induced Pluripotent Stem Cells from Human Cord Blood, 5 Cell Stem Cell 434, 2009.

Haedicke, Maximilian: Kein Patent auf Leben? – Grundlagen des Patentrechts und der Schutz biotechnologischer Erfindungen, JuS 2002, 113–119.

Halliday, Samantha: A Comparative Approach to the Regulation of Human Embryonic Stem Cell Research in Europe, 12 Medical Law Review 40, 2004.

Han, Xiao et al.: Lengdong Peitai de Lunli Wenti Yanjiu [An Analysis on the Ethical Problem of Frozen Embryos], 15 Kunming Ligong Daxue Xuebao [Journal of Kunming University of Science and Technology], 15, 2015.

Hansen, Matthias: Hände weg vom absoluten Stoffschutz – auch bei DNA-Sequenzen, Mitt. 2001, 477–485.

Hardee, Karen et al.: Family Planning and Women's Lives in Rural China, 30 International Family Planning Perspectives 68, 2004.

Harmon, Shawn H. E. et al.: Organ Transplantation in China und Beyond: Addressing the 'Access Gap', 10 Medical Law International 191, 2010.

Harn, Ren-How: Keeping the Gates Open for Human Embryonic Stem Cell Research, 13 Cardozo Public Law, Policy and Ethics Journal 525, 2015.

Hartmann, Marion: Die Patentierbarkeit von Stammzellen und den damit zusammenhängenden Verfahren, GRUR Int. 2006, 195–201.

He, Huanfeng: Daxuesheng Zhishichanquan Jiaoyu Tanxi – Yi Shandongsheng Daxuesheng zhishichanquan Yishi Diaocho wei Jichu [Analysis on the Education of Intellectual Property for College Students], 27 Journal of Shandong Youth University of Political Science 42, 2011.

Heidenreich, Matthias/*Zhang*, Feng: Applications of CRISPR-Cas systems in neuroscience. Nature Reviews, Neuroscience, 2016, 17 (1): 36–44.

Heins, Nico et al.: Derication, Characterization, and Differentiation of Human Embryonic Stem Cells, 22 Stem Cells 367, 2004.

Heller, Michael A.: The Boundaries of Private Property, 108 Yale Law Journal 1163, 1999.

Heller, Michael A.: The Tragedy of the Anticommons: Property in the Transition from Marx to Markets, 111 Harvard Law Review 621, 1998.

Heller, Michael A./*Eisenberg*, Rebecca S.: Can Patents Deter Innovation? The Anticommons in Biomedical Research, 280 Science 698, 1998.

Hellstadius, Âsa: A Comparative Analysis of the National Implementation of the Directive's Morality Clause, in: Aurora Plomer/Paul Torremans (eds.), Embryonic Stem Cell Patents: European Law and Ethics, Oxford University Press 2009.

Herdegen, Matthias: Die Patentierbarkeit von Stammzellenverfahren nach der Richtlinie 98/44/EG; GRUR Int. 2000, 859–864.

Hesketh, Therese et al.: The Effect of China's One-child Family Policy After 25 Years, 353 New England Journal of Medicine 1171, 2005.

Hoffman, David C.: Modest Proposal: Toward Improved Access to Biotechnology Research Tools by Implementing a Broad Experimental Use Exception, 89 Cornell Law Review 993, 2003.

Holden, Constance/*Vogel*, Gretchen: A Seismic Shift for Stem Cell Research, 319 Science 560, 2008.

Hoppe, Christian: Die Patentierbarkeit biotechnologischer Erfindungen, Pharma Recht 97, 392–404.

Hoxha, Eneda: Stemming the Tide: Stem Cell Innovation in the Myriad-Mayo-Roslin Era, 30 Berkeley Technology Law Journal 567, 2015.

Hu, Yuhong: Ren de Zunyan de Falü Shuxing Bianxi [An Analysis of the Legal Attributes of Human Dignity], 5 Zhongguo Shehui Kexue [Social Science in China] 101, 2016.

Huang, Kenneth G./*Murray*, Fiona E.: Does Patent Strategy Shape the Long-run Supply of Public Knowledge? Evidence From Human Genetics, 52 Academy of Management Journal 1193, 2009.

Hübel, Andreas: Patentability of pluripotent stem cells unlikely although they are not considered as embryo, Mitt. 2011, 494–501.

Hübel, Andreas et al.: General Issues of Biotech Patents, in: Ulrich Storz (ed.), Biopatent Law: Patent Strategies and Patent Management, Springer 2012.

Hübel, Andreas et al.: Limits of Patentability: Plant Sciences, Stem Cells and Nucleic Acids, Springer Science & Business Media 2012.

Hübel, Andreas/*Storz*, Ulrich/*Hüttermann*, Aloys: Limits of patentability. Plant sciences, stem cells and nucleic acids, Berlin, 2013.

Hurlbut, William B.: Ethics and Embryonic Stem Cell Research: Altered Nuclear Transfer as a Way Forward, 21 Biodrugs 79, 2007.

Ilic, Dusko et al.: Derivation of Human Embryonic Stem Cell Lines from Biospied Blastomeres on Human Feeders with Minimal Exposure to Xenomaterials, 18 Stem Cells and Development 1343, 2009.

Isasi, Rosario M./*Knoppers*, Bartha M.: Towards Commonality? Policy Approaches to Human Embryonic Stem Cell Research in Europe, in: Aurora Plomer/Paul Torremans (eds.), Embryonic Stem Cell Patents: European Law and Ethics, Oxford University Press 2009.

Isasi, Rosario M./*Knoppers*, Bartha M.: Mind the Gap: Policy Approaches to Embryonic Stem Cell and Cloning Research in 50 Countries, 13 European Journal of Health Law 9, 2006.

Jackson, Emily: Regulating Reproduction: Law Technology and Autonomy, Hart Publishing 2001.

Jackson, Vickson: Constitutional Dialogue and Human Dignity: States and Transnational Discourse, 65 Montana Law Review, 15, 17, 2004.

Jacobs, Philippe: Gene Patents: A Different Approach, 23 European Intellectual Property Review 505, 2001.

Jaffe, Adam B.: The U.S. patent system in transition: Policy innovation and the innovation process, Research Policy 2000, 531–557.

Jiang, Li: Regulating Human Embryonic Stem Cell in China: A Comparative Study on Human Embryionic Stem Cell's Patentability and Morality in U.S. and EU, Springer 2016.

Johnson, Martin H.: Human ES Cells and a Blastocyst from One Embryo: Exciting Science but Conflicting Ethics? 2 Cell Stem Cell 103, 2008.

Keay, Laura A.: Morality's Move within U.S. Patent Law: From Moral Utility to Subject Matter, AIPLA Quarterly Journal 2012, 409–439.

Keil, Gernot: Umweltschutz als Patenthindernis, GRUR 1993, 705–711.

Kelbel, Günter: Die Geheimerfindung, GRUR 1969, 155–167.

Kevles, Daniel: The Advent of Animal Patents: Innovation and Controversy in the Engineering and Ownership of Life, in: Max Rothschild/Scott Newman (eds.), Intellectual Property Rights in Animal Breeding and Genetics, 17, 21–22, 2002.

Kienle, Thomas: Die neue EU-Richtlinie zum Schutz biotechnologischer Erfindungen – rechtliche und ethische Probleme der Patentierung biologischer Substanzen, WRP 1998, 692–699.

Kim, Hee Sun et al.: Methods for Derivation of Human Embryonic Stem Cells, 23 Stem Cells 1228, 2005.

Kintisch, Eli: Groups Challenge Key Stem Cell Patents, 313 Science 281, 2006.

Kirkland, Russell: "Enhancing Life?" Perspectives from Traditional Chinese Value-Systems, 36 The Journal of Law, Medicine & Ethics 26, 2008.

Kitch, Edmund W.: The Nature and Function of the Patent System, 20 Journal of Law and Economics 265, 1977.

Kitch, Edmund W.: The Patent Policy of Developing Countries, 13 Pacific Basin Law Journal 166, 1994.

Klar, Martin/*Kunze*, Matthias/*Zahradnik*, Harold P.: Diskussion um den ethischen Status humaner Embryonen – Eine Zusammenfassung von zentralen Argumenten und Perspektiven, Journal für Reproduktionsmedizin und Endokrinologie 2007, 21–35.

Kleine, Tatjana/*Klingelhöfer*, Thomas: Biotechnologie und Patentrecht – Ein aktueller Überblick, GRUR 2003, 1–7.

Knoppers, Bartha et al.: Commercialization of Genetic Research and Public Policy, 286 Science 2277, 1999.

Ko, Yusing: An Economic Analysis of Biotechnology Patent Protection, 102 Yale Law Journal 777, 1992.

Kock, Michael/*Porzig*, Christian/*Willnegger*, Anna: Der Schutz von pflanzenbiotechnologischen Erfindungen und von Pflanzensorten unter Berücksichtigung der Biotechnologierichtlinie, GRUR Int. 2005, 183–188.

Koenig, Christian/*Müller*, Eva M.: EG-rechtliche Vorgaben zur Patentierbarkeit gentherapeutischer Verfahren unter Verwendung künstlicher Chromosomen nach der Richtlinie 98/44/EG, GRUR Int. 2000, 295–301.

Kollmann, Maite S.: Taking the Moral High Road: Why Embryonic Stem Cell Research Should be Strictly Regulated, 2 Faulkner Law Review 145, 2010.

Köllner, Maximilian/*Weber*, Peter: Trolls and their consequences – an evolving IP ecosystem. Mitt. 2014, 106–110.

Kranz, Wilhelm: Die Auswirkungen des 6. Überleitungsgesetzes vom 23. März 1961 auf § 1 Abs. 2 Nr. 1 des Patentgesetzes, GRUR 1962, 389–393.

Krauß, Jan: Die Effekte der Umsetzung der Richtlinie über den Schutz biotechnologischer Erfindungen auf die deutsche Praxis im Bereich dieser Erfindungen, Mitt. 2005, 490–494.

Krauß, Jan: Die richtlinienkonforme Auslegung der Begriffe "Verwendung" und "Funktion" bei Sequenzpatenten und deren Effekte auf die Praxis, Mitt. 2001, 296–301.

Krauß, Jan/*Engelhard*, Thomas: Patente im Zusammenhang mit der menschlichen Stammzellenforschung – ethische Aspekte und Übersicht über den Status der Diskussion in Europa und Deutschland, GRUR 2003, 985–990.

Krefft, Diedrich: Patente auf human-genomische Erfindungen, Schriftenreihe zum gewerblichen Rechtsschutz Band 122, 2003.

Kretschmer, Friedrich: Patentschutz für Gentechnik, GRUR 1992, 155–161.

Kumm, Alfred W.: Probleme der Geheimhaltung von technischen Erfindungen im Interesse der Staatssicherheit, GRUR 1979, 672–679.

Kunczik, Niclas: Die Legitimation des Patentsystems im Lichte biotechnischer Erfindungen. GRUR 2003, 845–849.

Ladas, Stephen P.: Patents, Trademarks, and Related Rights: National and International Protection, Harvard University Press 1975.

Laimböck, Lean/*Dederer*, Hans-Georg: Der Begriff des "Embryos" im Biopatentrecht. Anmerkungen zu den Schlussanträgen von GA Yves Bot vom 10. März 2011, Rs C-34/10 – Brüstle. Zugleich eine Kritik des Kriteriums der "Totipotenz", GRUR Int. 2011, 661–667.

Lander, Eric S. et al.: Adopt a moratorium on heritable genome editing, Nature 2019, 165–178.

Landry, Donald W./*Zucker*, Howard A.: Embryonic Death and the Creation of Human Embryonic Stem Cells, 114 Journal of Clinical Investigation 1184, 2004.

Langfang, Fei/*Peng*, Zhou: The Law Itself is not Above Human Beings: Comments on China's First Case on Frozen Embryos, 29 International Journal of Law, Policy and the *Family* 260, 2015.

Lanzendorf, Susan E.: Use of Human Gametes Obtained from Anonymous Donors for the Production of Human Embryonic Stem Cell Lines, 76 Fertility and Sterility 132, 2001.

Laurie, Graeme: Patenting Stem Cells of Human Origin, 26 European Intellectual Property Review 59, 2004.

Ledford, Heidi: Gene-editing surges as U.S. rethinks regulations, Nature 532 (7598) 158, 2016. Id.: CRISPR, the disruptor, Nature, 2015, 522 (7554), 2–24.

Lemley, Mark A. et al.: Life After Bilski, 63 Stanford Law Review 1315, 2011.

Lemley, Mark A./*Sampat*, Bhaven N.: Is the Patent Office a Rubber Stamp?, Emory Law Journal 2008, 181–209.

Leskien, Hermann: Gentechnologie und Patentrecht – Zum neuen Richtlinienvorschlag der Europäischen Kommission, ZUR 1996, 299–308.

Levenberg, Shulamit et al.: Endothelial Cells Derived from Human Embryonic Stem Cell, 99 Proceedings of the National Academy of Sciences 4391, 2002.

Levine, Robert J.: Federal Funding and the Regulation of Embryonic Stem Cell Research: The Pontius Pilate Maneuver, 9 Yale Journal of Health Policy, Law, and Ethics 552, 2009.

Levron, Jacob et al.: Male and Female Genomes Associated in a Single Pronucleus in Human Zygotes, 52 Biology of Reproduction 653, 1995.

Li, Chunliang et al.: Efficient Derivation of Chinese Human Embryonic Stem Cell Lines from Frozen Embryos, 46 In Vitro Cellular & Developmental Biology-Animal 186, 2010.

Li, Haiping: Lun Ren de Zunyan zai Woguo Xianfa Shang de Xingzhi Diwei [On the Qualitative Orientation of Human Dignity in the Chinese Constitution], 12 Shehui Kexue [Social Science] 101, 2012.

Li, Wei/*Cai*, Lisheng: The Scope of Patent Protection for Gene Technology in China, 32 Nature Biotechnology 1001, 2014.

Li, Yahong: Imitation to Innovation in China: The Role of Patents in Biotechnology and Pharmaceutical Industries, Edward Elgar 2010.

Liang, Puping et al.: CRIPR/Cas9-mediated Gene Editing in Human Tripronuclear Zygotes, 6 Protein & Cell 363, 2015.

Liang, Puping/*Xu*, Yanwen/*Zhang*, Xiya/*Ding*, Chenhui/*Huang*, Rui/*Zhang*, Zhen et al.: CRISPR/Cas9-mediated gene editing in human tripronuclear zygotes, Protein & Cell, 2015, 6 (5): 363–372.

Liddell, Kathleen: Immorality and Patents: The Exclusion of Inventions Contrary to Ordre Public and Morality, in: Annabelle Lever (ed.), New Frontiers in the Philosophy of Intellectual Property, Cambridge University Press 2012.

Lin, Laifan: Ren de Zunyan yu Ren'ge Zunyan – Jianlun Zhongguo Xianfa Di 38 Tiao de Jieshi Fangan [Personal Dignity and Personality Dignity: on the Interpretation of Article 38 of the Chinese Constitution], 3 Zhejiang Shehui Kexue [Zhejiang Social Sciences] 47, 2008.

Lindvall, Olle et al.: Stem Cell Therapy for Human Neurodegenerative Disorders – How to Make it Work, 10 Nature Medicine S42, 2004.

Liu, Chuntian: Intellectual Property Law, 4th edition, Zhongguo Renmin Daxue Chubanshe [China Renmin University Publishing] 2009.

Liu, Deming: Now the Wolf Has Indeed Come! Perspective on the Patent Protection of Biotechnology Inventions in China, 53 The American Journal of Comparative Law 207, 2005.

Liu, Deming: Reflections on Lack of a Patent System throughout China's Long History, 12 The Journal of World Intellectual Property 122, 2009.

Liu, Hua/*Ying*, Zhou: Woguo Shehui Gongzhong Thishichanquan Yishi Xianzhuang Diaocha Fengxi ji Duice Yanjiu [Survey of Chinese Public's IP Protection Awareness and Some Recommendations], 10 Zhongguo Ruankexue [China Soft Science] 103, 2006.

Liu, Jie/*Fan*, Daiming: Hepatitis B in China, 369 The Lancet 1582, 2007.

Liu, Qiang/*Sheng*, Wei: 3D Dayin Renti Qiguan Ke Zhuanlixing Yanjiu [The Patentability of 3D Printed Human Organs], 6 Keji yu Falu [Journal of Science, Technology and Law] 1098, 2015.

Liu, Yinliang: Shengwu Jishu de Falü Wenti Yanjiu [Studies on Legal Issues for Biotechnology], Kexue Chubanshe [Science Publishing House] 2007.

Locke, John: Second Treatise of Government, C. B. Macpherson (ed.), Hackett Publishing Company 1980.

Lovell-Badge, Robin: The Regulation of Human Embryo and Stem-cell Research in the United Kingdom, 9 Nature Reviews Molecular Cell Biology 998, 2008.

Luk, Bernard Hung-kay: Abortion in Chinese Law, 25 The American Journal of Comparative Law 372, 1977.

Machin, Nathan: Prospective Utility: A New Interpretation of the Utility Requirement of Section 101 of the Patent Act, 87 California Law Review 421, 1999.

Machlup, Fritz: An Economic Review of the Patent System: Study of the Subcommittee on Patents, Trademarks, and Copyrights of the Committee on the Judiciary, US Government Printing Office 1958.

Macklin, Ruth: Dignity is a useless concept, British Medical Journal, 2003, 327–336.

MacQueen, Hector et al.: Contemporary Intellectual Property: Law and Policy, Oxford University Press 2008.

Magnani, Thomas: The Patentability of Human-Animal Chimeras, 14 Berkeley Tech Law Journal 443, 444, 1999.

Mahalatchimy, Aurélie et al.: Exclusion of Patentability of Embryonic Stem Cells in Europe: Another Restriction by the European Patent Organization, 37 European Intellectual Property Review 25, 2015.

Mai, Qingyun et al.: Derivation of Human Embryonic Stem Cell Lines from Parthenogenetics Blastocysts, 17 Cell Research 1008, 2007.

Malpas, Jeff/*Lickiss*, Norelle: Perspectives on Human Dignity: A Conversation, Springer 2007.

Mandra, Raymond R./*Russo*, Alicia A.: Stem Cells and Patenting and Related Regulatory Issues: A United States Perspective, 7 Bio-Science Law Review 143, 2004.

Marshall, Eliot: Ethicists back Stem Cell Research, White House Treads Cautiously, 285 Science 502, 1999.

Marx, Karl: Theses on Feuerbach, Vol. 5, Karl Marx/Frederick Engels (eds.), Lawrence & Wishart 2010.

Maskus, Keith E.: The Role of Intellectual Property Rights in Encouraging Foreign Direct Investment and Technology Transfer, 9 Duke Journal of Comparative & International Law 109, 1998.

Mayer-Maly, Thomas: Was leisten die guten Sitten?, AcP 194, 1994, 105–111.

McCoy, Andrew: Biotechnology and Embryonic Stem Cells: A Comparative Analysis of the Laws and Politics of the United States and Other Nations, 8 Loyola Law and Technology Annual 63, 2008.

McDougal, Myres S./*Lasswell*, Harold D./*Chen*, Lung-chu: Human Rights and World Public Order: The Basic Policies of an International Law of Human Dignity, New Haven: Yale UP, 1980.

Menell, Peter S.: Forty Years of Wandering in the Wilderness and No Closer to the Promised Land: Bilski's Superficial Textualism and the Missed Opportunity to Return Patent Law to Its Technology Mooring, 63 Stanford Law Review 1289, 2011.

Meng, Yanjuan/*Meng*, Tiancai: Zhishi Jingji Shidai de Daxuesheng Zhishichanquan Yishi he Renzhi Zhuangkuang Yanjiu [A study on University Students' Awareness and Cognition of Intellectual Property in an Era of Knowledge-based Economy], 24 Journal of Nanjing University of Science and Technology 96, 2011.

Merges, Robert P.: Contracting into Liability Rules: Intellectual Property Rights and Collective Rights European Patent Organizations, 84 California Law Review 1293, 1996.

Merges, Robert P.: Intellectual Property in Higher Life Forms: The Patent System and Controversial Technologies, 47 Maryland Law Review 1051, 1987.

Merges, Robert P. et al.: Intellectual Property in the New Technological Age, Wolters Kluwer Law & Business 2007.

Mertes, Heidi: Understanding the Ethical Concerns that Have Shaped European Regulation of Human Embryonic Stem Cell Research, 1 Proceedings of the Belgian Royal Academies of Medicine 127, 2012.

Miller, Amy: The Effect of Federal Funding Restrictions for Embryonic Stem Cell Research on Colleges and Universities: The Need for Caution when Ethical Objections to Research are Raised, 41 Journal of College and University Law 147, 2015.

Mills, Oliver: Biotechnological Inventions: Moral Restraints and Patent Law, Revised edition, Ashgate Publishing Limited 2010.

Mireles, Michael S.: States as Innovation System Laboratories: California, Patents, and Stem Cell Technology, 28 Cardozo Law Review 1133, 2006.

Mitalipova, Maisam et al.: Human Embryonic Stem Cell Lines Derived from Discarded Embryos, 21 Stem Cells 521, 2003.

Mitnovetski, O./*Nicol*, D.: Are patents for methods of medical treatment contrary to the ordre public and morality or "generally inconvenient"?, Journal of Medical Ethics 2004, 470–475.

Moon, Shin Yong et al.: Generation, Culture, and Differentiation of Human Embryonic Stem Cells for Therapeutic Applications, 13 Molecular Therapy 5, 2006.

Moore, Keith: The Developing Human: Clinically Oriented Embryology, 9th edition, Elsevier Sauders 2013.

Moren, Jonathan D.: Will A Trump Administration Let Sleeping Cells Lie? 35 Nature Biotechnology 20, 2017.

Moses, Lyria Bennett: Understanding Legal Responses to Technological Change: The Example of In Vitro Fertilization, 6 Minnesota Journal of Law Science & Technology 505, 2004.

Moufang, Rainer: Patenting of Human Genes, Cells and Parts of the Body? – The Ethical Dimensions of Patent Law, 25 International Review of Industrial Property and Copyright law 487, 1994.

Mueller, Janice M.: Patenting Human Embryonic Stem Cells in the United States: The Legal and Ethical Debate, 14 CASRIP Newsletter 1, 2007.

Murray, Fiona: The Stem-cell Market – Patents and the Pursuit of Scientific Progress, 356 New England Journal of Medicine 2341, 2007.

Murray, Fiona/*Spar*, Debora: Bit Player or Powerhouse? China and Stem-cell Research, 355 New England Journal of Medicine 1191, 2006.

Murray, Thomas: Medical ethics, moral philosophy and moral tradition, Social Science & Medicine, Volume 25, Issue 6, 1987, 637–644.

Murray, Thomas H.: Ethical (and Political) Issues in Research with Human Stem Cells, 265 Novartis Foundation Symposium 188, 2008.

Muscati, Sina A.: "Some More Human than Others": Assessing the Scope of Patentability Related to Human Embryonic Stem Cell Research, Jurimetrics 201, 2004.

Nägele, Thomas/*Jacobs*, Sven: Patentrechtlicher Schutz indigenen Wissens, Mitt. 2014, 353–361.

Newell-McGloughlin, Martina: A Kinder, Gentler Jeremy Rijkin Endorses Biotech, or Does He?, 312 SCIENCE 1586, 1587, 2006.

Nie, Jing-Bao: Behind the Silence: Chinese Voices on Abortion, Rowman & Littlefield Publishers 2005.

Nie, Jing-Bao: The Problem of Coerced Abortion in China and Related Ethical Issues, 8 Cambridge Quarterly of Healthcare Ethics 463, 1999.

Nieder, Georg: Die gewerbliche Anwendbarkeit der Sequenz oder Teilsequenz eines Gens – Teil der Beschreibung oder notwendiges Anspruchsmerkmal von EST-Patenten, Mitt. 2001, 97–103.

Nordberg, Ana/*Minssen*, Timo: A "Ray of Hope" for European Stem Cell Patents or "Out of the Smog into the Fog"? An Analysis of Recent European Case Law and How it Compares to the US, 47 International Review of Intellectual Property and Competition Law 138, 2016.

Normile, Dennis: China sprints ahead in CRISPR therapy race, Science 2017, Vol. 358, Issue 6359, 20–21.

Novak, Atara et al.: Enhanced Reprogramming and Cardiac Differentiation of Human Keratinocytes Derived from Plucked Hair Follicles, Using a Single Excisable Lentivirus, 12 Cellular Reprogramming 665, 2010.

Ohly, Ansgar: Anmerkung zu einer Entscheidung des EuGH, Urteil vom 18.10.2011 (C-34/10); EuZW 2011, 908–912.

Olson, David S.: Taking the Utilitarian Basis for Patent Law Seriously: The Case for Restricting Patentable Subject Matter, 82 Temple Law Review 1, 2009.

Ooms, Casper W.: The Patent Provisions of the Atomic Energy Act, The University of Chicago Law Review 1948, 822–838.

Oppenheimer, Max Stul: Patents 101: Patentable Subject Matter and Separation of Powers, 15 Vanderbilt Journal of Entertainment & Technology Law 1, 2012.

O'Sullivan, Ella: International Stem Cell Corp v. Comptroller General of Patents: The Debate Regarding the Definition of the Human Embryo Continues, 36 European Intellectual Property Review 155, 2014.

Overwalle, Geertrui Van: Patenting Stem Cell Research in Europe and in the United States, in: W. Bender et al. (eds.), Crossing Borders: Cultural Religious and Political Differences Concerning Stem Cell Research, Agenda Verlag 2005.

Overwalle, Geertrui Van/*Berthels*, Nele: Patents & Venus: About Oocytes and Human Embryonic Stem Cells, in: Stem Cells and Women's Health – Cellules souches et santé des femmes – Stamcellen en vrounwengezondheid, Anthemis-Intersentia 2007.

Pan, Yuqiong et al.: In Vitro Neuronal Differentiation of Cultured Human Embryonic Germ Cells, 327 Biochemical and Biophysical Research Communications 548, 2005.

Papastefanou, Stefan: Die Bedeutung und Funktionalität von Menschenwürde im internationalen Patentrecht, in: Recht als Infrastruktur für Innovation, GRUR Junge Wissenschaft, 2018, 107–125.

Paradise, Jordan et al.: Patents on Human Genes: An Analysis of Scope and Claims, 307 Science 1566, 2005.

Pehlivan, C. N.: The Creation of a Single European Patent System: From Dream to (Almost) Reality, 34 European Intellectual Property Review 453, 2012.

Pelligrino, Edmund/*Merrill*, Thomas/*Schulman*, Adam: Human Dignity and Bioethics, University of Notre Dame Press 2009.

Peng, Yaojin: Patenting Human Embryonic Stem Cell Related Inventions in China, Singapore, 2018.

Peng, Yaojin: The Morality and Ethics Governing CRISPR-Cas9 Patents in China, 34 Nature Biotechnology 616, 2016.

Peng, Yaojin: The Patentability of Human Embryonic Stem Cell Technology in China, 34 Nature Biotechnology 37, 2016.

Pera, Martin F.: Human Embryonic Stem Cell Technology in China, 113 Journal of Cell Science 5, 2000.

Piao, Wenxuan: Daojia de Shengming Lunli he Ganxibao Yanju de Wenti [Ethical View of Life in Taoism and Stem Cell Research], 9 Wuhan Keji Daxue Xuebao, Shehui Kexue Ban, [Journal of Wuhan University of Science and Technology, Social Science Edition] 109, 2007.

Pinker, Steven: The Stupidity of Dignity, The New Republic 2008, 149–161.

Pins, Maria N.: Impeding Access to Quality Patient Care and Patient Rights: How Myriad Genetics' Gene Patents Are Unknowingly Killing Cancer Patients and How to Calm the Ripple Effect, 17 J. Intellectual Property Law 377, 379–380.

Plomer, Aurora: After Brüstle: EU Accession to the ECHR and the Future of European Patent Law, 2 Queen Mary Journal of Intellectual Property 110, 2012.

Plomer, Aurora: Human Dignity, Human Rights and Article 6(1) of the EU Directive on Biotechnological Inventions, in: Aurora Plomer/Paul Torremans (eds.), Embryonic Stem Cell Patents: European Law and Ethics, Oxford University Press 2009.

Plomer, Aurora: Towards Systemic Legal Conflict: Article 6(2) of the EU Directive on Biotechnological Inventions, in: Aurora Plomer/Paul Torremans (eds.), Embryonic Stem Cell Patents: European Law and Ethics, Oxford University Press 2009.

Plomer, Aurora et al.: Challenges to Human Embryonic Stem Cell Patents, 2 Cell Stem Cell 13, 2008.

Plomer, Aurora/*Torremans*, Paul: Embryonic Stem Cell Patents: European Law and Ethics, Oxford University Press 2009.

Pontin, Jake: The Genetics (and Ethics) of Making Humans Fit for Mars, Wired, 8 July 2018.

Porter, Gerard: Human Embryos, Patents and Global Trade: Assessing the Scope and Contents of the TRIPS Morality Exception, in: Aurora Plomer/Paul Torremans (eds.), Embryonic Stem Cell Patents: European Law and Ethics, Oxford University Press 2009.

Porter, Gerard: The Drafting History of the European Biotechnology Directive, in: Aurora Plomer/Paul Torremans (eds.), Embryonic Stem Cell Patents: European Law and Ethics, Oxford University Press 2009.

Porter, Gerard et al.: The Patentability of Human Embryonic Stem Cell Patents in Europe, 24 Nature Biotechnology 653, 2006.

Pralong, Danièle et al.: Cell Fusion For Reprogramming Pluripotency: Toward Elimination of the Pluripotent Genome, 2 Stem Cell Reviews 331, 2006.

Qiu, Jane: China Goes Back to Basics on Research Funding, 507 Nature 148, 2014.

Qiu, Jane: Stem-cell Research and Regenerative Medicine in China, 3 National Science Review 257, 2016.

Qiu, Renzong: Cong Zhongguo "Ganxibao Zhilia" Re Lun Ganxibao Linchuang Zhuanhua Zhong de Lunli he Guanli Wenti [Behind the Vogue for "Stem Cell Therapy": Ethical and Regulatory Issue in Clinical Translation of Stem Cells in China], 3 Kexue yu Shehui [Science & Society] 8, 2013.

Qiu, Renzong: Renlei Peitai Ganxibao Yanjiu de Lunli Wenti [Ethical Issues of Human Embryonic Stem Cell Research], 7 Qun Yan [Popular Tribune] 18, 2002.

Qiu, Renzong: Reshaping the Concept of Personhood: A Chinese Perspective, in: Gerhold K. Becker (ed.), The Moral Status of Persons: Perspective on Bioethics, Rodopi 2000.

Qiu, Xiangxing: Renlai Peitai Ganxibao Yanjiu Lunli Wenti de Diacho he Taolun [A Survey and Discussion on Ethical Issues of Human Embryonic Stem Cell Research], 25 Yixue yu Thexue [Medicine and Philosophy] 8, 2004.

Quan, Cao: Pige Mingjiao Zhuanli de Lunli Wenti, Zenme Jiejue [How to Solve the Problem concerning Patents upon the Methods of Using Leather Waste to Make Edible Gelatin], Xinjing Bao The Beijing News, A03, May 3, 2012.

Rabin, Sander: The Gatekeepers of hES Cell Products, 23 Nature Biotechnology 817, 2005.

Rabin, Sander: The Human Use of Humanoid Beings: Chimeras and Patent Law, 24 Nature Biotechnology 517, 2006.

Rabkin, Jeremy: Law and Human Dignity: What We Can Learn About Human Dignity from International law, 27 Harvard Journal of Law & Pub Pol'y 145.

Radick, Gregory: Discovering and Patenting Human Genes, in: Andrew Bainham et al. (eds.), Body Lore and Laws 63, 74, 2002.

Rai, Arti K.: Fostering Cumulative Innovation in the Biopharmaceutical Industry: The Role of Patents and Antitrust, 16 Berkeley Technology Law Journal 813, 2001.

Rai, Arti K.: The Information Revolution Reaches Pharmaceuticals: Balancing Innovation Incentives, Cost, and Access in the Post-Genomics Era, 2001 University of Illinois Law Review 43, 1998.

Rao, Mahendra/*Condic*, Maureen L.: Alternative Sources of Pluripotent Stem Cells: Scientific Solutions to an Ethical Dilemma, 17 Stem Cells and Development 1, 2008.

Regalado, A.: The DIY designer baby project funded with Bitcoin. MIT Technol. Rev., 1 February 2019.

Renesse, Dorothea v./*Tanner*, Klaus/*Renesse*, Margot v.: Das Biopatent – Eine Herausforderung für die rechtsethische Reflektion, Mitt. 2001, 1.

Resnik, David B.: Embryonic Stem Cell Lines From Human Blastocysts: Somatic Differentiation In Vitro, 18 Nature Biotechnology 399, 2000.

Resnik, David B.: Owning the Genome: A Moral Analysis of DNA Patenting, State University of New York Press 2004.

Revazova, Elena S.: Patient-specific Stem Cell Lines Derived from Human Parthenogenetic Blastocysts, 9 Cloning and Stem Cell 432, 2007.

Rigby, Barbarasy: Revocation of European Patent for Neural Progenitors Highlights Patent Challenges for Inventions Relating to Human Embryonic Stem Cells, 23 Expert Opinion on Therapeutic Patents 1397, 2013.

Riley, Margaret/*Merrill*, Richard A.: Regulating Reproductive Genetics: A Review of American Bioethics Commissions and Comparison to the British Human Fertilization and Embryology Authority, 6 Columbia Science & Technology Law Review 1, 2005.

Rimmer, Matthew: Intellectual Property and Biotechnology: Biological Inventions, Edward Elgar 2008.

Rimmer, Matthew: The Attack of the Clones: Patent Law and Stem Cell Research, 10 Journal of Law and Medicine 488, 2003.

Rogge, Rüdiger: Patente auf genetische Informationen im Lichte der öffentlichen Ordnung und der guten Sitten, GRUR 1998, 303–309.

Romandini, Roberto: Die Patentierbarkeit von menschlichen Stammzellen – Eine vergleichende Betrachtung des europäischen, deutschen und italienischen Patentrechts, Schriftenreihe zum gewerblichen Rechtsschutz, Carl Heymanns Verlag, 2012, Köln.

Rowlandson, Malene: WARF/Stem Cells (G2/06): The Ordre Public and Morality Exception and Its Impact on The Patentability of Human Embryonic Stem Cells, 32 European Intellectual Property Review 67, 2010.

Ruse, Michael/*Pynes*, Christopher A.: The Stem Cell Controversy: Debating the Issues, Prometheus Book 2006.

Salter, Brian: Patenting, Morality and Human Embryonic Stem Cell Science: Bioethics and Cultural Politics in Europe, 2 Regenerative Medicine 301, 2007.

Salter, Brian et al.: China and the Global Stem Cell Bioeconomy: An Emerging Political Strategy? 1 Regenerative Medicine 671, 2006.

Sandel, Michael J.: The Case Against Perfection: Ethics in the Age of Genetic Engineering, Belknap Press of Harvard University Press 2007.

Schacht, Hubertus: Commencement or Completion: What Constitutes a "Human Embryo" Within the Meaning of the EU Biotechnology-Directive? 26 European Intellectual Property Review 66, 2014.

Schatz, Ulrich: Öffentliche Ordnung und gute Sitten im europäischen Patentrecht – Versuch einer Flurbereinigung, GRUR Int. 2006, 879–889.

Schechter, Jody: Promoting Human Embryonic Stem Cell Research: A Comparison of Policies in the United States and the United Kingdom and Factors Encouraging Advancement, 45 Texas International Law Journal 603, 2009.

Schuster, Martina Ines: The Court of Justice of the European Union's Ruling on the Patentability of Human Embryonic Stem-Cell-Related Inventions (Case C-34/10), 43 International Review of Intellectual Property and Competition Law 626, 2012.

Schwartz, Steven D. et al.: Embryonic Stem Cell Trials for Macular Degeneration: A Preliminary Report, 379 The Lancet 713, 2012.

Schwartz, Steven D. et al.: Human Embryonic Stem Cell-derived Retinal Pigment Epithelium in Patients with Age-related Macular Degeneration and Stargardt's Macular Dystrophy: Follow-Up of Two Open-label Phase $^1/_2$ Studies, 385 The Lancet 509, 2015.

Séguin, Béatrice et al.: Genomic Medicine and Developing Countries: Creating a Room of Their Own, 9 Nature Reviews Genetics 487, 2008.

Seville, Catherine: EU Intellectual Property Law and Policy, Edward Elgar 2009.

Shamblott, Michael J. et al.: Derivation of Pluripotent from Cultured Human Primordial Germ Cells: 95 Proceedings of the National Academy of Sciences 13726, 1998.

Shroff, Geeta/*Hopf-Seidel*, Petra: Use of Human Embryonic Stem Cells in the Treatment of Parkinson's Disease: A Case Report, 17 International Journal of Emergency Mental Health and Human Resilience 661, 2015.

Simon, Brenda M./*Scott*, Christopher T.: Unsettled Expectations: How Recent Patent Decisions Affect Biotech, 29 Nature Biotechnology 229, 2011.

Sleeboom-Faulkner, Margaret E.: National Risk Signatures and Human Embryonic Stem Cell Research in Mainland China, 12 Health, Risk & Society 491, 2010.

Snead, O. Carter: The Pedagogical Significance of the Bush Stem Cell Policy: A Window into Bioethical Regulation in the United States, 5 Yale Journal of Health Policy, Law, and Ethics 491, 2005.

Snow, Nancy E.: Stem Cell Research: New Frontiers in Science and Ethics, University of Notre Dame Press 2003.

Spranger, Matthias T.: Ethische Aspekte bei der Patentierung menschlichen Erbgutes nach der Richtlinie 98/44/EG, GRUR Int. 1999, 595–602.

Spranger, Matthias T.: Indigene Völker, "Biopiraterie" und internationales Patentrecht, GRUR 2001, 89–95.

Spranger, Matthias T.: Zur Auslegung des Begriffs des menschlichen Embryos gemäß Art. 6 Abs. 2 Buchst. c EGRL 44/98 – Vorlage an den EuGH zur Vorabentscheidung, LMK 2010, 298400.

Sreenivasulu, Nese/*Raju*, Bhupathiraju: CB, Biotechnology and Patent Law: Patenting Living Beings, 1st edition, Manupatra 2008.

Staunton, Ciara: Brüstle v. Greenpeace, Embryonic Stem Cell Research and the European Court of Justice's New Found Morality, 21 Medical Law Review 310, 2013.

Stazi, Andrea: Biotechnological Inventions and Patentability of Life: The U.S. and European Experience, Edward Elgar 2015.

Sterckx, Sigrid: European Patent Law and Biotechnological Inventions, in: Sigrid Sterckx (ed.), Biotechnology, Patents and Morality, Ashgate Publishing 1997.

Sterckx, Sigrid/*Cockbain*, Julian: Exclusions from Patentability: How Far Has the European Patent Office Eroded Boundaries?, Cambridge University Press 2012.

Storz, Ulrich: The Limits of Patentability: Stem Cells, in: Andreas Hübel et al. (eds.), Limits of Patentability: Plant Sciences, Stem Cells and Nucleic Acids, Springer 2013.

Straus, Joseph: Abhängigkeit bei Patenten auf genetische Information – Ein Sonderfall?, GRUR 1998, 314–320.

Straus, Joseph: Anmerkung zum Urteil des Gerichtshofs der Europäischen Union vom 18.10. 2011 zum Ausschluss der Patentierbarkeit nach Art. 6 Abs. 2 Buchst. c der Richtlinie 98/44, GRUR Int. 2011, 1048–1052.

Straus, Joseph: Besprechung von Plomer/Torremans, Embryonic Stem Cell Patents – European Law and Ethics, GRUR Int. 2010, 1104–1109.

Straus, Joseph: Biotechnologische Erfindungen – ihr Schutz und seine Grenzen, GRUR 1992, 252–258.

Straus, Joseph: Ethische, rechtliche und wirtschaftliche Probleme des Patent- und Sortenschutzes für die biotechnologische Tierzüchtung und Tierproduktion, GRUR 1990, 913–917.

Straus, Joseph: Patentrechtliche Probleme der Gentherapie, GRUR 1996, 10–16.

Straus, Joseph: Produktpatente auf DNN-Sequenzen – Aktuelle Herausforderung des Patentrechts, GRUR 2001, 1016–1021.

Straus, Joseph: Völkerrechtliche Verträge und Gemeinschaftsrecht als Auslegungsfaktoren des Europäischen Patentübereinkommens, GRUR Int. 1998, 1–15.

Straus, Joseph: Zur Patentierung humaner embryonaler Stammzellen in Europa – Verwendet die Stammzellenforschung menschliche Embryonen für industrielle oder kommerzielle Zwecke?, GRUR Int. 2010, 911–915.

Sumikura, Koichi: The Issues Surrounding Patent Protection for Human-Embryonic Stem Cells and Therapeutic Cloning in Japan, in: Josef Drexl et al. (eds.), Patentschutz und Stammzellenforschung: Internationale und rechtsvergleichende Aspekte, Springer 2009.

Sun, Lingguo: Fuqi Jian Lengdong Peitai Chuli Nanti de Falü Jiejue [Legal Countermeasures of Issues in Frozen Embryo Disposition between the Couple], 23 Goujia Jiancha Guan Xueyuan Xuebao [Journal of National Prosecutors College] 110, 2015.

Suss-Toby, Edith et al.: Derivation of a Diploid Human Embryonic Stem Cell Line from A Mononuclear Zygote, 19 Human Reproduction 670, 2004.

Svendsen, Clive N./*Ebert*, Allison D.: Encyclopedia of Stem Cell Research, Vols 1 & 2, Sage Publications 2008.

Takahashi, Kazutoshi et al.: Induction of Pluripotent Stem Cells from Adult Human Fibroblasts by Defined Factors, 131 Cell 861, 2007.

Takahashi, Kazutoshi/*Yamanaka*, Shinya: Induction of Pluripotent Stem Cells from Mouse Embryonic and Adult Fibroblast Cultures by Defined Factors, 126 Cell 663, 2006.

Tan, Ying et al.: Nongcun gongzhong dui Zhishichanquan de Renzhidu ji Guanzhudu Yanjiu [Research on Plural Public's Awareness of and Attention to Intellectual Property Rights], 17 Journal of Northwest A&F University, Social Science Edition, 144, 2017.

Tännsjö, Torbjörn: Why No Compromise is Possible, 38 Metaphilosophy 330, 2007.

Taupitz, Jochen: Menschenwürde von Embryonen – europäisch-patentrechtlich betrachtet – Besprechung zu EuGH, Urt. v. 18.10.2011 – C-34/10 – Brüstle/Greenpeace, GRUR 2012, 1–5.

Taymor, Kenneth S. et al.: The Paths around Stem Cell Intellectual Property, 24 Nature Biotechnology 411, 2006.

Teschemacher, Rudolf: The Practice of the European Patent Office Regarding the Grant of Patents for Biotechnological Inventions, IIC 1988, 18–29.

Thomson, James A.: Embryonic Stem Cell Lines Derived from Human Blastocysts, 282 Science 1145, 1998.

Thomson, James A./*Odorico*, Jon S.: Human Embryonic Stem and Embryonic Germ Cell Lines, 18 Trends in Biotechnology 53, 2000.

Tian, Lupu: Shengming Xingshi Zhishi Chanquan ji Guojia Zhengce [Intellectual Property Right of Life Form and National Policies], Zhongguo Nongye Chubanshe [China Agriculture Press] 2003.

Tong, Rou: Zhongguo Minfa Xue MinFa Zongze [Chinese Civil Law Science: General Principles of Civil law], Zhongguo Gong'an Daxue Chubanshe [People's Public Security University of China's Press] 2003.

Torremans, Paul: The Construction of the Directive's Moral Exclusions Under the EPC, in: Aurora Plomer/Paul Torremans (eds.), Embryonic Stem Cell Patents: European Law and Ethics, Oxford University Press 2009.

Trips-Hebert, Roman/*Grund*, Martin: Die Früchte des verbotenen Baumes? Die Patentierung von Stammzellen nach dem Brüstle-Urteil des Bundespatentgerichts und mögliche Fernwirkungen für die pharmazeutische Industrie, PharmR 2007, 397–402.

Tronser, Ursula: Ziele und Grenzen des Patentrechts – Dürfen Erfindungen patentfähig sein, die lebende Materie, auch höhere Lebewesen, und den Menschen oder menschliche Bestandteile betreffen?, DRiZ 2000, 281–288.

Trüstedt, Wilhelm: Patentrecht und Gentechnologie, GRUR 1986, 640–645.

Turovets, Nikolay et al.: Derivation of Human Parthenogenetic Stem Cell Lines, in: Philip H. Schwartz/Robin L. Wesselschmidt (eds.), Human Pluripotent Stem Cells: Methods and Protocols, Springer 2011.

Tur-Sinai, Ofer: Cumulative Innovation in Patent Law: Making Sense of Incentives, 50 Idea 723, 2009.

Vakulskas, Christopher A./*Dever*, Daniel P./*Rettig*, Garrett R./*Turk*, Rolf/*Jacobi*, Ashley M./*Collingwood*, Michael A. et al.: A high-fidelity Cas9 mutant delivered as a ribonucleoprotein complex enables efficient gene editing in human hematopoietic stem and progenitor cells, Nature Medicine, 24, 2018, 1216–1224.

Varju, Marton/*Sándor*, Judit: Patenting Stem Cell in Europe: The Challenge of Multiplicity in European Union Law, 49 Common Market Law Review 1007, 2012.

Vazin, Tandis/*Freed*, William J.: Human Embryonic Stem Cells: Derivation, Culture, and Differentiation: A Review, 28 Restorative Neurology and Neuroscience 589, 2010.

Verlinsky, Yury et al.: Cytoplasmic Cell Fusion: Stembrid Technology for Reprogramming Pluripotentiality, 2 Stem Cell Reviews 297, 2006.

Viens, Alexander M.: Morality Provisions in Law Concerning the Commercialization of Human Embryos and Stem Cells, in: Aurora Plomer/Paul Torremans (eds.), Embryonic Stem Cell patent: European Law and Ethics, Oxford University Press 2009.

Vitzthum, Wilhelm: Die Menschenwürde als Verfassungsbegriff, JZ 1985, 201–210.

Vogel, Horst Günther: Gewerbliche Anwendbarkeit und Wiederholbarkeit als Patentierungsvoraussetzung, München, 1977.

Volokh, Eugene: The Mechanisms of the Slippery Slope, 116 Harvard Law Review 1026, 2003.

Vorwerk, Volkert: Patent und Ethik, GRUR 2009, 375–378.

Vossius, Volker: Der Beurteilungsmaßstab für die Neuheit einer Erfindung nach deutschem und europäischem Patentrecht, in: Festschrift für Rudolf Nirk zum 70. Geburtstag, 1992, 103–118.

Vossius, Volker: Patentschutz für Tiere – "Krebsmaus/Harvard", GRUR 90, 333–339.

Vossius/Grund: Patentierung von Teilen des Erbguts – Der Mensch als Sklave? – Einspruchsverfahren gegen das Relaxin-Patent, Mitt. 1995, 339–344.

Wagner, Klaus R.: Heilverfahren als nicht patentierbare Behandlungsverfahren?, GRUR 1976, 673–679.

Walsh, Patrick: Stemming the Tide of Stem Cell Research: The Bush Compromise, 38 John Marshall Law Review 1061, 2004.

Walter, Carrie F.: Beyond the Harvard Mouse: Current Patent Practice and the Necessity of Clear Guidelines in Biotechnology Patent Law, 73 Indiana Law Journal 1025, 1997.

Waltz, Emily: Gene-edited CRISPR mushroom escapes U.S. regulation, Nature 532, (7599), 2016.

Wang, Luozhong: Woguo Zhuanxingqi Gonggong Zhengce Guochengzhong de Gongmin Canyu Yanjiu – Yizhong Liyi Fenxi de Shijiao [Study on the Participation of Citizens in Public Policy Making During China's Transition: From the Interest Analysis Perspective], 8 Zhongguo Xingzheng Guanli [Chinese Public Administration] 86, 2005.

Wang, Nian: Guangxi Shehui Gongzhong Zhishichanquan Renzhidu Diaocha yu Fenxi ji Silu Tantao [The Survey, Analysis, and Discussion on Public Perceptions of IP in GuangXi], 3 Xiandai Shangye [Modern Business] 175, 2016.

Warnock, Mary: Report of the Committee of Inquiry into Human Fertilization and Embryology, HM Stationary Office 1984.

Warren-Jones, Amanda: A Mouse in Sheep's Clothing: The Challenge to Patent Morality Criterion Posed by "Dolly", 20 European Intellectual Property Review 445, 1998.

Warren-Jones, Amanda: Vital Parameters for Patent Morality – A Question of Form, 2 Journal of Intellectual Property Law & Practice 832, 2007.

Weber, Max et al.: The Religion of China: Confucianism and Taoism, Collier Macmillan 1964.

Whitehill, Joshua: Patenting Human Embryonic Stem Cells: What is so Immoral? 34 Brooklyn Journal of International Law 1045, 2008.

Whitman, Jackson: The Two Western Cultures of Privacy: Dignity Versus Liberty, 113 Yale Journal of Law 1151, 1161, 2004.

Wiebe, Andreas: Gentechnik als Patenthindernis, GRUR 1993, 88–95.

Wing-Tsit, Chan: A Source Book in Chinese Philosophy, Princeton University Press 1973.

Winter, Gerd: Gentechnik als Rechtsproblem, DVBl 1986, 585–591.

Wu, Handong: Zhishi Chanquan Zhanlüe Shishi de Guoji Huanjing yu Zhongguo Changjing [The International Environment of Implementing Intellectual Property Strategy and China's Situation], 2 Faxue [Law Science] 3, 2012.

Wu, Handong: Zhongguo Zhuanli Fa de Fazhan Daolu: Xiandaihua, Guojiahua yu Zhanlüenhua – Zai Zhongguo Zhuanli Fa Banbu 30 Zhounian Zuotanhui Shang de Fayan] The Development Paths of the Chinese Patent Law: Modernizing, Internationalizing, Strategizing – An Address in Colloquia "the Issuing of the Chinese Patent Law" 30th Anniversary], 3 Zhishi Chanquan [Intellectual Property Journal] 10, 2014.

Wu, Yuehui/*Yu*, Siluan: Jinping Xi: Chuangxin Ganwei Tianxia Xian [Xi Jinping: Innovation, Dare to be the First in the World], Renmin Ribao [People's Daily] 2, 2017.

Xi, Jingping: Xi Jinping Tan Zhiguo Lizheng [Xi Jinping: the Governance of China], Waiwen Chubanshe [Foreign Languages Press] 2014.

Xu, Chongde: Zhonghua Renmin Gongheguo Xianfa Shi [History of the Constitution of the People's Republic of China], Fujian Renmin Chubanshe [Fujian People Press] 2003.

Xu, Haiyan: Lun Tiwai Zaoqi Renlei Peitai de Falü Diwei ji Chufen Quan [The Legal Status of Early Embryos and the Right of the Disposition of Frozen Embryos], 29 Faxue Luntan [Legal Forum] 146, 2014.

Xu, Yu et al.: Prevalence and Control of Diabetes in Chinese Adults, 310 Jama 948, 2013.

Yin, Xintian: Zhongguo Zhuanlifa Xiangjie [Introduction to the Patent Law of China], Zhishi Chanquan Chubanshe [Intellectual Property Press] 2011.

Young, Susan: CRISPR and Other Genome Editing Tools Boost Medical Research and Gene Therapy's Reach, MIT Technology Review, 2014.

Yu, Junying et al.: Induced Pluripotent Stem Cell Lines Derived from Human Somatic Cells, 318 Science 1917, 2007.

Yu, Peter K.: Building the Ladder: Three Decades of Development of the Chinese Patent System, Drake University Law School Research Paper, 2012.

Yu, Peter K.: From Pirates to Partners: Protecting Intellectual Property in China in the Twenty-first Century, 50 American University Law 131, 2000.

Yuan, Weiping et al.: Stem Cell Science On the Rise in China, 10 Cell Stem Cell 12, 2012.

Zaninovic, Nikica et al.: Derivation of Human Embryonic Stem Cells (hESC), in: Zev Rosenwaks/Paul M. Wassarman (eds.), Human Fertility: Methods and Protocols, Springer 2014.

Zhang, Jian-Hua/*Pandey*, Mritunjay/*Kahler*, John F./*Loshakov*, Anna/*Harris*, Benjamin/*Dagur*, Pradeep K. et al.: Improving the specificity and efficacy of CRISPR/CAS9 and gRNA through target specific DNA reporter, Journal of Biotechnology, 2014, 189, 1–8.

Zhang, Joy Yueyue: The Cosmopolitanization of Science: Stem cell Governance in China, Palgrave Macmillan 2012.

Zhang, Ping: Shengwu Yixue Lingyu zhong de Zhishi Chanquan Baohu [Intellectual Property Protection in the BioMedicine Field], 39 Journal of Peking University, Health Sciences 101, 2007.

Zhang, Qianfan: Xianfa Xue Daolun [Introduction to Constitutional Jurisprudence], Falü Chubanshe [Law Press, China] 2004.

Zhang, Qingkui: Yiyao ji Shengwu Jishu Lingyu Zhishi Chanquan Zhanlü Shiwu [Strategy and Practice of Intellectual Property in the Fields of Medicine and Biotechnology], Zhishi Chanquan Chubanshe [Intellectual Property Press] 2008.

Zhang, Xiadu: Zhanli Shizi Tiaojian [Substantial Requirements for Patent], Chengsi Zheng (ed.), Law Press 2002.

Zhang, Xin et al.: Derivation of Human Embryonic Stem Cells from Developing and Arrested Embryos, 24 Stem Cells 2669, 2006.

Zhao, Jing: Zhuanli Xingfa de Sikao [Preliminary Study on the Morality Exclusion in Patent Examination: Thinking from Two Gelatin Patents], 3 Zhoungguo Faming yu Zhuanli [China Invention & Patent] 92, 2013.

Zhao, Tongbiao et al.: Immunogenicity of Induced Pluripotent Stem Cells, 474 Nature 212, 2011.

Zhao, Xu: Renlei Peitai Ganxibao Yanjiu de Lunli Guan Fenxi [A Study on Ethical Values of Human Embryonic Stem Cell Research], 1 Lunli Xue Yanjiu [Studies in Ethics] 82, 2012.

Zhao, Yuanguo: Zhongguo Zhuanlifa de Yunyu Yu Dansheng [The Drafting History of the Patent Law of China], Zhishi Chanquan Chubanshe [Intellectual Property Publishing House] 2003.

Zheng, Xianwen: Gongxu Liangsu Yuanze zai Zhongguo Jindai Minfa Zhuanxing zhong de Jiazhi [The Value of the Principle of Public Order and Good Morals in the Transformation of the Civil Law of Modern China], 11 Faxue [Law Science] 87, 2017.

Zhou, Chenlin et al.: Comprehensive Profiling Reveals Mechanisms of SOX2-mediated Cell Fate Specification in Human ESCs and NPCs, 26 Cell Research 171, 2016.

Zhou, Di et al.: Establishment and Maintenance of Three Chinese Human Embryonic Stem Cell Lines, 46 In Vitro Cellular & Development Biology-Animal 192, 2010.

Zhou, Qi et al.: Mianxiang Weilai de Xin Yilun Yiliao Jishu Geming – Ganxibao yu Zaisheng Yixue Yanjiu Zhanluexing Xiandao Keji Zhuanxiang Jinzhan [Confronting Coming Medical Renovation: Progress on Stem Cell and Regenerative Medicine Research], 30 Zhongguo Kexueyuan Yuan Kan [China Academic Journal Electronic Publishing House] 262, 2015.

Zhou, Qi et al.: Zhongguo ji Zhongguo Kexueyuan Ganxibao yu Zaisheng Yixue Yanjiu Gaishu [An Overview of Stem Cell and Regenerative Medicine in China and at Chinese Academy of Sciences], 28 Chinese Bulletin of Life Sciences 833, 2016.

Zhou, Yan: Woguo Ganxibao Yanjiu Zhong de Lunli Weiji yu Falü Kunhuo jiqi Guojia Guanli de Yanjiu [Research on Ethical Crisis and Legal Issues Related to Stem Cell Research and National Regulatory Framework in China], Di San Junyi Daxue [Third Military Medical University of Chinese PLA] 12, 2009.

Zippelius, Reinhold: Wertungsprobleme im System der Grundrechte, Berlin, 1962.

Index

Afghanistan War 46
Agreement on Trade-Related Aspects of Intellectual Property Rights 55
Anti-personnel mines 41
Anti-sensor system 47
Applied ethics 26

Bayh-Dole Act 158
Beta thalassemia 36
Bio-piracy 61
BRCA1 and BRCA2 DNA 162
Brüstle (ECJ decision) 23, 79

Case Group Solution 137
CCR5 gene 38
Chakrabarty (US Surpreme Court decision) 88
Chinese State Intellectual Property Office 185
Class dignity 84
Commercial Exploitation 56
Composition of matter 92
Convention on the Prohibition of the Use, Stockpiling, Production and Transfer of Anti-Personnel Mines and on their Destruction 45, 47
Conventional Weapon Technology 43
CRISPR 17, 22, 34
Customs 107

Deceptive devices 152
Descriptive ethics 26
Devices with mischievous tendencies 152
Dictatorship of values 110
Directed-energy system 44

EPO Boards of Appeal 73
EPO Examining Division 73
EU Biotech Directive 27

European Convention for the Protection of Human Rights and Fundamental Freedoms 73
European Patent Convention 58
European Unitary Patent 27
European Unity 104

FRAND licensing 131
Fruit of the forbidden tree-doctrine 86

Gambling devices 149
Genetic identity 95
Geneva Convention 45
Genome editing 34
German Animal Protection Act 125
German Embryo Protection Act 81
German Federal Court of Justice 81
German Federal Patent Court 81
Germline editing 34

Harvard OncoMouse 170
Heat Ray 46
Humane Genome Project 95

In vivo 35
International Campaign to Ban Landmines 59
Ionizing radiation 49, 50

Krebsmaus 101

Laser Weapon Systems 42
Law of nature doctrine 165
Lethal Autonomous Robots 41

Median perception of morals 111
Meta-ethics 26
Moral utility doctrine 148
Multi-potent cells 80

Normative ethics 26

Office of Technology Assessment   91
Oxydonor   153

Pain Ray   46
Patent secrecy   27
Patent utility requirement   148
Photon radiation   49
Pluri-potent cells   80
President's Council on Bioethics   172
Public policy doctrine   156
Public welfare   57

Radar speed control identifier   154
Railgun   43
Range-finding device   47
Rifkin, Jeremy   147, 159

Social contract   28
Social disorientation   98
Social morality   107
Special beneficial utility doctrine   151

Special Respect Theory   192
Stem-cell research   38
Subject Matter Doctrine   161

Target illuminator   47
Temporary Statue on Technology Reward   186
Toti-potent stem cells   38

Uniform European patent standard   65
United Nations Convention on Certain Conventional Weapons   41, 46
United States National Academics of Sciences, Engineering and Medicine   37
University of Utah Research Foundation   163
US Bill of Rights   110
US Food and Drug Administration   37

Wertidee   109

Bernadette Makoski

Die Einrede der doppelten Inanspruchnahme

Eine Untersuchung zum Doppelschutz im Patentrecht

Die Einrede der doppelten Inanspruchnahme und der Doppelschutz sind auf die europäische Patentreform zurückzuführen. Diese steht für die Einführung einer einheitlichen europäischen Patentgerichtsbarkeit in Gestalt des Einheitlichen Patentgerichts und die Schaffung eines europäischen Schutztitels, des europäischen Patents mit einheitlicher Wirkung. Aus Anlass der europäischen Patentreform wurde u. a. das Begleitgesetz vorgeschlagen, das die Anpassung der nationalen Vorschriften zum Gegenstand hat. Es sieht als Novum die Einführung eines Doppelschutzes durch ein nationales Patent und einen europäischen patentrechtlichen Schutztitel vor. Gleichzeitig wird der Doppelschutz durch die Einrede der doppelten Inanspruchnahme beschränkt. Die Arbeit widmet sich der wissenschaftlichen Untersuchung beider Institute und gelangt zum Ergebnis, dass mehr und die besseren Argumente für die Einführung des beschränkten Doppelschutzes sprechen.

Beiträge zum Europäischen Wirtschaftsrecht, Band 81
2., korrigierte Aufl., 1 Abb., 247 Seiten, 2022
ISBN 978-3-428-18538-2, € 79,90
Titel auch als E-Book erhältlich.

www.duncker-humblot.de